# Cornbread Nation 6

## The Best of Southern Food Writing

**Edited by Brett Anderson**
**with Sara Camp Arnold**
**General Editor, John T. Edge**

Published in association with
the Southern Foodways Alliance
and the Center for the Study of Southern Culture
at the University of Mississippi

The University of Georgia Press ■ Athens

Publication of this work was made possible, in part, by generous gifts from
the Atticus Trust and the University of Georgia Press Friends Fund.

Acknowledgments for previously published material appear on pages
291–94, which constitute a continuation of this copyright page.

Published by the University of Georgia Press
Athens, Georgia 30602
www.ugapress.org
© 2012 by the Southern Foodways Alliance, Center for the Study of
Southern Culture, University of Mississippi
All rights reserved
Designed by Anne Richmond Boston
Set in 10.5 Adobe Minion Pro by Graphic Composition, Inc., Bogart, Ga.
Manufactured by Thomson-Shore
The paper in this book meets the guidelines for permanence and
durability of the Committee on Production Guidelines for Book
Longevity of the Council on Library Resources.

Printed in the United States of America
16  15  14  13  12  P  5  4  3  2  1

Library of Congress Cataloging-in-Publication Data

Cornbread nation 6 : the best of Southern food writing / edited by Brett Anderson
    with Sara Camp Arnold ; general editor, John T. Edge
        pages cm
    Published in association with the Southern Foodways Alliance and the
    Center for the Study of Southern Culture at the University of Mississippi.
    ISBN 978-0-8203-4261-0 (pbk.) — ISBN 0-8203-4261-0 (paperback)
        1. Food writing. 2. Food habits—Southern States. I. Anderson, Brett, editor.
    II. Title: Cornbread nation six.
    TX644.C693 2012
    394.1'20975—dc23          2011046505

# Contents

■ ■ ■ ■ ■ ■ ■ ■ ■ ■ ■ ■ ■ ■ ■ ■ ■ ■ ■ ■ ■ ■ ■ ■ ■

## MESSING WITH MOTHER NATURE

## SOUTHERN CHARACTERS

## SOUTHERN DRINKWAYS

## IDENTITY IN MOTION

## THE GLOBAL SOUTH

# Introduction
## Of Memes and Munificence

### Brett Anderson

A Spanish-speaking woman fed Florida sugarcane into a growling juice extractor at the Brazilian Market & Café in Kenner, Louisiana, a twenty-minute drive from my home in New Orleans. While we had ordered plenty of food, including two of the chicken-stuffed pastries called coxinhas, I was looking forward to the cane juice most of all. The last time I'd tried it was in an interactive lesson in junior high school, during which time my teacher endeavored to enlighten young Midwesterners about the crops once tended by enslaved Africans.

Sampled plain, sugarcane juice could generously be described as a naturally occurring soft drink, less charitably as Sprite gone flat.

But it tasted refreshing alongside the esfira, which in the Market's rendering tastes like Brazil's answer to the meat pies of Natchitoches, Louisiana. I ate mine with alternating squirts of housemade hot sauce and Sriracha, the fiery Southeast Asian–style condiment found everywhere from your favorite Vietnamese pho house to the window ledge at Vaughan's on Thursday night in New Orleans, where it's set out for revelers to spice up their red beans during the regular set by trumpeter and showman Kermit Ruffins.

The story is worth retelling not because it's exotic, but because it's the opposite. The lunch described was a pit stop on the way out of town, prompted by information shared as casually as the score of a football game. We stopped at the Market because it was en route to where we were heading, and we were hungry.

A meme of contemporary Southern food writing is that Southern cities offer a virtual buffet of foods that previous generations would never consider Southern. When you consider how much the off-the-grid culinary explorations of chefs, writers, and television personalities have enlivened the content of the nation's culinary entertainment-industrial complex, the same sentence would actually be true if you replaced *Southern* with *American*. It's one of the reasons the meme exists, at least in the South: to kick up evidence that the region is not just like the rest of the country, but just as good—progressive, open, diverse, tolerant, and everything else that cosmopolitanism implies.

Fully appreciating food in the South today requires some fluency with Southern history, warts and all. That history is baked into the stories you'll find in this sixth edition of *Cornbread Nation*. Some of them cast light on the darkest days of the South's past, none more so than Jessica B. Harris's unsettling investigation of the slaves' larder. Others, like Andrea Nguyen's celebration of the Viet-Cajun crawfish tradition, underscore Southern cuisine's life-affirming virtue as a grand diversion. Either should erase any doubt as to why it's a small triumph whenever a person of one race unconditionally embraces the food of another, particularly below the Mason-Dixon Line. If the embrace is subconscious, a habitual function of everyday life, well, the victory tastes even sweeter.

At least that's the view of this Minnesota-born, reluctant-cum-enthusiastic Southerner, a view that for the purposes of this book is relevant, and not just because I edited it (with the indispensable partnership of Sara Camp Arnold, to whom it would be impossible to pay proper gratitude in this space). Writing well about Southern food is a multifront battle where the past and present are fought, disentangled, and embraced in measures dictated by the personal concerns of the writer. Southern food offers anyone inclined to consume and ponder it the gift of discovery. These stories offer a path to that gift, and they are unified by it.

"How do you describe Southern food?" Bill Addison asks the question in a piece collected here, and like every writer whose work surrounds his, Addison digs in with both hands, which he acknowledges is the bare minimum required for the rewarding, if predictably futile, task at hand. The story leads off a chapter called "Identity in Motion." The title alludes to Southern cuisine's amorphous personality, which shifts from year to year, state to state, town to town, and cook to cook.

In these pages, the personal is often subtextual. When Calvin Trillin, the great existential comic of American letters, makes his way south to Mosca's, you feel the Midwestern–New Yorker's relief in what he discovers at the legendary Creole-Italian roadhouse whose heady fragrance survived even Hurricane Katrina. In the chapter entitled "Southern Characters," a profile of Edna Lewis reveals as much about the author, the *New York Times* writer Kim Severson, as it does about Lewis, who at the time of the story's writing was barely able to communicate. The respectful observance of dignity's twilight, boundless love, and amazing fried chicken opens a new corridor in Southern food writing's life-lesson wing. In "Messing with Mother Nature," a chapter as concerned with the human victims and perpetrators of said messing as with the environment, Francis Lam, an Asian American living in Queens, finds random family among a group of Cajun fishermen gathered around boiled crawfish in the ruins of East Biloxi, Mississippi.

Southern food may be the ultimate manifestation of Southern munificence, but the regional temperament, as ornery and defiant as it is generous, resides on the underside of the welcome mat, too. In "On the Menu," a chapter that probes Southern cooking's many subsets and dishes, two stories come down on opposite sides of the argument over competitive barbecue. One, by Brett Martin, the Brooklyn-born journalist currently squatting in New Orleans, finds a force for good. The other, by the sportswriting stud Wright Thompson, a Mississippi native, advocates dousing the flames.

Elsewhere, you can almost hear Besha Rodell buckling her holster as, prompted by a handful of Tweets, she defends Atlanta as worthy of savoring on its own terms. Rodell's treatise—like Hanna Raskin's serrated critique of the Dallas food scene—carries insights available only to nonnatives, Southern food's most effective change-agents as well as some of its fiercest advocates. Rodell's piece also doubles as a mash note to the New South beacon of Atlanta, her adopted home.

Again, Southern identity exposes itself as a moving target; often, race and ethnicity are not the half of it. A powerful case in point is embodied in Todd Kliman's story in the chapter "Southern Drinkways," which touches on bourbon but doesn't stop there. Kliman tells of spiritual deliverance reached through the wonders of modern medicine, spurred by enchantment with a native Southern wine grape as stubborn as Andrew Jackson.

"Global South," the book's final chapter, further scrambles Southern food's complicated map. Here you'll learn what ravioli has to do with country music and how African-born rice cookery made its way from South Carolina to Philadelphia. It's also where you'll find Bill Smith drinking beer and eating chicharrones in Celaya, Mexico, wondering why he fits in so well with the immigrant friends he's made in the kitchen of Crook's Corner, the iconic Southern restaurant in Chapel Hill, North Carolina. Rather than dwelling on the mystery, the chef basks in his good fortune. Smith's trips to Mexico summon background music of global geography and personal history for much the same reason visits to a South American grocery store in suburban New Orleans do something similar for this writer. The rewards of Southern food don't begin at the plate. Sometimes they don't end there, either.

Happy reading.

# Menu Items

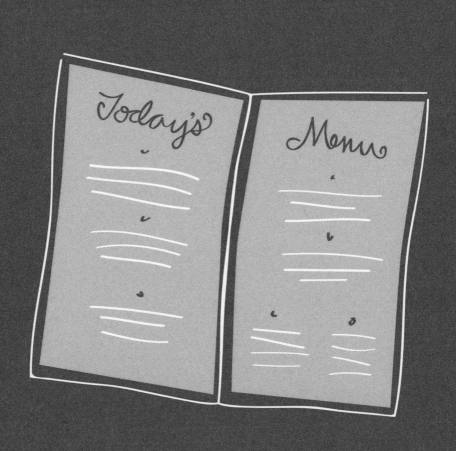

*Alison Cook is the James Beard Foundation Award–winning restaurant critic at the* Houston Chronicle.

# Why Chile con Queso Matters

## Alison Cook

If Tex-Mex is our state's tribal nursery food—a truth that I hold to be self-evident—then chile con queso is our mother's milk.

Who among us has not sought solace in the balm that is runny melted cheese dip, gently souped up with morsels of green chile and tomato? Few reversals of fortune cannot be salved with a molten bowl of queso (our shortened term of endearment) scooped up with fistfuls of crisp tortilla chips. Job loss, breakup, writer's block, what have you: all seem smoothed and softened as the magical potion coats our gullets, slicking down the day's rough edges.

"Queso is the golden currency of heaven above, flown down to us by nude cherubs so that we might find a small plot of happiness in our lifetime," insisted the Austin food blog *Dishola* not long ago. It was an exaggeration, but not by much. Some future scientist will, I feel certain, discover that chile con queso has a mysterious and beneficent effect on serotonin levels.

All quesos, of course, are not created equal. You can have the high-rent, artisanal versions; I'll take the low road. Snobbery has no place in my personal connoisseurship, since my quesos of choice are (almost) invariably made of processed cheese.

There, I said it. Unfashionable it may be in these days of green this and sustainable that, but Velveeta and its various unnatural commercial cousins are engineered for meltability. And with queso, texture is king. The dip needs to be runny but not too thin; viscous but not too thick. Smoothness is paramount. Like mother's milk, you should be able to suck queso out of a baby's bottle.

"But what of flavor?" the food snobs will protest. I submit that an assertive cheese taste subverts the mild charms of your old-school Tex-Mex queso. I seek a substance that makes no demands on my palate or my brain cells: just that slightly salty bloom of milky dairy-tude on the tongue, as infantile a pleasure as milk and cookies.

Sure, there are worthy Texas restaurant versions of chile con queso that echo the northern Mexico original, made with melted asadero or Chihuahua cheese, but the handstands and back flips a cook must use to produce a suitably runny dip out of "natural" cheese strike me as vaguely preposterous. All that béchamel-ing, all that roux-stirring, all that gradual folding and whisking and angst. For what? Only to fail at reproducing the texture of the processed stuff, generally ending in a queso that clumps and seizes up rather than oozing its way into the sweet spot.

High-toned chefs tend to fall afoul of chile con queso, the ultimate in democratic people's food. Robert del Grande may have helped to invent the "New Southwestern Cuisine" with his landmark Cafe Annie, but his chile con queso at downtown Houston's The Grove is a sludgy, dispiriting thing. Arnaldo Richards, one of Houston's most gifted interpreters of interior Mexican cuisine at Pico's Mex-Mex, excels at queso flameado (the melted white cheese with add-ins that is rolled into flour tortillas). But his chile con queso—buried deep on page 5 of his menu, under the scolding description "100% real cheese, the way it should be"—is so salty it assaults the palate rather than cosseting it. That's a chile con queso no-no.

A discriminating food professional of my acquaintance recently tried to work out the perfect chile con queso recipe for his establishment. He's a guy who haunts the farmers' markets, grows his own vegetables, drives hours to forage for raw milk. Let's call him Mr. Punctilious. Mr. P began with a natural-cheese, béchamel-based formula worked out by Lisa Fain, who writes the wonderful *Homesick Texan* blog and who contends that her recipe is as easy to make as if it used processed cheese. Using asadero and Chihuahua and cheddar and longhorn and goodness knows what else, Mr. P produced batch after batch of unsatisfactory queso. Finally, in despair, he turned to Land O' Lakes Extra Melt, a processed product that's widely used by Texas restaurants as an enchilada cheese. Bingo. Results good enough to satisfy his own palate and to serve at his place of business.

The fact that Mr. P is slightly embarrassed by his choice—reluctant to be identified—mirrors the conscientious Texas foodie's conflicted relationship with our funky chile con queso birthright. My advice, to Mr. P and others: Give it up. Embrace your inner infant. Find joy in the semireprehensible.

I certainly have. One of the first old-school chile con quesos I can remember wanting to wallow in—literally—was the proudly down-market version served forth at Fiesta Loma Linda, a profoundly old-fashioned Tex-Mex joint near my neighborhood on Houston's near East End. The molten dip arrived (as it does to this day) in a tan plastic cafeteria bowl, and it was escorted by a saucerful of pickled jalapeño slices and finely minced onions that seemed to have been sweated, they were so mild and sweet. I'd meet a couple of friends there at the end of a work week to commiserate, gossip, and chortle while attacking our bowl of queso so avidly we'd end up clashing our thin, crackly tortilla chips over the last few bites. It was a life-affirming group ritual, all that dipping repetitive and somehow comforting, that I held close long after they moved off to Baltimore and another world.

It wasn't the best chile con queso, maybe. But it was our chile con queso: customized with just enough savory onion and sharp hot jalapeño to balance mild dairy innocence with experience. That's the chile con queso dance, whether "experience" comes in the form of canned green chiles or more ambitious roasted fresh poblanos; via spicy canned Rotel tomatoes (that favored Texas party hostess's queso add-in) or diced fresh tomatoes and a hefty spoonful of salsa.

I've never been one for adding the taco meat, picadillo, or brisket that some restaurants tout as ingredients in their signature quesos. For me, meat muddles that soothing dairy message and sends the queso from the realm of mother's-milk liquid toward big-kid solid. But as someone who firmly believes chile con queso should be in a protected class of foodstuffs, immune to normal critical standards, it would be hypocritical for me to naysay these mutations.

I may flinch when I come across chile con queso recipes that call for such ingredients as Crisco, evaporated milk, Worcestershire sauce, or garlic powder. I may quail at the very thought of the famous chile con queso once served by Houston's Felix restaurant, a cupful of floury, roux-based sludge riddled with rivulets of grease. That Felix queso was much beloved by a close friend who misses it still and who rejoiced when the recipe was revived recently at the El Patio restaurant on Westheimer. I may not approve, but I understand.

In the end, we Texans love our chile con queso of choice with a fierce and childlike attachment that flouts reason. It is consolation in a cup, a sacrament conveyed on a triangle of crackly corn. And housed in its one-for-all bowl, on restaurant table and party buffet alike, chile con queso is one of the few communal food experiences left to us.

Long may it ooze, and drip, and make life better.

*Molly O'Neill, a contributing editor to* Saveur *magazine, is the author of five books, including the memoir* Mostly True: A Memoir of Family, Food, and Baseball. *For a decade, she was a reporter and food columnist for the* New York Times, *and her work has appeared in the* New Yorker *and the* Columbia Journalism Review. *This story comes from her latest cookbook,* One Big Table: A Portrait of American Cooking.

# The Ceremony

## Molly O'Neill

At the Day at the Docks Festival in Hatteras, a group of soft-spoken elders wearing bifocals and designer running suits were eager to talk about the fish they had caught, the fish they had cooked, and the fish they had eaten over the past eighty years on the Outer Banks of North Carolina. Their stories were dappled with references to "Mama," "Daddy," "the cook," "our girl." But when one of the women said, "But ole drum, now that just isn't right," the happy mood at the picnic changed.

Red drum is North Carolina's state saltwater fish. It is also called red-fish, channel bass, drum, and spot-tail, one of a big family of fish whose best-known members include black drum, croaker, kingfish, saltwater silver perch, white sea bass, and weakfish. Red drum that weighs less than ten pounds and is less than three years old is called redfish or puppy drum. Puppy drum is meaty and delicately flavored, and was the cheapest and most plentiful fish in the surf along the south Atlantic and Gulf coasts until Paul Prudhomme invented blackened redfish at his restaurant in New Orleans. Once it became famous, the cost of the fish jumped from pennies to dollars a pound, and within a decade, the wild stocks were seriously diminished.

Farmed versions helped fill the demand for smaller redfish. But genera-tions of Outer Bankers considered the older, bigger drums to be the real prize. The reason for this is unclear. Old drum is a big, tough, sinuous fish, fine for slow-cooked soups or stews but otherwise not great eating. The pas-sion for old drum may be historic. Or maybe it is born of the American belief that bigger is always better.

The fish generally weigh twenty to thirty pounds, but the largest on record (caught off Hatteras Island) tipped the scale at just over ninety-four. In 2007,

George W. Bush designated redfish a protected game fish and encouraged a ban on commercial harvest. To its aficionados, the president might as well have outlawed apple pie.

In the Outer Banks, people of a certain age speak longingly of old drum. Some are sad; others area angry; all considered eating the big old fish an inalienable right as well as an act of patriotism. Many have a Robin Hood tale of full moons and secluded coves and outrunning game wardens in order to bring "the old people" the fish they loved.

"We would like you to join us for The Ceremony," one courtly gentleman whispered. I didn't ask for details, but the following evening, as I approached his grand house, I wondered precisely what sort of "ceremony" this was. As I walked up to the back door, I heard muffled sounds not unlike the suck-giggle-shush noises that are sometimes overheard outside a room in which illegal substances are being smoked. Were the Elegant Elders up to no good?

Au contraire. "Welcome," whispered the Courtly Gentleman, who opened the door before I knocked. I stepped inside and an intense odor rolled over me. The place smelled like low tide and fried pig. The aroma became more pronounced as I followed my host through a long, darkened hallway toward a glowing doorway. The dining room was lit with at least 100 small candles. Dressed in evening attire, they were standing behind their chairs around the Chippendale banquet table looking as bright and expectant as they must have been at their first midnight cotillion. The chargers were silver, as were the eight pieces of flatware that flanked each place, and in the center of the table, a huge silver platter proudly held twelve thick white slabs of old drum. The platter was surrounded by bowls of boiled potatoes, chopped raw onion, chopped hard-cooked egg, and cubed and fried pork fatback. Six gravy boats contained hot grease; four silver castor sets held salt, pepper, and white vinegar. The precision of the table felt like an altar.

"I don't appreciate a society that outlaws my fish," murmured the Courtly Gentleman after helping me to my place near him at the head of the table. "Do we look like criminals? Should we have to worry about going to jail? Worry that our grandchildren would see our names in the paper? We're just a bunch of old geezers keeping The Ceremony alive."

The gentleman on my right leaned toward me and whispered: "His daddy had a speakeasy. That old acorn hasn't fallen far from the oak."

The scrupulously scripted ritual of eating old drum began. Each person placed two boiled potatoes on his or her plate and used the fork at the far left to mash it. The next fork in was used for flaking the fish over the potato. This deconstructed fish cake was then topped with raw onion, chopped egg, and a mound of cracklings. Finally, a river of pork grease was poured over the entire arrangement. Some people sprinkled vinegar on old drum; others used salt and pepper. When everyone had completed building his stack of fish, a short prayer of thanksgiving was offered.

It took about the same time to eat old drum as it does to boil it: 90 to 120 minutes.

After all the evidence of the crime had been cleared from the table and the chess pie and demitasse had been served, the Courtly Gentleman said, "The driver will take you home." When I reminded him that I had my car, he smiled patiently and said, "You should not operate heavy machinery after The Ceremony."

Jessica B. Harris is a food historian and a professor who lives in New York and New Orleans. This piece is adapted from her book High on the Hog: A Culinary Journey from Africa to America.

# In Sorrow's Kitchen

## Jessica B. Harris

Slavery's duration in the North did not equal its longevity in the South. During the colonial period, blacks made up 61 percent of the population of South Carolina and 31 percent of that of Georgia. But at the time of the American Revolution, fewer than 10 percent of the total population of enslaved in the United States lived in the North. Their numbers, however, continued to grow in the South. In 1680, slaves made up a tenth of the Southern population; by 1790, they made up a third of the population. Following the American Revolution, the slave population exploded in the South, and between 1790 and 1810 the population of enslaved almost doubled. By the late seventeenth century, however, attitudes were changing in the North. Slave labor, which had been largely involved in agriculture in the North, was being eliminated as inefficient in the rapidly industrializing area.

Vermont outlawed slavery in 1777. Pennsylvania banned it in 1780, and it was outlawed in Massachusetts in 1783. Gradual emancipation began in Rhode Island, a former leader in the slave trade, in 1784. New York State began to abolish slavery in 1799, although the process did not end until July 4, 1827. New Hampshire became the last of the Northern states to end enslavement, in 1857. The Southern states were left with the "peculiar institution" — an economic system that increasingly put them at odds with the world and with their former slaveholding countrymen in the North. The slave system, though, continued to grow and prosper in the South.

Most Americans today base their ideas of the antebellum South on images created in popular culture that have little to do with the realities of history. Despite a national tendency to generalize slaveholding into North and South, there was no monolithic South even in the antebellum period. The region was divided into upland and coastal, and then subdivided further into the Up South, the Carolinas and Georgia, the Deep South, and the Gulf South. The mountainous spine of the Appalachians further bisected the region and was an area in which slaveholding was minimal. Each area had a unique experience with enslavement. Our blue-versus-gray vision of slavery is further complicated by popular imagery of white-columned plantation houses manned by a flotilla of enslaved blacks hauling and toting and doing the bidding of Massa and Miz Ann. In fact, even in slaveholding areas, in many cases hard-pressed whites had only a few helpless slaves; and in more than a few cases, owners were apt to be working in the fields alongside their one or two slaves. Less than one-quarter of white Southerners held slaves, and half of those held fewer than five. Only 1 percent of Southerners owned more than one hundred, and a miniscule number owned more than five hundred and had the large spreads that we imagine; they lived mainly in South Carolina, Georgia, and Louisiana. In 1860, the average number of slaves residing together was about ten. These realities, though, in no way mitigate the horror of enslavement. "Plantation," in most cases in the South, was just a fancy word for the farm on which slaves toiled for their masters.

The work done by the enslaved was mainly agricultural and varied from locale to locale. Different crops—tobacco, rice, indigo, cotton, and sugar—produced different working environments, and the enslaveds' daily tasks and degree of autonomy varied from crop to crop. In Virginia and the Upper South the crop tended to be tobacco or the Tidewater triad of corn, wheat, and tobacco. Coastal South Carolina and Georgia had rice-based economies where slaves had a particular task to perform, and once it was completed, their time was their own. As slavery progressed from North to South and onward toward the West, it became even more arduous. J. S. Buckingham, an Englishman who journeyed through the slave states of the South in 1839, recounted,

> All the slaves have a great horror of being sent to the south or the
> west,—for the farther they go in either of these directions, the
> harder they are worked, and the worse they are used.

The cotton kingdoms of the Deep South were the ones that have provided us with most of our mental images. The sugar empires of the Gulf Coast offered different systems based on the Caribbean models, in which life was cheap and the enslaved were often simply worked to death then replaced. Whatever the crop or the system, all were horrific in that the enslaved, whether under a beneficent or a harsh master, had no control over their destinies. A gambling debt to be paid, a wedding in the master's family, a bequest given, or something as simple as an argument or a whim could result in a slave family being broken up forever.

Slaves, whatever their number in a household, were omnipresent, and they were dependent on their master for the essentials of life: housing, clothing, and especially food. Throughout the period of enslavement, discussion raged about how to feed the slaves. As the agricultural backbone of the region, the slaves not only produced the cash crops; they also were tasked with growing and processing most of the food that was consumed by all on the plantations, whether white or black. Feeding the enslaved, however, had of necessity to be an economically viable process. Rations had to be sufficiently nourishing to allow the enslaved to perform their tasks but could not be so lavish as to be unprofitable. In some cases, however, rations were so parsimonious as to be tantamount to starvation. On plantations of some size, there were basically two different systems of food distribution: one in which the enslaved were fed from a centralized kitchen somewhere on the plantation, and another wherein the enslaved were given their rations on a schedule and allowed to prepare them in their own cabins or within whatever communities they might have created for themselves. The former system was more common in the early years of enslavement, when the enslaved were often housed in dormitories and lived communally. Distributing rations became more common as the slave populations grew.

In almost all cases, the enslaved supplemented their rations by hunting and trapping. The nocturnal habits of the opossum made it a prime target for the enslaved, who had to hunt after the work of their daylight hours. There was also fishing for catfish, porgies, mullet, and other denizens of the creeks and rivers to supplement the rations. Foraging in nearby woods allowed the enslaved to add wild greens like watercress to their diets, as well as such items as ramps, chives, and wild garlic. In more than a few cases, there was also pilfering and poaching from their master or the masters of others. Theft from masters' fields was so prevalent that the enslaved on one Mississippi plantation even created a song about it.

> Some folks say dat a nigger won't steal,
> I caught two in my own corn field,
> one had a bushel,
> one had a peck
> an' one had rosenears [roasting ears]
> strung round his neck.

On some plantations that followed a more Caribbean model, the slaves were given provision grounds to raise their own crops, including vegetables like okra, chili peppers, and eggplant, which harked back to an African past. The slave gardeners were so successful that they occasionally sold produce back to their masters. At Monticello, Jefferson purchased items from his slaves and duly noted them down in his account books. Slave gardeners raised plants that they liked to eat and items they knew would sell, so it is telling to find on the listings of things grown in the provision grounds such crops as watermelon, cabbage, and greens—foods that even today remain totemic in the cooking of African Americans. They also raised cucumbers, white potatoes, and squash. Gardening was done in the little free time that the enslaved had after their daily work of running the plantation had been completed. This free time was usually on Sunday—a day of little work—or on weekdays after the sun went down. The oral history record suggests that animal fat and tallow were burned in old iron cooking pots to illuminate the gardens and enable the slaves to work after their day's labor. Alternately, they worked by the light of the moon. The quest for food, and enough of it, was a daily obsession for many of the enslaved, if the numerous mentions of food and eating found in the slave narratives of the antebellum period are to be believed. Slave rations were never fixed by national law in the United States, as they were in the French territories, where the Code Noir (Black Code) of 1685 legislated the amount of cassava meal, beef, or fish to be given to all adult slaves over eighteen years of age. The lack of such uniformity in the United States meant that amounts were often established by individuals who were more interested in controlling costs than providing nourishment. George Washington, deemed a benign if not beneficent master, fed his slaves adequately. However, during the 1790s, after the Revolution, he reduced their rations and estimated that eleven pounds of corn, two pounds of fish, and a pound and a half of meat were sufficient weekly rations for each of the twenty-three slaves on one of his farms. Not a lot when compared with those rations remembered by John Thompson, who had been enslaved on a plantation in Maryland: "The provision for each slave, per week, was a peck of corn, two dozens of herrings, and about four pounds of meat."

Even those amounts were lowered by the antebellum period on some plantations. James W. C. Pennington, enslaved to a wheat planter in Washington County, on Maryland's western shore, gave a more detailed account of his rations in his 1849 narrative:

> The slaves are generally fed upon salt pork, herrings, and Indian corn.
> The manner of dealing it out to them is as follows—
> Each working man, on Monday morning goes to the cellar of the master where the provisions are kept, and where the

overseer takes this stand with someone to assist him, when he, with a pair of steel yards, weighs out to every man the amount of three-and-a-half pounds to last him till the ensuing Monday—allowing him just half a pound per day. Once in a few weeks, a change is made, by which, instead of the three-and-a-half-pounds of pork, each man receives twelve herrings allowing two a day. The only bread kind the slaves have is that made of Indian meal. In some of the low counties, the masters usually have to give their slaves the corn by the ear; and they have to grind it for themselves by night at hand-mills. But my master had a quantity sent to the grist mill at a time, to be ground into coarse meal, and kept in a large chest in his cellar, where the woman who cooked for the boys could get it daily. This was baked into large loaves called "steel poun bread." Sometime as a change it was made into "Johnny Cake," and then at others into mush.

The slaves had no butter, coffee, tea, or sugar; occasionally they were allowed milk, but not statedly; the only exception to this statement was "harvest provisions." In harvest, when cutting the grain, which lasted for two to three weeks in the heat of summer, they were allowed some fresh meat, rice, sugar, and coffee; also their allowance of whiskey.

Solomon Northup, a free black who had been illegally captured in New York City and sold in the South in 1841, bitterly recalled that all that was allowed the slaves on the Louisiana plantation where he was enslaved for twelve years was

corn and bacon, which is given out at the corn-crib and smokehouse every Sunday morning. Each one receives, as his weekly allowance, three and a half pounds of bacon, and corn enough to make a peck of meal. This is all—no tea, coffee, sugar and with the exception of a very scanty sprinkling now and then, no salt. I can say from a ten year's residence with Master Epps, that no slave of his is ever likely to suffer from the gout, superinduced by excessive high living.

Unlike Pennington's plantation, where the master distributed cornmeal already ground, on the Epps plantation, where Northup was enslaved, the corn was given by the ear. So the slaves had to process it, shell it, and grind it into meal on their own time, which added to their already overburdened schedules. Northup's account gives a sense of the never-ending, bone-numbing labor slaves did day in and day out. He notes that after the work in the fields was over, the slaves still had to attend to their other chores—feeding the animals, cutting wood, and the like—before they could finally go to their own cabins to build their own fire, grind the corn, and then prepare their meager suppers as well as the midday meal to take to the fields the next day. This midday meal was usually a form of corn ash cake with bacon. By the time all this was accomplished, he states simply, "it is usually midnight." The dreaded horn or the equally hated bell, depending on the plantation, rang before daybreak, calling them back to the fields for another day's toil. On the Epps plantation and many others, being caught in the quarters after daybreak was cause for flogging.

The midday meal was often taken to the fields and eaten there or was distributed by others so the rhythm of fieldwork wasn't interrupted. Often superannuated slaves who could no longer do hard labor were selected to distribute meals. John Brown, who had been a slave in Virginia in the first half of the nineteenth century, noted that the first full meal at the plantation on which he was enslaved was served in the field at noon after the cotton was weighed. It was a soup made from cornmeal and potatoes, called "lob-lolly" or "stirt-about." A pint of it was served in a tin pan that each slave carried at his waist, and, as Brown remembered, "the distribution and disposal of the mess did not take long."

Young children were usually fed communally. They were given a mash of cornmeal and milk in a communal kitchen by women who were too old or too infirm to be otherwise useful. Fannie Moore of South Carolina remembered the midday meal in a 1930s account recorded by the Works Progress Administration (WPA):

> My granny cooked for us chillums, while our mammy away in the fiel'. Dey warn't much cookin' to do. Jes' make co'n pone an' bring in de milk. She hab a big bowl wif enough wooden spoons tro go 'roun'. She put milk in de bowl an' break it [the cornbread] up. Den she put de bowl in the middle of de flo' an all de chilluln grab a spoon.

Slave narratives generally agree that the location for eating evening meals was the slave quarters. Many recalled that after the labor on the plantation was finished, the yard that was common ground in the quarters would begin to hum with life as individuals and families began to prepare evening meals, socialized, and savored what few minutes of private time they had. The chimneys in the slave cabins, although frequently made of daub and wattle and not stone, served for heating and cooking, which was done indoors in the winter when fires were necessary for warmth. In the summer, when the additional heat would be oppressive, cooking was done outdoors over a fire of some sort in the plantation yard.

Fanny Kemble was the reluctant mistress of a Southern plantation. A British actress, she met and married Pearce Mease Butler, scion of an illustrious South Carolina family with plantations in the Sea Islands, following a successful American tour. Her visit to the plantations and the journal that she kept during her almost fifteen-week stay offers a view of the meals of the enslaved from the other side of the social spectrum. The meals on her plantation were distributed from a communal kitchen.

> The second meal in the day is at night, after their labor is over, having worked, at the *very least*, six hours without intermission of rest or refreshment since their noonday meal (properly so-called, for 'tis *meal* and nothing else). Those that I passed today sitting on their doorsteps, or on the ground round them eating were the people employed at the mill and threshing floor. As these are near to the settlement, they had time to get their food from the cookshop. Chairs, tables, plates, knives, forks, they had none; they sat, as I said, on the earth or doorsteps, and ate either out of their little cedar tubs or in an iron pot, some few with broken spoons, more with pieces of wood, and all the children with their fingers. A more complete sample of savage feeding I never beheld.

All the enslaved were not in the miserable conditions Kemble describes. On some plantations, they were assigned their own tin pans or were able to barter for wooden utensils. Archaeologists began to look intensely at the remains of slave quarters for the first time in the 1960s, and they have been a remarkable source of information. In the slave quarters at Mount Vernon they have found items ranging from white and brown glazed stoneware to Chinese porcelain to Rhenish stoneware that must have come from the Big House—possibly they'd been cracked or broken. Of the pieces found, slipware and white salt-glazed stoneware seem to predominate, but the most intriguing sherds are those called colonoware. These pieces of hand-thrown, low-fired, unglazed earthenware were once thought to be Native American pottery, but increasingly evidence has pointed to the creation of colonoware by African American potters as well. More interesting, the African American forms of colonoware seem to resemble pottery still made in parts of Western Africa and used in cooking and serving food there. Many of the pieces found in both Virginia and South Carolina are from bowls that would have been used to hold the African-inspired one-pot soupy stews and porridge-like mashes that were the enslaveds' daily fare.

The cooking of the slave yard inadvertently allowed the enslaved to maintain an African tradition of one-pot meals sopped with starches and stews of leafy greens seasoned with smoked or pickled ingredients. Ingenuity was called upon to relieve the forced monotony of the slave diet and inspired whatever creativity could be wrung from a peck of corn and three pounds of salt pork. Hunting by slave women and men after their hours of plantation labor allowed them to add new meats such as possum, turkey, raccoon, and rabbit to the pot.

Foraging and gardening in provision grounds produced greens and food-stuffs with the taste of Africa, like okra, eggplant, and chilies. The culinary monotony would change only at holiday time, most notably at Christmas, and occasionally at family weddings and harvest time. Then all but the most miserly master allowed the enslaved some modicum of feasting. Solomon Northup writes:

> The table is spread in the open air, and loaded with varieties of meat and piles of vegetables. Bacon and cornmeal at such times are dispensed with. Sometimes cooking is performed in the kitchen on the plantation, at others in the shade of wide branch-ing trees. In the latter case, a ditch is dug in the ground, and wood laid and burned until it is filled with glowing coals, over which chickens, ducks, turkeys, pigs, and not unfrequently the body of an entire wild ox, are roasted. They are furnished also with flour, of which biscuits are made, and often with peach and other preserves, with tarts, and every manner and description of pies . . . Only the slave who has lived all the years on his scanty allowance of meal and bacon, can appreciate such suppers. White people in great numbers assemble to witness the gastronomical enjoyments.

The feasting was followed by general merriment including dances, and on some plantations the enslaved were given hard cider or whiskey as well.

Harriet Jacobs, the first female slave to write a narrative, in 1858, describes the Johnkannus, bands of slaves masquerading in rags who played music on an instrument known as a "gumbo box." In an African parallel to European caroling, they would go from plantation to plantation, begging for Christmas donations, which they received in the form of money or liquor.

Christmas is a day of feasting, both white and colored people. Slaves who are lucky to have a few shillings, are sure to spend them for good eating; and many a turkey or pig is captured without saying, "By your leave, sir." Those who cannot obtain these, cook a 'possum, or a raccoon, from which savory dishes can be made. My grandmother raised poultry and pigs for sale; and it was her established custom to have both a turkey and a pig roasted for Christmas dinner.

Other occasions of relative feasting for the enslaved were harvest time or corn-shucking time. At these times and generally when there were guests or celebrations like birthdays, weddings, or other large gatherings at the Big House, there might be barbecues. The cooks for these events were black men, who used their talents to create the iconic Afro-Southern dish.

Night befo' dem barbecues, I used to stay up all night a-cooking and basting de meats with barbecue sass. It was made of vinegar, black and red pepper, salt, butter, a little sage, coriander, basil, onion, and garlic. Some folks drop a little sugar in it. On a long pronged stick, I wraps a soft rag or cotton for a swab, and all de night long, I swabs de meat til it drip into de fire. Dem drippings change de smoke into seasoned fumes dat smoke de meat. We turn de meat over and swab it dat way allnight long till it ooze seasoning and bake all through.

The Christmas holiday, which might last as long as a week, was a welcome respite. When the holidays were over and the festivities ended, it was back to the work routine of up before the dawn bell, back after dusk, and meals that rang in all possible changes on monotonous rations of corn and hog with whatever additions could be found, foraged, or filched. The world of plenty, however, was never far away. It existed in the Big House, where the master and his guests dined nightly on foods raised, processed, prepared, served, and cleaned up by the enslaved. The Big House kitchen was where the tastes of Africa truly began to colonize those of Europe.

The Big House kitchen was one of the centers of power during the antebellum period in the South; from it, the cook, solo or in conjunction with the mistress of the house, fed the master's family and often oversaw the feeding of all on the plantation. At some of the loftier plantations there could be twenty or more guests to dinner every evening. By the early eighteenth century, it had become custom in the South for the kitchens at plantation houses to be placed in a building that was separate from the main house. John Michael Vlach, a specialist in the architecture of the Southern plantation, suggests that "the detached kitchen was an important emblem of hardening social boundaries and the everyday society created by slaveholders that increasingly demanded clearer definition of status, position, and authority." Other reasons were more practical. If the kitchen was removed from the house, any kitchen fire would not endanger the Big House complex.

The Big House kitchens were the epicenter of food preparation on the plantation. They were equipped with massive hearths, complete with turning spits and an array of pots and pans and the people to tend them. Mariah Robinson, who must have had intimate knowledge of hearth cooking, recalled these kitchens in the 1930s WPA slave narratives:

> Dere wuzn't any stoves long slavery times. And de chimbleys
> wuz made special to cook an'warm by dem. De built dem out of
> rock or stick an'dirt. Ledges wuz lef' on each side an' a long heavy
> green pole wuz put 'cross from one ledge to another. Dis wuz
> high up in the chimbley to keep it from burning in de flames.
> On dis rod wuz hooks and chains to hang pots an' things to
> cook with. Dey call dese pot hooks, pot hangers, pot claws, and
> crooks. Dey wuz hung at different lengths so as to cook hot or jes
> warm. Effen dey wuzn't careful, dis long log would burn through
> an' spill everything an' bend or break de cooking vessels. Some-
> times dey would burn a person when dey spilled.
>
> Some of the pots and kettles had legs an' de skillets an' sauce
> pans had slim legs, so dat day could be placed wid deir food
> on little beds of coals which had been raked to one side of the
> hearth. Dere was a trivet to set skillets and pots on over the coals.
> Dese trivets had [three] legs, some shot to put de pot right on de
> fire to cook quick, an' some had long legs so dat de food would
> jes keep warm and not cook much.

The hearth cooking that went on in these kitchens was an arduous endeavor punctuated by lifting heavy cast-iron pots and spiders, bending and arranging and maintaining flame levels, and hauling buckets of ash and used charcoal. In addition, there was always the omnipresent fear that the women's long skirts would sweep up a spark and catch fire. All this was accomplished under the watchful eye of the mistress, who, on any plantation of size, did none of the heavy lifting.

Usually, this world was presided over by a slave cook, who was under the direction of the mistress and in charge of all food preparation. The Big

House slave cook was a trusted individual who was given the allowance of ingredients for the meals to prepare and made responsible not only for their preparation but also for overseeing the folks required to do it. The role was one of favor, as house servants occasionally had access to more food. However, the position of Big House cook as one to be envied was not always the case, as remembered by Harriet Jacobs. She recalled the eagle eye with which her mistress, the dyspeptic and aptly named Mrs. Flint, watched over her provisions. The raw materials that were allotted to her grandmother for the preparations of the household's food were "weighed out by the pound and ounce, three times a day. I can assure you she gave them no chance to eat wheatbread from her flour barrel. She knew how many biscuits a quart of flour would make, and exactly what size they ought to be." Jacobs reminded that Mrs. Flint would "station herself in the kitchen and wait till [the meal] was dished, and then spit in all the kettles and pans that had been used for cooking. She did this to prevent the cook and her children from eking out their meager fare with the remains of gravy and other scrapings." Other narratives confirmed that such mean-spiritedness on the part of a mistress was not an isolated act.

The Big House cooks wielded a fair amount of power. They were usually women, except on some very large plantations. (In southern Louisiana near New Orleans, however, there was a Gallic tendency to give the word *chef* a masculine article and more male chefs were found there.) They ruled their domains with iron discipline and often garnered praise for their culinary expertise from white visitors. R. Q. Mallard of Georgia wrote of one plantation where "French cooks are completely outdistanced in the production of wholesome, dainty and appetizing food; for if there is any one thing for which the African female intellect has a natural genius, it is for cooking." Male or female, the results that came from Big House kitchens were overwhelmingly praised by whites. Stereotypes of the time suggested that, to whites, blacks were born cooks, and several even suggested that it was a racial talent. Louisianan Charles Gayarré echoed the prevailing sentiment of the time in an article in an 1880 issue of *Harper's* magazine: "The Negro is a born cook. He could neither read nor write, and therefore he could not learn from books. He was simply inspired; the god of the spit and the saucepan had breathed into him; that was enough." Throughout the period of enslavement, black cooks gradually had their way with their masters' palates, and dishes that had the mark of the cabin and of Africa, whether through ingredients or method, became an established part of the Southern culinary lexicon.

In 1824, when Mary Randolph published *The Virginia House-wife*, she was certainly unaware that the ingredients that she called for, such as field

peas, eggplant, and okra, arrived in this country from the African continent. Yet in her book there are recipes aplenty using what must have been
new ingredients. They include fried eggplant, a field pea (black-eyed pea)
cake fried in lard and garnished with thin bits of bacon, and a simple dish
of boiled okra called "Gumbs—A West India Dish," which she pronounces
"very nutricious [sic] and easy to the digestion." Her "ochra" soup—requiring okra, onions, lima beans, squash, chicken (or veal knuckle), bacon, and
peeled tomatoes and thickened with a flour and butter roux—could pass for
a form of chicken andouille gumbo anywhere in southern Louisiana. She
even suggests it be served with an accompaniment of boiled rice. There's
also a recipe for young greens. All are culinary refinements of dishes that
certainly came from the slave quarters and were transformed in the hands
of Big House cooks.

The 1839 *Kentucky Housewife*, by Lettice Byran, continues the pattern and
includes a recipe for boiled field peas to be eaten with baked or boiled pork.
There is also one for stewed eggplant that seems to be a variant of Randolph's
recipe and an early recipe for watermelon-rind pickles. There is another okra
soup recipe; this one calling for beef, veal, or chicken broth as a base into
which thinly sliced okra and tomatoes are placed. The whole is heated, and
when ready, it is sieved and seasoned with cayenne pepper. Finally it's served
over toast in a tureen.

Sarah Rutledge's 1847 *The Carolina Housewife* includes another of the
seemingly ubiquitous okra soups. This one, though, is roux-less and similar
to the roux-less Charleston gumbo that is still served today. A groundnut
soup seasoned with a "seed pepper" and a bennie soup prepared from sesame seeds using the same method also have a decidedly African feel. Rutledge's recipes are wider ranging than the other two collections and include
dishes like groundnut cheesecakes, a confection of ground peanuts and puff
pastry topped with grated sugar. There's a Guinea squash recipe for baked
eggplant, a New Orleans gumbo thickened with filé, and a Seminole soup of
squirrel and hickory nuts served with filé, or the tender top of a pine tree,
which "gives a very aromatic flavor to the soup." The book offers the first
hints of the elaborate rice kitchen that had been developed in the Lowcountry under the watchful eye of the African Big House cooks who had experience with the grain. There is also a selection of recipes for rice cakes, rice
breads, rice confections, and other dishes.

The sieved-okra soup of *The Kentucky Housewife*, the delicate roux-less
gumbo of *The Carolina Housewife*, and the simple boiled okra of *The Virginia House-wife* all point to the ubiquity of okra dishes on the developing
Southern table. Others calling for ingredients such as field peas, benne (ses-

ame), greens, and eggplant hint at a cross-pollination of culinary cultures. These dishes and others like them most certainly made an appearance in other less-sophisticated guises in the quarters before gracing the masters' tables. Seasonings changed in African hands as well, and Southerners developed a taste for more highly seasoned food, as indicated by the frequent use of "seed pepper" and cayenne. The Big House kitchens were slowly having Africa's way with the tastebuds of the South in what historian Eugene Genovese called "the culinary despotism of the slave cabin over the Big House." The Africanizing of the Southern palate outlasted the reign of Baron Tobacco, King Cotton, and Empress Sugar and defined the taste of the American South.

*This observation of Maryland in the 1830s, written by the ex-slave, writer, editor, and abolitionist Frederick Douglass, was reprinted in the 2011 food issue of Lapham's Quarterly.*

# Blood-Bought Luxuries

## Frederick Douglass

As a general rule, slaves do not come to the quarters for either breakfast or dinner but take their "ash cake" with them and eat it in the field. This was so on the home plantation, probably, because the distance from the quarter to the field was sometimes two and even three miles.

The dinner of the slaves consisted of a huge piece of ash cake and a small piece of pork, or two salt herrings. Not having ovens, nor any suitable cooking utensils, the slaves mixed their meal with a little water to such thickness that a spoon would stand erect in it, and after the wood had burned away to coals and ashes, they would place the dough between oak leaves and lay it carefully in the ashes, completely covering it—hence the bread is called ash cake. The surface of this peculiar bread is covered with ashes to the depth of a sixteenth part of an inch, and the ashes, certainly, do not make it very grateful to the teeth nor render it very palatable. The bran, or coarse part of the meal, is baked with the fine, and bright scales run through the bread. This bread, with its ashes and bran, would disgust and choke a Northern man, but it is quite liked by the slaves. They eat it with avidity and are more concerned about the quantity than about the quality. They are far too scantily provided for and are worked too steadily to be much concerned for the quality of their food.

The close-fisted stinginess that fed the poor slave on coarse cornmeal and tainted meat, that clothed him in crashy tow linen and hurried him on to toil through the field in all weathers—with wind and rain beating through his tattered garments—that scarcely gave even the young slave mother time to nurse her hungry infant in the fence corner, wholly vanishes on approaching the sacred precincts of the great house, the home of the Lloyds. There the scriptural phrase finds an exact illustration: the highly favored inmates of this mansion are literally arrayed "in purple and fine linen" and fare sumptuously every day! The table groans under the heavy and blood-bought luxuries gathered with painstaking care, at home and abroad. Fields, forests, rivers, and seas, are made tributary here. Immense wealth and its lavish expenditure fill the great house with all that can please the eye, or tempt the taste. Here appetite, not food, is the great desideratum. Fish, flesh, and fowl are here in profusion. Chickens of all breeds, ducks of all kinds, wild and tame, the common and the huge Muscovite. The graceful swan, the mongrels, the black-necked wild goose; partridges, quails, pheasants, and pigeons. Beef, veal, mutton, and venison of the most select kinds and quality roll bounteously to this grand consumer. The teeming riches of the Chesapeake Bay, its rock, perch, drums, crocus, trout, oysters, crabs, and terrapin are drawn hither to adorn the glittering table of the great house. The dairy, too, probably the finest on the Eastern Shore of Maryland—supplied by cattle of the best English stock, imported for the purpose—pours its rich donations of fragrant cheese, golden butter, and delicious cream to heighten the attraction of the gorgeous, unending round of feasting. Nor are the fruits of the earth forgotten or neglected. The tender asparagus, the succulent celery, and the delicate cauliflower; eggplants, beets, lettuce, parsnips, peas, and French beans, early and late; radishes, cantaloupes, melons of all kinds; the fruits and flowers of all climes and of all descriptions, from the hardy apple of the North to the lemon and orange of the South, culminated at this point. Baltimore-gathered figs, raisins, almonds, and juicy grapes from Spain. Wines and brandies from France, teas of various flavor from China, and rich, aromatic coffee from Java all conspired to swell the tide of high life, where pride and indolence rolled and lounged in magnificence and satiety.

*Lonnée Hamilton is a writer and editor who lives in Pasadena, California. This story originally appeared in* Saveur.

# Green Goddess
## Why We Love Collard Greens

### Lonnée Hamilton

There were some soul food dishes that my family did not eat. Chitlins were spoken of in hushed, horrified tones. Pig's feet? No, thank you. We left those back at the plantation. But collard greens were different. Stewed in a cauldron, the big, tough-looking leaves become wonderful and delicious, tender and emotional.

When I was growing up in Pasadena, California, my mother cooked collard greens once a month or so. The dish was a departure from our mainstream American diet, which consisted largely of the convenience foods that so many people ate in the 1970s: Tater Tots, frozen vegetables, and Chung King–brand Chinese food. But collards were a family recipe. My grandparents had left Louisiana in the 1930s to escape segregation and Jim Crow, and while they didn't talk much about life the South, we did hear a lot about the food. My Nana told me that back when she was a little girl in Minden, Louisiana, a small town outside of Shreveport, her aunt Athelene had a big farm. They would go out and pick vegetables from the field for their dinner, including what Nana called "tree collards." "Most people, you would go to their house and you'd see these big stalks of greens," she told me recently. "The stalk would be about six feet tall."

When I was young, Mom showed me how to clean the leaves—which wasn't a delicate activity; they held a good deal of sand and grit. Then she would braise them in a stockpot over low heat, and the broad, leathery greens would take on a silky, sleek texture. When they were ready, I would break up corn bread into pieces and mix it in. The bitterness of the greens and the sweetness of the bread combined to make an earthy, fragrant stew.

After I left home, collards followed me. In my college days at Berkeley, I worked as a waitress at the Blue Nile, an Ethiopian restaurant, where one of the most requested dishes was *ye'abesha gomen*, collard greens stewed with a spiced butter called *nit'r qibe*, eaten with torn-off pieces of *injera* flat bread. A stint in a Brazilian restaurant introduced me to that country's staple collard dish: *sopa de fubá*, a savory porridge threaded with collards and thick with cornmeal and sausage. Once I had my own family, I started to cook collards for my children. I learned that the robust leaves were just as delicious chopped into ribbons and quickly sautéed with olive oil, yielding a dish that was as crisp and brightly colored as my mother's was soft and subdued. The versatility of the greens, and the many preparations I'd encountered, led me to wonder about collards' origins. I'd always considered them the birthright of the American South, but where had they actually come from?

Some say the connection to collards is hardwired in black people because the plant helped us survive slavery times. For slaves, meat was often a luxury, rationed out in stingy portions by their owners. Greens, when cooked with a smoked ham hock, took on the richness of the meat. The pork would fall off the bone, its taste imparted to the potlikker—the nutritious broth created by stewing the collards that replenished the body after a long day of labor in the fields. From deprivation came something delicious.

The humble profile of collard greens in America and the affinity slaves had for them have led to a misconception that Africans brought them to the New World. The plant, a non-heading cabbage—which means that its leaves are loosely gathered, rather than tightly bound—is most likely native to southern Europe, where it has been cultivated for thousands of years. Genetically, it is more closely related to cabbage than it is to kale, though all are part of the vegetable species known as *Brassica oleracea*, which also includes cauliflower, kohlrabi, and Brussels sprouts. The ancient Greeks and Romans grew kale and collards, making no distinction between the two. The term that described them both, "coles," appeared in European writing as far back as the first century. In the Americas, the earliest reference to "coleworts," the Anglo-Saxon word for cabbage plants that was the precursor to *collards*, dates to 1669.

While Africans did not introduce collards to the New World, they did bring the technique that produces the potlikker. "It's the drinking of the potlikker that is African in origin," explains Jessica B. Harris, author of the cookbook *Iron Pots & Wooden Spoons: Africa's Gift to New World Cooking*. I spoke to my grandmother, who remembers the practice from her own childhood. "In the olden days, they used to get the juice from the greens and give it to the babies," she told me. "They'd say that all your vitamins were in the potlikker." I'd known the term when I was young, but it had seemed outdated and quaint. I hadn't realized its importance.

Back in the days of slavery, and again during the Great Depression, many families made it through tough times by eating greens grown in a back-yard collard patch. Collards' hardscrabble hardiness probably explains why they are associated with good luck. Southern tradition holds that a New Year's Day meal of collard greens and black-eyed peas will bring prosperity throughout the year. The green leaves are said to represent dollar bills, and the peas coins.

Of course, in the South, collards are revered by blacks and whites alike, and the plant is one of the most widely grown crops in the region. It's there that you find a good assortment of collards, too, as many farmers grow and sell heirloom varieties, some with thinner ribs, others with more-ruffled leaves. Many collards lovers believe that the best time to eat them is in winter, right after the first frost, when the leaves are at their sweetest.

Nowadays, I use collards every which way at home: I make salads out of the baby leaves, when I can find them; I sauté them; I cook them in soups and stews. It's mostly on the holidays that we cook them the traditional Southern way. At Thanksgiving, my family congregates in the Las Vegas house owned by Nana and my aunt Carol. Collards cooking duty alternates between my relatives. Each person's recipe is slightly different, but no matter who is responsible, the greens are always tender, with a bit of smoked ham hock and some onion.

Thanksgiving in Las Vegas seemed unusual to me at first, but the combination of family, good food, and Wheel of Fortune slots at the Suncoast is hard to beat. After all, collards are supposed to bring good luck. I think I'll have another bowl.

*Wright Thompson is a senior writer for ESPN.com. He lives in Oxford, Mississippi.*

# The Fatback Collective

## Wright Thompson

Before a man with one leg got women to take their shirts off while he poured liquor into their mouths via an ice luge; before the wild-eyed guy who provides the pigs to the French Laundry walked around the party slipping packages in people's hands, which at least two of us thought were 8-balls of cocaine but turned out to be bacon; before Donald Link's boudin for lunch and John Currence's andouille for happy hour and Sean Brock's soft-shell crab for dinner; before we waited to hear if we'd made the finals of the Memphis in May World Championship Barbecue Cooking Contest; before the revolutionary act of creating an all-star team that included four James Beard award–winning chefs, three old-school Southern pit masters, and one boozehound writer; before any of that, there was a pretentious but earnest idea: Could we rescue a barbecue contest, and maybe even barbecue itself, from a crushing sameness?

The line was drawn. On one side, us: a cooking team called the Fatback Collective, organized by barbecue industrialist Nick Pihakis, who founded the Jim 'N Nick's Bar-B-Q chain of restaurants. On the other, Memphis and its world-famous barbecue contest, entering its thirty-fourth year. Now, Memphis in May is many things: a place for Parrotheads to gather between nautical-pun tours, a grown-up frat party with a hundred thousand pledges, a place where friends commune over a smoking pig, and, maybe most important, a driver of where our barbecue culture will go. Here's what it isn't: a reflection of where our barbecue has been. We wanted to turn back the clock.

Maybe that's silly. Maybe that's an idea fueled by ten cases of whiskey and two thousand Jell-O shots, but from the belly of the beast, surrounded by what many of us consider to be the enemy of authentic barbecue—lean pigs, tricked out with injections, cooked not as a reflection of a family or place, not as a connection to our vanishing past, but, rather, gamed to the strange tastes of the Memphis judges—we all realized the mission of the Fatback Collective: redemption.

Redemption and about seventeen thousand calories a day, most of them liquid.


## READY, SET, STRIP

It all starts with a screaming buzz saw and the smell of burning pig bone.

A hog is splayed out, gutted, with a half dozen hands reaching inside its carcass. Pat Martin, a Nashville pit master, revs the blade and digs into the backbone. Pig shrapnel flies around the tent.

When the job is done, the truly heartbreaking part begins, trimming out pounds of glorious, expensive, and carefully cultivated fat. Our team is consulting with a former grand champion, someone who is gracefully helping us understand the intractable customs of Memphis in May. He points at the thick layers of white.

The chefs look at each other, then at the pig. Reluctantly, they start stripping. Every so often, they'll make eye contact with each other and shake their heads. Someone mutters. Sean stands to the left of the pig, and Donald on the right, each cutting back ribs to expose more shoulder meat. A pile of fat forms on the table.

"Too much," says Ryan Prewitt, the chef de cuisine at Herbsaint in New Orleans.

Stephen Stryjewski, the chef at Cochon who won his Beard award just four days ago, asks the competition expert once more if he's *sure*.

"They don't want to see that marbling?" he asks.

"You don't find that in other hogs," the former grand champion says. "Technically, they don't want to see that."

"That's so one hundred and eighty degrees to what I do every day," Stephen says.

Donald, the mind behind Cochon and Herbsaint, watches in silence. This is what he's thinking: *ARRRGH!* I'm a little stunned. There are all these Beard winners with their hands in the hog, but something is being lost in translation. Amateurs wrestle food into submission, but chefs are more like ushers. Their job is to cook food that stays true to the essence of the ingredients. The job of a Memphis in May contestant is to deliver what the judges want, and, more important, to stay away from things they don't. Here, as best as I can tell, are some of the things the judges don't like:

1. Fat
2. Spice
3. Pork that tastes like pork, as opposed to pork that tastes like it got pistol-whipped by MSG and sugar
4. Puppies

## GAMING THE SYSTEM

The more I learn, the more I realize that winning this thing has very little to do with great barbecue and more to do with anticipating the judges. They like sweet. They don't like spice. They like tenderloin. They don't like belly. On and on. So competitors study past winners, then go Mr. Wizard on the pigs. They fill the cavity with bricks of cold butter. They pack iced pillowcases around their tenderloins to stop the cooking. Some pigs are souped up with culinary nitrous oxide: fat-laden injections.

This isn't happening in a vacuum. These traveling cooking teams are the face of Southern barbecue. Not the guys, like the pit masters on our team, who cook pigs three hundred days a year. The most wonderful thing about barbecue has always been its regional differences. Each pig told a story. Rodney Scott uses wood he chops himself. Pat Martin was born in Mississippi but worked as a bond trader in Charlotte before realizing his calling, and his Beach Road 12 sauce, with the Carolina tang and a touch of the Memphis sweet, is a reflection of his own journey to the pit. Barbecue changes from town to town, an entire style morphing at the Tennessee River, or at the Piedmont, or when you sweep down onto Highway 61 from Memphis to Clarksdale, Mississippi. Memphis in May, the most important barbecue event in the world, rewards homogeny. It encourages the worst in 'cue while punishing the best and it reflects a trend our team wants to stop. If you live in the South, as I do, maybe you've noticed how hard it's becoming to find a good, simple barbecue sandwich. Real barbecue is dying as competition barbecue is rewarding smoke and mirrors. These things cannot be unrelated.

So while we do cut away some of the fat, more fat than the chefs would have liked, there is still plenty left on the hog. I've never seen pigs like this (we're putting two on the coals). It's marbled, laced with thin lines of fat. It looks like a rib eye steak. There are fewer than a thousand Mangalitsas in North America, and this is the first time, to the best of everyone's knowledge, that one has ever been barbecued. It could put a new face on barbecue or, more accurately, give barbecue its old face back. The guys shake on a rub, the extent of the doctoring, and look down at the pit-ready pig.

"I think we should do a shot of bourbon," says Drew Robinson from Jim 'N Nick's.

There are murmurs of agreement. Hell, yeah. Breakfast.

"I'll get the Pappy Van Winkle," says Sean Brock, chef/owner of Husk in Charleston, South Carolina.

Pappy is poured into those flimsy cone-shaped water cups. I hold mine over the pig and knock it back.

"Bourbon and pigs," Donald says.


## THE WEE HOURS


Bourbon and pigs. That fairly sums up my next twenty hours. The pit doors shut and smoke rolls out. Nothing to do but wait. The chefs and pit masters hold little summits, conversations that food nerds would freak out over, trading tips and hints and stories. There is laughter. There is boudin and soft-shell crabs and oysters and crawfish. There are trays of Jell-O shots, and big cups of bourbon, and people dance until the speakers overheat. There is some drama at the pig; the fire gets too hot, but Rodney Scott finesses the coals, brings the temperature down. There's no pit problem he can't fix. You've seen *Pulp Fiction*? He's the Mr. Wolfe of pork.

I pass out in a chair by the pit and later move to a couch. I wake up around 4:30 a.m. to find Rodney and Sean still awake. Sean and I tag out, and I settle in next to Rodney. He's bulletproof. I'm not. The Pappy is gone. There's a dead tall boy of Pabst and a cashed bottle of Patron on a table, along with the empty shell casings of Jell-O shots.

"We look rough," says Sarah Johnson from Jim 'N Nick's.

"I feel rough," Sean says.

Rodney puts R&B on the speakers. Al Green brings us back to life. The last hours pass quickly. We've been goofballs for the past two days, but when the end comes, it's all business.

"Do you feel good about this?" Nick asks.

Sean nods.

It's time to create the Box. We've talked about the Box endlessly, lending it the importance of an advanced policy initiative, which seems slightly ridiculous, given that the Box is a Styrofoam container of cooked pig. But the Box is for the most important part of judging, the blind taste test, so there are four Beard-winning chefs on the Jim 'N Nick's mobile smoking rig. Everyone is calm, quiet, with a few jokes and short, precise comments. The Box has to go at noon. Donald has a knife in his hand. Some of the Beach 12 sauce is in a jug; abstract ideas and theories are great, but these guys didn't become who they are by *trying* to lose. Some of my snark evaporates as I realize every team is doing this exact same thing.

"It's 11:50, guys," John Currence, from City Grocery in Oxford, Mississippi, says quietly.

What follows is a damn impressive ten minutes. My boys are stone cold. Nobody ever raises his voice or appears to rush, and I realize that before these guys were famous, they spent their lives in hot, anonymous kitchens, cranking out dinner night after night after night. All thirty-four other whole-hog teams are equally concerned with sticking the landing.

The Box is off, and three in-person judges are coming through. They are given the Gospel According to Fatback. Pat Martin does most of the talking. They hear about the Mangalitsas, about the pit masters and the chefs, about Pat's dream of a win at Memphis in May changing the arc of the pig industry, replacing the flavorless factory hogs with ones more like our grandparents ate. His son, he testifies, might one day enjoy the results of our work today. Finally, the last judge leaves, and Rodney walks back to the pit. Sam Jones, whose joint, the Skylight Inn in Ayden, North Carolina, grew out of a family barbecue tradition that dates back two hundred years, is standing there.

"We are so full of it," Rodney says.

"Full of what?" Sam asks.

"Truth," Rodney says.


FATBACK GLORY


Nick is worthy of love for many reasons, for his generosity, for his terrible dancing, and for his creation of the Fatback Collective. But the moment I really want to spoon him is when he arranges for $500 worth of Gus's World Famous fried chicken to be delivered to the tent just after the judges leave. People make *love* to that chicken, coming up for air with faces and fingers covered in grease—"That's my last meal," Sean gushes, orbiting the tables like some sort of bird of prey—and I eat, very quickly, four chicken thighs and two pieces of Wonder bread. So, we're pigging out, and someone is telling Drew that bad news comes via a messenger on foot, but if you make it to the finals, a judge will arrive in a golf cart. At that exact moment, a golf cart pulls up.

"You mean like that?" Sean asks.

The Fatback Collective is in the final three.

The last group of judges arrive, four this time, and the show is smooth. They eat the pig and head back out to make their decision. The confidence is palpable. People are flocking to the pit to pull out meat. Word has spread that the team of ringers has the greatest barbecue ever cooked. There are judges coming by just to eat. One tells me: *You've got it in the bag.* A feeling arises.

"If we win this thing," Nick says, "people are gonna look at pork differently."

We go stand by the stage. Someone there has a pig's head on a stake, with a cigarette in its mouth, a picture of excess that defines much of Memphis in May.

"This is the old model," says one observer.

"This dies tonight," I say back.

However, we are not entirely innocent. We consulted a past champion. We did a taste test on various sauces. We tried to game the judges, too, while preserving our integrity. We came here wanting to change this competition but now, in the last moments, we want to win it. The grizzled chefs' nerves are palpable. I haven't even cooked anything—my role is to be a hyper-partisan observer (and eater)—and even I want to win. I've rolled my eyes for the past two days at the other teams, and now I realize my ire is misplaced. Everybody else isn't trying to educate the judges—they are trying to kick ass. And, as one look at the tense Fatback Collective confirms, so are we. Finally, the results are announced. The winner is the same team that won last year.

Fatback Collective is third.

We shuffle to the stage, trying to smile. The crowd cheers, and all our hopes of stopping the homogeneous 'cue train suddenly feels like sour grapes. We are lots of things, but we are not sore losers. Pat takes the microphone and tells the other cooks that we all respect the hell out of what they do. Those are his exact words, and after, teammates slipped up to him to tell him he'd nailed it. We go back to the tent, and there is talk of how great it is to finish third in our first year, and hugs, and drinks, but the DJ cuts to the heart of the feelings in the tent. We are serenaded with "Auld Lang Syne."


TRUTH IN BARBECUE


After Sean Brock grew up "dirt, dirt, dirt poor," with a dream that seemed impossible from the forgotten corner of Virginia he called home; after he won his Beard medal at the age of thirty-two and hid with his cell phone in a Lincoln Center bathroom, weeping, calling to tell his mama: *I did it*; after Donald Link did for boudin what Arnold Palmer did for golf; after Sam Jones tended his pit the same way his ancestors did two hundred years ago; after Rodney Scott showed up to man the fires at midnight the night he graduated from high school; after John Currence learned to cook on a tugboat the morning after his high school graduation; after we traveled to Memphis to try to change the way people think about barbecue; after we succeeded, and also failed; after all of that, I can't shake an image that I'll cherish long after my cardiologist buys a new ski boat with the money he'll make off the weekend: Pat Martin, our loud, opinionated mouth of the South, sitting in the corner, waiting to find out if we've won.

He's quiet now, with his little boy on his lap. They have the same haircut. Pat gives his son a kiss and rubs his forehead. He holds him tight. Something becomes clear in this moment. The real barbecue we love, that we pretentiously and earnestly came to save, might be under siege, but it isn't dead. It lives in anyone who believes in doing things the way their grandfathers did them, who believes that what we eat tells a story about who we are. It lives in anyone who cares enough to sit all night with a hog. It lives in the fading notes of "Auld Lang Syne" and in the sparks popping off the burn barrel past midnight. It lives in the way a father holds his boy when the cooking is done.

*Brett Martin is a correspondent for* GQ. *His work has appeared in* Bon Appetit, Vanity Fair, *the* New York Times, Best Food Writing 2006 *and* 2010, *and on public radio's* This American Life. *He embedded with a competition barbecue team in 2005.*

# I Was a Texas Rib Ranger

## Brett Martin

Bill Milroy, chief cook of the Texas Rib Rangers, is waiting astride the road at the 2005 Pork & Brew BBQ State Championship, in Rio Rancho, New Mexico, to welcome me to the world of competitive barbecue. Rio Rancho is a sprawling suburb northwest of Albuquerque, and the festival is held on a stretch of road surrounded by high plains desert out by the high school. The row of tents and trailers stretches out in a thin line under vast Southwestern skies, like a squatter's camp. The faint haze of smoke hanging overhead tells a different story: Oak. Hickory. Mesquite.

A Texan man of Texan proportions who once worked security for professional wrestlers, the forty-nine-year-old Milroy is wearing a fleece jacket over a vivid orange and teal muscle shirt. It depicts a steer, in cowboy hat and Lone Star belt buckle, holding aloft a fork and knife. By the standards of the barbecue circuit, this practically qualifies as formal wear.

His team, stationed around a huge trailer across the road, are more in the spirit of things. Charlie, who heads up the team's vending operation and anticipates Milroy's every need with eerie Radar O'Reilly–like precision, is serving racks of ribs while wearing an enormous yellow foam ten-gallon hat. Kristie, another team member, is in a chicken hat that frames her head as though it were an emerging egg. Nearby, Page Skelton, who's joined the team from North Carolina this weekend, is preparing a snack of chicken drumsticks wrapped in thick-cut bacon; periodically, he pauses to ring a huge triangle and holler, "Texas Rriib Rraangers!" at passersby. Milroy's wife, Barbara, is washing individual leaves of lettuce to be used as garnish for tomorrow's competition; she wears a mother hen's expression of long acquaintance with boys and their games. When I head over, Skelton drapes a shiny necklace of plastic chili peppers over my head. "Welcome to the party," he says. Simultaneously, someone pulls a four-inch-diameter buffalo sausage—black and oozing fat—from one of the smokers perpetually at work in front of the trailer and places it in front of me. I think, "I believe I'm going to like it here."

■　■　■

There is great dignity in barbecue—the age-old art of transforming meat, smoke, and spice into the perfect food—but it is not a quiet dignity. Later that night, I join Milroy, Skelton, and Chip Hearn, another team member and owner of ribsandrubs.com, one of the nation's largest hot sauce and condiment distributorships, at the main judging tent, where the weekend's fifty competing teams are gathering for a contestants' briefing. Funny hats abound, as does creative facial hair; barbecuers may be single-handedly responsible for keeping the mustache-wax industry alive. T-shirts tend toward garish chili pepper motifs and grinning, minstrel-like, anthropomorphic pigs, all but slathering their own rumps in sauce and offering up a slice.

The teams—mostly male and all but exclusively white—sit around folding tables trading shop talk and browsing free copies of *The Bullsheet*, the house organ of the Kansas City Barbecue Society (KCBS), one of three major sanctioning bodies that govern the U.S. competitive barbecue circuit. That scene now includes some three hundred events scattered far and wide around the country and upwards of $1.5 million in annual prize money. (Barbecue's laid-back ethos seems to prohibit anyone from keeping precise numbers.) The Grand Champion of this event—who garners the highest aggregate score in the four major categories: pork ribs, pork, brisket, and chicken—wins an automatic bid to the KCBS's premiere showcase, the American Royal International BBQ Championship, held in Kansas City every October.

Milroy sits, Buddha-like, at a table near the corner, exchanging greetings with nearly everybody that passes by. He has been involved in competitive barbecue since its earliest days, in the late '70s. Subsidized by the vending operation and their line of Texas Rib Rangers sauces and rubs, he and Barbara have been on the circuit full-time since 1995—one of only a handful of teams able to do so.

Before coming to New Mexico, I had made the mistake of asking Milroy to send over a list of the Rib Rangers' awards. It ran to twelve pages and nearly blew out my fax machine's toner cartridge. With countless divisions ("Best Vinegar-Based Sauce, Hot," "Best Vinegar-Based Sauce, Mild," "Best Spicy Rub," "Best Cajun Rub," "Best Mediterranean/Herb Rub") and prizes for the top ten entrants in each, the circuit can seem a bit like Little League, where everybody brings home a trophy. Still, with first places at the American Royal, the Jack Daniels World Championship Barbecue Contest, and from the National Barbecue Association, it's an impressive resume.

"Bill's the master," Skelton told me, as we waited for the meeting to begin.

Until two years ago, Skelton, who has a master's degree in information science, was a global accounts manager at WorldCom in Chapel Hill; he left during the company's legal troubles to market his own line of Cackalacky sauces and rubs, which had been successful at several sauce competitions. Skelton and Milroy had been brought together by Chip Hearn, who markets Cackalacky and Texas Rib Rangers products, along with those of several other champions. Skelton, thirty-seven, is a distant relative of Red Skelton and the son of longtime Missouri congressman Ike Skelton; he has both an entertainer's charm and a politician's instinct for pressing the flesh. Already, he had given me a nickname: Burnt Ends, after the Kansas City delicacy of blackened brisket tips.

Like Skelton, I, an enthusiastic novice with a newly acquired home smoker, had come to study at the feet of the master. I was drawn to barbecue for all the same peculiarly American, peculiarly male reasons as most: Because of the shameful need to turn even the most benign hobby into an obsession and a competition. Because of the irresistible combination of geeky technical know-how and artistic flair. Because you get to buy cool equipment. Because it involves playing with fire and drinking beer. Because (and this is barbecue's great, dirty secret) it's *easy*—at least relative to the amount of admiration and gratitude it generates. And because, when you're done, you get to eat barbecue.

I was of course aware of those that damn the competition circuit as somehow demeaning of those who have practiced an age-old folk art since time immemorial. Such objections, I couldn't help but think, were based more than anything on a kind of fish-in-the-barrel snobbishness about competition barbecue's garish superficialities. Certainly I had yet to see a crime that rose above the level of an aesthetic one. Or, for that matter, anything to suggest there was a zero sum game between competition and "real" barbecue. To the contrary, it seemed to me that the phenomenon was a rising smoke cloud that seasoned all flanks; judging by the guest appearance schedule at festivals throughout the year, it appeared that the circuit was a chance for older legends of barbecue to finally get the respect and recognition—and, one hoped, money—they deserved, much as musicians like Muddy Waters and Bo Diddley once did from a new group of vulgar and inauthentic acolytes.

In any event, I think we can all agree, as a matter of principle, that our threshold should be pretty high indeed when it comes to discouraging any activity men use to experience pleasure, foster community, give meaning to their lives, and generally while away the long march toward oblivion—as long as it isn't war, or violence, or hatred. Or, you know, golf.

■   ■   ■

Already, I've committed a faux pas, grabbing a beer to go with the dinner of enchiladas and taquitos the festival's organizers have laid out. (The great tragedy of hanging around barbecue folk is that they tend to be sick and tired of eating barbecue; between that and the fact that most teams aren't licensed to serve the public, it's quite possible to go hungry at a barbecue competition.) Turns out, Milroy doesn't drink during competitions. "Let everybody else get drunk, please," he says. "I'm in the zone right now."

I slowly push my beer away.

Talk around the Rib Rangers' table turns in the direction it almost always does: to food. Hearn, a Delaware man of Texan proportions, describes a creation he's working on: deep-fried Twinkies crusted with crushed Cap'n Crunch. "This weekend, we're gonna Cap'n Crunch something," he promises me. The team is also fond of throwing odd things on the smoker: octopus, doughnuts, an entire pig's ass, complete with tail.

"The octopus was chewy, but the mesquite sort of compensated for the texture," Skelton says thoughtfully. "I like to use stuff that's indigenous to the area. Like, what about cactus?"

"There's an outfit out here that sells rattlesnake," Hearn says.

"I've smoked rattlesnake before," says Milroy. Nobody expresses surprise.

"I wonder if tumbleweed is carcinogenic," asks Skelton.

"Maybe Brett can catch a road runner."

I'm envisioning myself in prison for violating the Endangered Species Act when the briefing begins. Two KCBS representatives run through the rules: Ribs can be either spares or baby backs. Pork is defined as whole shoulder, picnic, or Boston butt. Each meat must be submitted to the blind judging in an unmarked Styrofoam container. Garnish is limited to green leaf lettuce and parsley. Entries will be rated by six judges for taste, tenderness, and appearance. No propane or electricity is permitted; everything must be cooked on a wood, charcoal, or pellet smoker or grill. This includes such ancillary categories as seafood, beans, dessert, and "Anything But," which covers the rest of the conceivable food universe. Turn-in deadlines are absolute and inviolable. One second late will be cause for disqualification. The teams all synchronize their watches.

By the time the meeting is over, it's getting on 9 p.m., which means it's time to get to work. "Let's go," says Milroy, hauling himself to his feet. Skelton is still musing as we file out of the tent. There's a teenage volunteer taking a smoke break by the door.

"Hey," he asks her. "What do you know about tumbleweed?"

■   ■   ■

This much is commonly accepted about barbecue: It is the process of taking tough pieces of meat and cooking them at very low heat for a very long time, adding flavor with smoke. Nearly everything else is up for debate. Wet or dry? To baste or not to baste? Rub early or rub late? Hickory or mesquite? These and a thousand other fine points are debated with the intensity of your average Mideast summit. Even the spelling of barbecue (*BBQ*, *Bar-B-Q*, *Barbeque*, etc.) is cause for debate, as one Howard L. Taylor made clear in a lengthy exegesis in a recent *Bullsheet*. ("Does it matter how we spell it?" Mr. Taylor asks, before answering in the affirmative. Among other reasons, he points out, "Your child or grandchild could lose points on a report or test . . . if he/she spelled barbecue with a 'q.'")

Bill Milroy certainly has his preferences. He believes in steaming his ribs by wrapping them in foil during the last stages of cooking, a technique some Easterners look down on as "the Texas crutch." And he is deeply dubious of the aberrant Carolina habit of serving coleslaw with pork. "Coleslaw is what we feed rabbits," he says. Still, Milroy's style of barbecue could most accurately be described as "competition barbecue." His meat is designed to win championships.

When we get back to the trailer, he strips to his muscle shirt, pulls up a chair, and sets to work on two briskets—one a rectangular "flat," the other a pointed "crown." The flavor of the fattier crown may be better, but the judges like neat, symmetrical slices, so Milroy heaps more attention on the flat. Methodically he works at the meat with a short Santoku knife, finding pockets of fat and tendons invisible to the naked eye.

"The rule is, you never put anything on a judge's plate that a lady would have to take out of her mouth," he says.

Next, Milroy takes a flour sifter filled with his spicy rub and covers the briskets in a thick dusting. "Now, if you'll excuse me, you spank your meat," he announces, vigorously patting the beef until the soft snowfall of rub turns a dark red. Then he places the briskets on one rack of the smoker, there to sit for the next twelve hours.

It's now fully dark and in tents all up and down the fairway, by the flickering light of their cookers, men are bent silently over the same task. One by one, the smoker doors open and close for the night. And when Milroy puts the last pieces in and we head off for a few hours sleep, it's hard not to dream of the meat sitting there, alone in the smoky dark, quietly, inexorably, doing its job.

■   ■   ■

By 7:30 the next morning, the camp is wide awake. Teams are preparing breakfast and getting their ribs ready for the cookers. It feels like a small village. Walking the length of the road, the diversity of smoking devices is remarkable—from simple kettle grills to bullet-shaped R2D2 units to odd egg-shaped pods to blackened behemoths, mounted on their own trailers, that look like stranded locomotives.

The Rib Rangers are using two sleek, rectangular units called Fast Eddys. They resemble steel refrigerators and are fueled by compressed wood pellets the size and shape of guinea pig feed. Controlled by a thermostat, they can be left alone for hours. There are purists who turn their noses up at such innovations, but the fact is that barbecue today is better than it has ever been.

"In the old days, you just threw a log in there and smoked the meat for as long as possible. There was no way to control it," Milroy says. "For the next two weeks, every time you farted, it smelled like smoke."

Still, for all the fancy technology, Milroy makes a point of checking in on his smokers during the night. This morning, the team is glad for that caution. When I arrive at the trailer, Skelton tells me that he and Milroy came by at about 3:45 a.m., en route to a local TV appearance. They discovered that, for mysterious reasons, Skelton's cooker had gone out while they slept and the meat had gone cold. A neighboring team had awoken and offered to let Skelton use a shelf on their cooker—a gesture characteristic of the circuit's camaraderie—but it would still be a race to get the brisket up to temperature in time for the 1:30 p.m. turn-in. I'm beginning to see the benefits of operating without a hangover.

Milroy appears, looking surprisingly chipper. "I love my job," he grins.

Even with this morning's headaches, it's not hard to believe. It sometimes seems that there are two factors to thank for the rise of competitive barbecue: shitty jobs and wonderful wives. Milroy's first taste of barbecue competition came in 1976, when he participated in an ad hoc contest staged by the local volunteer fire department—basically a bunch of guys in their 4×4s drinking beer and massacring briskets. In the early '80s, he helped form the North Texas Barbecue Cookers Organization, which was the first group to codify rules for competitions. He even tried his hand at starting a restaurant.

Then he discovered his first wife fooling around with one of his barbecue buddies at the restaurant and that was it for a few years. "I didn't even want to smell barbecue," he says. When he met Barbara, in 1986, he was working as a delivery driver for a bread company. At Barbara's urging, the couple started dabbling in competitions again, but Milroy's work dominated his time.

"One day, I called Barbara up and told her that this job was taking my life away. She said, 'Come home. Just come home.'"

By 1995, they were on the road as many as thirty-six weeks a year. Each year, from mid-February to mid-November, they crisscross the country in their F350 pickup with Charlie and Kristie trailing behind in a second truck.

"Most people wait until they retire to do what we do," Barbara says. "We're just not the kind of people who can just sit around and watch TV."

■  ■  ■

There will be a turn-in every forty-five minutes this afternoon, and the Rib Rangers area is abuzz. Chicken is first and Kristie, the designated runner, heads off to the judging tent, precariously balancing Milroy's Styrofoam box filled with rich, golden thighs. She's wearing her chicken hat, though she'll cycle through pigs and cows as the day goes on, depending on her cargo.

As the 12:30 rib turn-in approaches, Skelton is frantically preparing his garnish, fussing with bits of parsley. Milroy, who has his own ribs to turn in, is nowhere to be seen. "How's my time?" Skelton yells to Hearn. "You've got twenty minutes," Hearn tells him.

Skelton chooses a rack of ribs and places them nervously on a bed of lettuce. He carefully dabs the meat with sauce on a paper towel, making them glisten. A drop splashes on the Styrofoam lip and he hurriedly wipes it off. Then he dashes off towards the judging tent.

That's when Milroy emerges lazily from the trailer. It is 12:15. With infinite calm, he unwraps his ribs and inspects them, looking for those with the straightest bones. Then he cuts two slabs, paints them with sauce and throws them briefly on the grill, letting the sugar caramelize and form a glaze. Every step of the process is torturously slow.

At 12:21, Milroy takes his finished ribs inside the trailer and carefully begins arranging one of the slabs in its box. Kristie waits by the door in her pig hat. Milroy appears to finish, starts to lower the lid and then stops. He's noticed something—a bare spot of bone, an errant drop of sauce, God only knows—that he doesn't like.

"Get me one of those other slabs," he tells Barbara. Hearn stares at his watch in silent horror.

Milroy replaces the slab, finally closes the box. It is 12:26. "I can run," says Kristie.

"DON'T RUN," Barbara and Hearn say, simultaneously.

"Charlie," Milroy says, almost inaudibly. Charlie is suddenly in the doorway.

"You're going to have to clear a path for her," says Milroy, mercifully closing the container at last.

Charlie grins: "That's what I'm good at."

They take off, navigating through baby carriages and blissfully unaware festivalgoers. A few minutes later, they're back, having made it with seconds to spare. "Didn't you cut that a little close?" I ask Milroy. He just grins.

The next few hours are a blur as container after container is turned in: pork, brisket, a chocolate raspberry-filled cake that Barbara has prepared in the smoker. True to his word, Hearn has Cap'n Crunched his "Anything But" entry of shrimp stuffed with crabmeat. My duties are limited to hovering like a jackal around the perimeter, hoping for a stray bite here and there and trying to stay out of the way.

At 3 p.m., the last dish is delivered and everybody exhales. You can almost hear beer tops popping open up and down the camp. The Rib Rangers have done all they can do and the contest is now in the hands of the judges.

"Anybody who's been around knows it's a crapshoot. You can cook something the best you possibly can, and lose," Milroy says. "And then stuff you'd like to throw in the garbage gets a good score."

It's time, then, to concentrate on the other rewards of life in barbecue. Milroy dons a fuzzy armadillo hat and an apron fashioned to look like a satin nightgown, complete with breasts that squeak, and clowns around with festivalgoers. Skelton talks shop with neighboring teams. Hearn falls asleep in a chair.

This time around, such reminders of how much better life is when you're not delivering bread or sitting behind a corporate desk will have to suffice. The best the team scores is a respectable fifth place in ribs.

Charlie starts packing up the trailer and we say our goodbyes. The Rib Rangers will travel several thousand miles before I see them again, at one of barbecue's biggest events, the so-called Super Bowl of Swine, the Memphis in May World Championship Barbecue Cooking Contest.

"Let me tell you," Milroy says, as I head off. "It's going to be real different down there."

■　　■　　■

These are the things I can see while standing in one spot in front of the main stage at Memphis in May: a large sunburned man wearing a green tie-dyed skirt and a massive collection of Mardi Gras beads the size of Christmas ornaments; a barbecue team's booth that features a portable air conditioner, a collection of garden gnomes, and an entire second floor; a camera crew from the Food Network, zipping around in golf carts—competitive barbecue making for successful TV programming lately, despite the fact that it consists almost entirely of waiting patiently.

On stage, competitors in the "Ms. Piggy Contest," for best barbecue-related performance, are step-dancing to blaring hip-hop while wearing leprechaun, wizard, and pig costumes; earlier, a different team had enacted an entire elaborately staged opera on the theme of Best Sauce. A few rows of booths south of here, there's a giant blood-red pig, fashioned from an industrial boiler and covered in what I'm told is "nuclear-grade" insulation; at the press of a remote control button, the belly of this cooker slides open on hydraulic casters, revealing an entire hog smoking inside.

No, Mr. Milroy, I don't think we're in Rio Rancho anymore.

Each year, in an attempt to promote cross-cultural understanding, Memphis in May—at which some 247 teams will compete—chooses a sister nation to honor. This year, it's Ireland, which participants seem to have taken as a mandate to dress in green, make Lucky Charms references, and get seriously loaded. It's a record ninety-two degrees on the banks of the Mississippi and smoke and particulated fat hang in the air, clinging to my skin.

Along with the American Royal, Jack Daniels, and the Houston Livestock Show and Rodeo, Memphis in May belongs in what you could call the barbecue Grand Slam. It is also a giant corporate hospitality gangbang, at which seemingly every business in greater Memphis fields a team—from the NRA to Bell South Yellow Pages to Protank Liquid Handling Products (yum).

I beat a retreat to the relative calm of the Rib Rangers' booth. Hearn and Skelton are trying to keep cool in front of several small fans. Skelton is eating Cheerios in soy milk and casually lets drop the bomb that, when he's not on the barbecue trail, he's essentially a vegan. I ask him to take off his sunglasses and repeat that while looking me in the eye, but it appears to be true.

Milroy arrives, walking with a limp. He blew out his knee on a vending stop at the Texas Motor Speedway last week. Last year, he had surgery for a hernia. With the hours, the heat, and the heavy lifting, there's a decent case to be made for barbecue as an extreme sport.

Between the injury and truck trouble that's had Charlie driving back and forth between Dallas and Texarkana for the past two days, Milroy isn't in the best of moods. He's no great fan of the pageantry of Memphis in May, especially since it extends to the judging of barbecue. In addition to submitting a blind box, teams must make an in-booth presentation to three separate judges. "It's a dog and pony show," Milroy says.

This week, there's no vending for the Rib Rangers. And while they'll turn in several side entries (Hearn is Cap'n Crunching some conch) the main competition event will be ribs. I'm intent on being of more use this time around, though my nerves keep getting in the way. It takes me twenty full minutes to spread a tablecloth on the table at which we'll seat the judges.

At midday, I volunteer to turn in the team's entry for hot wings. I've seen the judging tent; how hard can it be? But when I leave the Rib Rangers booth, Styrofoam cups of sauce balanced precariously in one hand, I'm suddenly disoriented. Identical leering pigs and grinning leprechauns surround me in all directions. Panicked, I stumble around in the heat until happening upon the tent, where I shove the container into a volunteer's hands. And when I'm catching my breath there, I'm asked to sit in as a judge of the vinegar-based sauce competition.

It's not unusual for noncertified judges to participate at barbecue competitions (at Rio Rancho about half had never judged before) but it is further proof of the arbitrariness of the process. I'm seated at a table with three other judges. We're given cups of four different sauces, which we carefully spoon out onto plastic plates. Just looking at them, it's clear we'll be comparing apples, oranges, pineapples, and grapes. One is thick and burgundy color, another watery and orange; the third is speckled with chili pepper flakes and the last tar black.

The scoring is confusing. We're told to judge based on overall impression, aroma, flavor, and spice compatibility, though it's unclear exactly how this last category differs from flavor. Furthermore, the selection of sauces are meant to be judged against each other, not against an ideal. So, in each of the categories, one of the four in front of me will have to score perfectly on a scale of six to ten.

"A six is if they don't turn in at all," the supervisor says. "So, if you can put it in your mouth, that's a seven. And if you can keep it there, it's probably an eight."

It doesn't help that all my sauces are pretty awful—one sickeningly sweet, another like spicy orange juice. I pick the least offensive of them and am forced to give it a glowing score. What's amazing, I think as I walk away, isn't that Milroy's outrageously good barbecue is sometimes shut out, but that such an arbitrary and subjective process *ever* gets it right.

■   ■   ■

Back at the booth, Barbara has set a table with a centerpiece and china. Skelton is sweeping the Astroturf floor while Milroy puts the finishing touches on his ribs. Hearn, a championship bullshit artist, will be in charge of the presentations when the judges arrive, shepherding each to the smokers for a Q&A with Milroy and then to the table. Skelton will act as waiter. My job is to mind the clock; judges' visits last fifteen minutes, no more and no less, and I'm given an elaborate set of hand signals to keep Hearn on top of time.

"We'll let them cut one rib and depending on how that goes, that'll be the story," Milroy says. "Either it will be 'See how nicely that slid off the bone, it's perfect,' or, 'You don't want it to just fall off the bone, do you? See how these have a nice little tug to them?'"

On the phone the week before, Milroy had asked me my shirt size (which in Texas seems to mean how many Xs before the L) and mentioned that he'd already secured my pants. This worried me; rightly as it turned out. The T-shirt is within the normal bounds of fashion—the Rib Rangers logo augmented with a shamrock and some Celtic designs—but Hearn has also procured a set of the most eyeball-meltingly ugly trousers imaginable: oversized black pajama pants with hideous red and orange flames shooting up the legs and licking at the crotch. They make me absurdly proud. Skelton tops this off with a gift from the team: a cowboy hat with "Burnt Ends" emblazoned on it in rhinestones. I feel I might weep.

As planned, we burst into applause when the first judge arrives. She's a middle-aged woman from Memphis wearing maybe thirty barbecue pins. She's been a judge for fifteen years.

"Love your pants," she says.

Hearn brings her back to Milroy at the cookers and he talks her through his technique. Then Hearn steers her to a seat. Skelton, towel draped over arm, offers water. Hearn picks up a dish of Texas Rib Rangers rosemary and herb seasoning, one of Milroy's secret weapons. "Let me tell you about this herb *concept*," he says, almost purring. "It allows the flavors to surf back and forth across your tongue." The judge nods politely. I flash Hearn a single finger—only five minutes down.

Skelton gently places a rack of ribs in front of the judge. Milroy never tastes his barbecue before submitting it to judging, only gauges its quality by sight and feel. This time, he gets unlucky. The first rib the judge cuts into is just the tiniest bit tough.

"Taste is much more important than falling off the bone, don't you think?" Hearn coos. Two fingers; still five minutes to go.

The judge picks away at the rack. The rest of the ribs are more tender and she compliments their flavor. But before I can even flash my three finger signal that there's one minute left, she stands, thanks Hearn and Milroy and goes.

"God. *Fifteen years* as a judge," Hearn says, mopping his brow. "I couldn't bullshit her at all."

"She got a tough rib," Milroy says, matter-of-factly.

The second judge arrives, another longtime veteran in a straw cowboy hat. He and Milroy instantly hit it off and the conversation is nice and breezy. "That was great," Hearn says, when he's gone. "He was a good old boy and Bill nailed it."

The third judge sports a red-blonde bouffant. At the cooker, she tries to trap Milroy. "Do you take ribs from the top shelf or bottom shelf first?" she asks.

"I take them from the center, ma'am," Milroy answers, correctly.

At the table, the judge accepts Skelton's offer of wine. She takes a bite of a rib and nods, inscrutably. Then she stops eating and starts to talk. For what seems like an eternity, she discusses how she got into barbecue, how her husband and son are both police officers, the best thing about Memphis—nearly everything imaginable except what's on her plate. Hearn keeps an eye on the rib, held delicately between two fingers to better gesticulate with the other hand. I flash one finger, then two.

Finally, she returns to the food. "Mmm, that's just wonderful, honey," she says. Everybody relaxes. Skelton offers more wine, which is readily accepted. By the time the fifteen minute mark rolls around and she totters off, all is well.

Now, we wait. Skelton strums an acoustic guitar. Milroy goes back to check the smokers. The field of 111 rib contestants will be narrowed to three finalists. If we make it, he'll have to have a whole new set of ribs ready for yet another round of judges. Slowly, news starts to drift in from the other areas of the festival, where the pork shoulder and whole hog competitions are taking place. The Food Network crew zips back and forth, wanting to be on hand for the announcement of the finalists.

Eventually, the word comes. We didn't make the finals.

"Hey, man," Milroy says, when he sees my face. "It's a game. It ain't nothin' but a game."

Almost instantly, the team starts packing up. It's early in the season yet. In the coming weeks and months the Rib Rangers will bring their barbecue to Hickory and Tryon and Lincolnton, North Carolina (where Milroy will take Reserve Grand Champion and Skelton come in third with his whole hog); to Warminster, Maryland, and Lawrenceburg, Tennessee; and then Youngstown, Ohio; Rockford, Illinois; Mason City, Iowa; Mankato, Minnesota; Lincoln, Nebraska; Buffalo, New York; and a dozen other towns across America, before heading back to Texas and getting ready to start again.

I won't be with them; I have to go home, back to work. But there's time yet for me to sneak away and eat a few more ribs, the ones the finals judges will never taste. I open a foil package. The meat is gorgeous—covered in a thick, glistening, deep red bark. My teeth sink into the flesh and it is moist and firm, smoky and meaty, salty and sweet, all in perfect proportion. At the moment it also tastes of other things—of hard work and good company and second chances and adventure on the open road. To spend one's days creating, perfecting, and sharing such a thing, it occurs to me, would be a happy and noble use of one's time. It tastes like the good life.

*This story first appeared in the* Economist. *Jon Fasman is the magazine's Atlanta correspondent.*

# Fire in the Hole

## Jon Fasman

It is a noun, not a verb. You do not barbecue meat; you smoke it until it becomes barbecue. And it is not a meal so much as a meditative process, perched somewhere between science and art, dependent on reserves of judgment. The science lies in building a fire that will smoulder steadily without flaring, and in constructing a vessel that will bathe the meat in smoke without subjecting it to too much heat. The art lies in the butchering and seasoning. The judgment comes in knowing precisely when a cooking process that may last as long as 18 or 24 hours should end. Barbecue is the art of turning tough cuts tender ("Need no teef to eat my beef" is a popular boast among smokemasters). None of these facts brook disagreement, but here the unity ends.

American barbecue falls into four broad geographic categories—and understand, letter-to-the-editor writers, that this is a crude sketch, not holy writ. In North Carolina pork, either whole hog or shoulder, is seasoned minimally if at all. The sauce, applied at table, varies. In the eastern part of the state it is usually nothing more than cider vinegar, salt and red pepper flakes. In the west it may include a bit of tomato. North Carolina barbecue at its best is as austere and perfect as a bowl of properly cooked Japanese rice. As with rice, however, perfection is exceptionally difficult to achieve, whereas mediocrity is easy. Mediocre Carolina pork will bring back memories of school dinners and premonitions of the nursing home.

Memphis is known for ribs and shoulder, the former often served "dry", with just a rub of spices, and the latter often served pulled, on a sandwich, with coleslaw as an essential element rather than an option. Unsurprisingly, the ranching state of Texas prefers beef to pork. The brisket is cooked "low and slow" and often served with nothing more than Saltine crackers or white bread, raw onions and pickles. Texas also displays strong German influences, seen in the prevalence of barbecued sausage in the region just east of Austin, as well as Mexican ones, seen in covered-pit barbacoa, traditionally made from cows' heads.

Kansas City barbecue slathers both beef and pork in a sweet, tomato-based sauce: This style of barbecue, probably because it is easiest to do tolerably well and because people always love a sweet sauce, has become the default broad American style. If you order ribs in a chain restaurant in Buffalo or Minneapolis, say, you will probably get them doused in sweet tomato sauce. There are regional quirks throughout the country—western Kentucky prefers mutton to beef or pork, South Carolina's sauce is mustard-based while northern Alabama's is an abomination based on mayonnaise, and Chicagoans display a fondness for rib tips (unwieldy, delicious bits of meat, bone and cartilage). But those are the four main categories.

Yet beyond that rough classification lie deeper questions: What is barbecue? What does it mean? What is its proper venue? These are not mere culinary questions. Barbecue in America, particularly in the American South, is like red wine in Bordeaux or maize in Mexico. More than just something to consume, it is an expression of regional and perhaps even national identity. In "Smokestack Lightning", a delicious book about barbecue, Lolis Eric Elie explains, "Barbecue alone encompasses the high- and lowbrows, the sacred and the profane, the urban and the rural, the learned and the unlettered, the blacks, the browns, the yellows, the reds and the whites."

Mr Elie's book, punctuated by Frank Stewart's photographs, is an account of a summer spent driving around America in search of first-class barbecue. It is the sort of book that makes a reader look across the table at spouse and children, and think, "They'll be all right without me for a few months, won't they?" Writer and photographer traverse the rural South and Texas before turning north into Kansas City and Chicago, cities with barbecue traditions shaped by the Great Migration of African Americans northward from the rural South in the early 20th century. It is a tour of barbecue's redoubts.

Yet even as Mr Elie and Mr Stewart were writing, and photographing, barbecue was spreading from its roots. It is now America's food in the same way that jazz and blues are its music. All were formed from the interplay of African, European and native cultures. Barbecue at its best has a depth and complexity that, say, hotdogs and hamburgers never could; they are Elvis Presley to barbecue's Louis Armstrong. And, like jazz and blues, barbecue is easy to water down. In culinary terms that may mean parboiling meat, then coating it with sweet barbecue sauce flavoured with Liquid Smoke rather than taking the time to cook it slowly over a wood fire.

Whereas great barbecue tastes great, even mediocre barbecue tastes pretty good. And mediocre barbecue demands far less time, attention, discipline and labour. It can also be aimed at the broadest possible section of palates, offending few but delighting few as well (for the same reason, one is more likely to hear the music of Kenny G than Miles Davis while on hold). For many years—particularly to those smokehounds trapped in the northeast, or some other benighted and barbecue-deprived corner of the world, forced by cravings to order a rack of baby-back ribs in a middle-of-the-road, non-barbecue establishment, only to be presented with spongy, tasteless meat dripping with smoky ketchup—this danger has long seemed especially perilous. Mr Elie's writing is sharp but markedly elegiac.

Nearly two decades later, however, he has cause—so have we all—for joy. The forces of smoke and time are fighting bravely against prefabricated red sauce and parboiling. Inspired by writers such as Michael Pollan, Alice Waters and Hugh Fearnley-Whittingstall, diners have grown increasingly concerned about the route their food takes from farm to table. There has been a boom not just in organic food but in what can be called "vernacular food". And the country has seen the spread not merely of barbecue, but of first-rate and even inventive barbecue.

Some of the credit belongs to restaurateurs such as Danny Meyer. Mr Meyer is a native of St Louis, whose unique contribution to barbecue is the snoot sandwich, which is just what it sounds like. He opened Blue Smoke in 2002 in Manhattan, an island blessed with many things, barbecue not among them. That absence proved liberating: "In any of the real barbecue destinations of the world," Mr Meyer explains, "it's heresy to veer from what local tastes have dictated for ever." But in New York local tastes have dictated nothing, which means nobody (other than finicky expats, who will presumably be too busy stuffing their faces to talk) will object if a restaurant serves Texas-style brisket with a bottle of eastern Carolina vinegar sauce. And indeed Mr Meyer's restaurant, rather than being steeped in a single tradition, is an homage to barbecue's catholicity. Yet befitting its Manhattan location, it has a drinks menu that extends beyond RC Cola and Bud Light. "The worst thing we could have done", says Mr Meyer, "is to pretend that we were a 'barbecue joint' rather than a New York restaurant."

If Blue Smoke is barbecue's greatest-hits collection, Jim & Nick's, a chain of barbecue restaurants, is more "Kind of Blue": a stylistically coherent album that is not tied to any particular region. Nick Pihakis, an Alabaman who started the chain with his father 25 years ago, boasts that none of his 28 restaurants has a freezer. Their barbecue is hardwood-smoked, low and slow, the right way; the side dishes, biscuits and pie dough are made from scratch. It is neither Memphian nor Texan, but a sort of hybrid of the two, with nods to the traditional southern table as well.

Messrs Pihakis and Meyer, like smokehounds outside the South, have at some point had to face the question every art form faces: is it authentic? Lauded today, Blue Smoke opened to rocky reviews. What happened, explains Mr Meyer, "was that a small number of 'gastronauts' felt they had all the knowledge in the world. It was important to them to say 'I know what authentic is, and this isn't authentic.'" It is easy to defend good barbecue from those who would debase it, but how do you protect a living practice from those who would, in its defence, smother it? Art needs iconoclasts and bold fusions of distinct traditions. Otherwise it stagnates.

Consider the way that music—notably, in America, jazz and hip-hop—developed both distinct regional flavours as well as an overarching hybrid style. Some may prefer, say, New Orleans jazz to the less regional schools of bebop or free jazz, but nobody would seriously argue for the superiority of one over the other. It is comforting to believe in the purity of isolation, and to believe that good barbecue exists only in a remote tarpaper shack, or in obscure blues clubs in Memphis, but it is a fiction. Barbecue, like jazz, develops from conversation, from talking and listening, from eating and thinking. As Duke Ellington said of music, there are really only two kinds of barbecue: good and bad.

Those afflicted by nostalgia for the music of the past can listen to Louis Armstrong or Miles Davis and lament how far the world has fallen. In visual art, too, we have old prints, and in literature we have old books. Food has an advantage that those art forms lack. Every time fire touches flesh it is reinvented: there is nothing to compare it to. The man who had that restaurant, long shuttered, on that corner in West Memphis, Arkansas, where weeds now grow may have been a great cook. His rub might have contained spices unheard of and perhaps his sauce would not have been out of place at the table of Kublai Khan. He may well in fact have been the best that ever was, but all there is to prove it is talk. The past is gone. In fact, it is eaten.

Greg Alan Brownderville, whose first collection of poems, entitled Gust, was published in 2011 by Northwestern University Press, is a native of Pumpkin Bend, Arkansas, and a professor of English at Lincoln University in Jefferson City, Missouri.

# Carlo Silvestrini on the Hog Slaughter

## Greg Alan Brownderville

Hog-killing day, wind face-chap cold.
    Fever got me good, woozing up my thought.
    I seeing triple, hunger-fangs take a hold.

Fire over water in a big black pot,
    Papa slit hog throat, rope him round the head,
    hang him from a gum tree, douse him right hot,

shave him cleany pink. Next part I dread.
    Stab hog in the heart, let bright blood.
    For blood pie sake, save a pail a red.

Rain, sleet, snow blows up, make shitty mud.
    Stray mutt twitchy from the swamp, slobber beard,
    coughing like a brimstone preacher mongst the crud.

One dog, see, make three to me. I get skeered.
    Papa toss him hog gut slime. Sky's dark guts
    ooze out, turn the light blue weird.

Papa clean intestines and, checking for cuts,
    blow them up a like balloons. Mash B-grade meat
    for sausage links and the salt-skin gobbets

dry to cracklins. Tongue, lips, ears, and feet
    pickled or ground to hogshead cheese.
    Ain't too much here a man can't eat.

Loin for *lonza*, quarters for *prosciutto*. Sugar, yeast,
    meal, and raisin make cake out of boiled backbone.
    Drop liver, heart, and kidney fresh in a grease,

sizzle with some pepper, salt, and onion.
    Scramble brains with eggs and fry.
    Cut fat and skin in bits, boil them in a cauldron

for the family lard—year supply.
    Muddy man-shadows making rag soap, scald
    waste fat and mix it up with lye.

Only hair, hoof, intestine goop, and teeth get culled.
    No smokehouse, no stable,
    so we move inside. Papa rub a thick coat a salt

in a fat slab. We store it on the cypress table
    in my leaky room, where it smells
    up my dreams. Dirty snow buries my Bible,

chills my bed. Through knotholes
    in the floor of my head, I see a red-eye rabid dog
    and I'm skeered every night when the black blanket falls,

I'll feed a snorting ghost ripped from a hog.

*Elizabeth Engelhardt, associate professor of American Studies and Women's and Gender Studies at the University of Texas, Austin, writes about food, gender, race, and class in the U.S. South. She is lead author of* Republic of Barbecue: Stories Beyond the Brisket *(2009) and author of* A Mess of Greens: Southern Gender and Southern Food *(2011).*

# An Oyster by Any Other Name

## Elizabeth Engelhardt

On a late February Saturday night in Galveston, Texas, I stood shoulder to shoulder with a hundred fellow conspirators, tasting two thousand oysters from all along the Gulf Coast. It was the first symposium hosted by Food-ways Texas, an organization dedicated to preserving, promoting, and cel-ebrating the state's diverse food cultures. We took over a room at Gaido's, a century-old restaurant that has served its share of succulent oysters. As revelers drank and cheered, Mardi Gras parade floats, barely visible through the early spring fog, advanced noisily down the seawall.

Our targets—a consideration of oyster appellations and a revaluing of fish previously dismissed as trash—intermittently floated up through the thick fog of history, and industrial-scientific rhetoric, raising as many questions as answers. Sweet, fat, briny, buttery, and luscious, the oysters were a phenom-enon of excess and local flavor, a bacchanalia fitting the surrounding party.

*Mad Island, Elm Grove, Todd's Dump, Possum Pass, Bayou Cook, Pepper Grove, and Ladies Pass.* The sheer number of oysters in one place was notable. Rather than numeric codes in fine print designating the bed from which oys-ters were harvested, rather than a tag lumping all together as from the Gulf, for one night the oysters stopped being generic. The Texas oyster beds got their names back. (Laminated nametags accompanied each sampling of oys-ters.) We compared the taste of Mad Island versus Pepper Grove. We debated the salinity of Possum Pass versus Bayou Cook. We found the provenance, and we located and glimpsed the history in the names.

*Ribbonfish, Almaco Jack, Big Eyes, Rainbow Runners, and Drills.* Oysters were not the only food to regain their names at the Foodways Texas Gulf Coast gathering. A panel took on monocultural fishing practices driven by market forces, practices that value one product and dismiss everything else that comes up in the nets or on the line as "trash." If Redfish are selling, then Ribbonfish get trashed, along with Rainbow Runners.

But if we rename the trash as by-catch, and find someone like P. J. Stoops, a Texas-born encyclopedia of the names and qualities of Gulf species, then we might compare the Almaco Jack with the Big Eyes and not throw either away. By restoring the names and the balance, we also might find similarities between predators such as oyster drills and delicacies such as escargot, and discover that devotees of snails in butter and delicate herbs also may like oyster drills—kissing cousins to the land snails—prepared the same way. Such practices could help protect the oyster beds from at least one threat.

*Anahuac, Lonesome, Desperation, Moses Gate, Resignation, Mary's, Slim Jim, Frenchy's.* For this North Carolina native, Texas is the perfect place to examine questions of cultures, landscapes, and artifacts. Now, thanks to the work of food historians like Robb Walsh, who have dug up old maps and newspaper stories from the days before the beds were scientifically coded and classified by number, we're able to establish place names for oysters and restore nineteenth-century reef names, too.

We heard the poetry in old names used by local fishermen and women. (Stoops, who studied English in college, favors vernacular by-catch names over Latin ones.) The long history of erasure of the local by nationalizing or industrializing scientific rhetoric took a small step back. Even if we do not know how lonesome, desperate, or resigned some early oystermen and women were, we glimpsed stories of families and lives memorialized by names. From the restoration of narratives came a celebration of cultures, people, and places.

*Confederate, Dollar, Gaspipe, Dryhole, Snake Island, Redfish.* Names and narratives can be fraught. We can use them to romanticize an untroubled past, one without gas pipes draining into the bay waters and without traces of civil war and its racial divides carved into the coast. We can use nostalgia to forget our responsibilities in the present. Dollars seem quaint rather than profoundly influential on a working bay.

Oyster and fish names can stand in place of the names of the men, women, and children who historically worked in the canneries and factories, on the boats, and in the crews—often for little pay, in brutal conditions. Efforts to restore histories and cultures can fetishize products, price them out of their blue-collar roots, and harvest them out of a healthy balance in the ecosystem.

*Lonetree, Little Bird, Eagle Point, Buckshot.* Amid contemporary habits of quantifying and generalizing, perhaps the fondness for storytelling demonstrated on that February weekend in Galveston addresses a gap. If food and drink can be thoughtfully combined with narratives and bonding across experiences, then names may make a difference. If we root ourselves and our foods in places, connect people and time, and reflect on cultural exchanges, we might build new commitments and political alliances.

Did the oyster appellation experiment cut through the night's soupy fog? Does the by-catch renaming transform our relationship with the seas? Do I now know a truth about oysters, an essential worth of fish not discarded? I am not sure. I do know that since the gathering a few Texas restaurants have begun hosting tastings organized by appellation. A by-catch booth at a Houston farmers' market Tweets lists of species and possibilities—and followers flock in. Perhaps restoring narratives to products previously obscure, unfailingly fresh, and newly valued will strengthen the connections between stories, oysters, fish, and cultures, and even create space for stories untold. That might be worth a celebratory parade.

*Sara Roahen is an oral historian and the author of* Gumbo Tales: Finding My Place at the New Orleans Table. *This story first appeared in* Garden & Gun.

# Adventures of a Boudin Junkie

## Sara Roahen

Back out in the parking lot at Legnon's Boucherie, a meat market in New Iberia, I set a brown paper sack on the trunk of my Toyota and begin to unpack its contents: a bottle of root beer; a bag of cracklins; and a hot link of boudin blanc, which at Legnon's is always dense with roughly ground pork, shored up with long-grain rice, enriched with pork liver, and peppered to impress. The white-hot heat of a Louisiana afternoon in August penetrates from all angles like a microwave oven, but I take my time. It's a two-hour drive back to New Orleans, and sustenance is in order. Even before I free the sausage from its white paper wrapping, I hear a low voice call out, "You got you some boudin, baby?" I turn to see a man lounging in the driver's seat of a white minivan parked beside me. As if offering a lesson in boudin enjoyment, the man leans hard into his reclined seat, tips back his head, and using his fingers and his front teeth empties the innards of a boudin link into his mouth. "This place is the best," he says, chewing with obvious satisfaction.

Boudin, a super-seasoned soft pork and rice sausage, is fast food, not given to pomp. Fuel stations are a primary source for it in southwest Louisiana; between ringing up Marlboro hard packs and scratch-off lottery tickets, cashiers use kitchen tongs to lift the warm links from Nesco ovens or slow cookers, snip them into manageable pieces with scissors, wrap them in paper, charge you just slightly more than a pack of gum costs, and send you on your way.

In Acadiana, the region of prairies and bayous where the Acadians (today called Cajuns) settled after 1755, having been expelled from Nova Scotia, you find boudin at supermarket deli counters and at the area's manifold festivals. A place like Legnon's, where the meat case glows with the rubies and roses of seven steaks and freshly ground chicken patties, is about as high-end as boudin shopping gets.

The absence of pretension in its packaging might prompt you to unwrap your boudin as I did, atop the closed trunk of your car (or, even more regionally appropriate, on the tailgate of your pickup truck). Go ahead! If you manage to make it to a seated position, as my new friend in the parking lot did, it's within the cultural norm to squeeze the sausage into your mouth as you drive. You may eat the casings, most of which are pure pork products, but pressing the peppery filling onto saltines, or into hollowed-out bell peppers for baking, is equally acceptable. Boudin can be cocktail party food, wedding food, and Super Bowl buffet food, but if its presentation ever gets stuffier than a napkin and a toothpick, something's fishy.


BONDING WITH BOUDIN


I first started eating boudin some seven years ago, once I'd lived in New Orleans long enough to need a breather from urban living and began exploring outside the city's limits. I experienced my first link ever at Poche's Market in Breaux Bridge, a town I've since come to regard as a boudin hotbed because of its several irresistible destinations: Poche's for livery links; Charlie T's for milder, green-onion-spiked specimens; the restaurant Café des Amis for boudin-stuffed omelets; Babineaux Slaughter House for increasingly difficult-to-find boudin rouge (blood boudin); and Bayou Boudin & Cracklin' for innovative white bean and tasso boudin, as well as fantastically seasoned cracklins.

Some newcomers to boudin country require periods of palate adjustment. The liver component is too exotic, or the soft texture is off-putting, or the deliberate seasonings are challenging (for seasoning-phobes, Floyd Poché, the market's proprietor, suggests trying a balanced Cajun seven-course meal: one pound of boudin plus a six-pack). Perhaps thanks to my late grandfather's liverwurst-and-raw-onion sandwich habit, or perhaps because eating in New Orleans had prepared my palate for boudin's riches, my affection for the sausage was immediate. Acadiana is rural and removed enough—from New Orleans, as well as the rest of the country—that even its largest town, Lafayette, has an old-fashioned charm; the liver in Poche's boudin seemed to be an edible expression of that. Ditto the boudin's simple wrapping, its made-today freshness, and its take-it-or-leave-it seasoning. I took to it without condition.

My easy bonding with the sausage was fortunate, as a few years later I got a job gathering interviews for the Southern Foodways Alliance's Southern

Boudin Trail oral history project. This work, which is ongoing, has changed my life in at least two ways. First, I never leave the city without an ice chest in the car anymore. Second, I Google *gout symptoms* more often than I ever imagined would be necessary for a former vegetarian who hasn't yet turned forty.

To date, we've accumulated roughly thirty interviews for the Boudin Trail, a preservation project archived at the University of Mississippi in Oxford that also exists on the Web as a resource for scholars, tourists, and the plain interested. Most of our subjects are boudin makers, but I've also chatted with rice growers, folklorists, historians, and one meat inspector. So many voices. Some of them still speak the Cajun-French dialect that began to disappear from dinner tables in Acadiana two generations ago—many subjects have told me that their parents were punished with slaps and spanks for speaking French in school. I'm short on female voices—boudin making is a man's world—though nearly every boudin maker credits his momma or MawMaw (grandmother) as a culinary inspiration.

Besides the boudin, there's one constant, one thread that connects all of the interviews: place. Boudin is so of Acadiana that it's nearly impossible to find it two hours away in New Orleans, or in Shreveport, or in Monroe. Which means, lucky me, that a boudin documentarian must go to it.


## LOST IN SAUSAGE COUNTRY

Acadiana is a marvel of surreally shaped marshland cut through with snaking bayous, forested with sugarcane stalks and sprouting rice, and populated by birds—egrets, terns, gulls—whose stark whiteness glows against the fervent green backdrop of nature. But development in this part of Louisiana has occurred without much ceremony. Ask a Cajun for directions to his favorite boudin stop, and the answer will likely involve landmarks that do not, to put it politely, suggest a depth of culture. Hunting for boudin in Lafayette recently, I jotted down, "Keep straight to the third stoplight—Hooter's on one corner, Sam's Club on the other." In Eunice it was "Take a left at the Burger King."

No, the romance of boudin is not about architectural context or rituals of service. Rather, boudin is about people, the people of Cajun country. People like Bubba Frey, a sausage maker, restaurateur, self-taught fiddle player, poultry farmer, and the owner-operator of the only general store in Mowata. Frey leaves the liver out of his boudin. A former rice and crawfish farmer (and, clearly, a Cajun Renaissance man), he uses long-grain rice, explaining that "short grain will mush up."

Also, people like Rocky Sonnier, the sausage maker at Bayou Boudin & Cracklin' forty miles southeast of Mowata who does use liver, at a ratio of fifty pounds of pork to fifteen pounds of liver for a standard batch. Sonnier prefers medium-grain rice—and can't imagine how boudin could hold together with long grain. When I sat down with him for an interview, Sonnier mentioned that he'd heard about a new boudin shop in the area where the cooks were using long grain. The way he saw it, the new place had two options: "They might switch to medium grain, or they might just close up."

To a person, my oral history subjects tell me that boudin is simple food. You make a gravy, stir it into some rice, pump it all into casings, and admire your profit margins. And yet even simple foods—especially those embedded in a culture, as boudin is in Acadiana, or chile verde in New Mexico, or bagels in New York—provoke heated opinion. While on the Boudin Trail, I've tasted boudin prepared with various amounts of liver, from farmy to faint. I've happily seared my tongue on boudin fired with red pepper, and I've enjoyed boudin so mildly peppered that even my own Northern seasoning-wary peoples could love it. I've watched a boudin maker pass raw white onion through the meat grinder, never cooking it, and another who didn't use any white onion in his boudin at all. Some cooks add celery and green bell pepper. Almost everyone uses green onions. These days, commercial boudin makers tend to use pork shoulder meat or Boston butts; pork picnics, which include some skin, are also popular. Bubba Frey, the Cajun Renaissance man, bolsters his liver-free boudin's porcine flavor with temple meat from the pig's head.

DON'T ASK WHAT'S IN IT

Frey, whose ancestral lines stream from both France and Germany, understood cultural preservation at a particularly early age. He learned to make boudin as a boy from his great-uncle Lawrence Frey. "I knew that one day I was going to make boudin myself because these people weren't going to be around anymore," he says. "I was going to have to learn how to do it, or it was going to be shoved underneath the table and forgotten forever."

The boudin lessons Frey received from his uncle took place on the family farm during an era when agriculture was Acadiana's primary industry and when many families raised the animals that would later feed them. Hogs held less market value than cattle, they fattened quickly, and their rendered lard offered an invaluable medium for preservation. Cold-weather hog killings, to this day called *boucheries* in Acadiana, were central to existence. It takes only one man to kill a hog, but in the days before reliable refrigeration, it took several pairs of hands to dress out a single animal's meat. Boucheries were community events—feasts—and sausage called boudin was a staple at them even before Louisiana rice production gained steam in the mid- to late 1800s. Other traditional Cajun preparations, many of them still called by their French names, were also born of the boucherie: *reintier de cochon* (backbone stew), *chaudin or ponce bourré* (stuffed pig's stomach), *gratons* (cracklins), *ti salé* (a peppered salt pork), and *fromage de tête cochon* (hogs head cheese).

These days it's cheaper and easier for Cajun families to visit the neighborhood supercenter's meat department for precut chops and steaks trucked in from the Midwest. Even reputable markets like Legnon's don't process whole animals anymore, with the exception of custom game slaughtering during hunting season. Instead, market owners purchase boxed meat from distributors and add value to it by stuffing it, marinating it, grinding it, or turning it into sausage or tasso (a highly seasoned ham-like product). And yet, while adjusting for convenience and modern economics, Cajuns do still hold tight to their culinary traditions. For evidence, take the abundance of boudin vendors in Acadiana, as well as places like Ruby's Café in the pork-centric town of Eunice, which I have a difficult time avoiding. Especially around lunchtime.

Propped out front of Ruby's on a recent visit, a dry-erase board enticed passersby with Wednesday's lunch specials: fried chicken with rice dressing, meatball stew, beef and sausage sauce piquant, and *ponce*, a remnant of the boucherie. Sometimes called *paunce*, that last dish translates to pork stomach stuffed with seasoned ground beef. The ponce at Ruby's is smoked, and the kitchen serves it in meatloaf-like slices, each bound by a tender cuff of the stomach. For seven dollars, the plate also heaves with cream potatoes, turnip greens slicked with bacon fat, and the consummate Cajun side dish of rice and gravy.

Opened in 1957 by Ruby Mott and resurrected a couple of times since her passing in 2001, Ruby's is a food tourist's Disneyland—Thursday there's stuffed beef tongue and pork ribs overlaid with a topcoat of cracklins—and yet on Wednesday I was the only nonregular who didn't seem to know whether you're meant to *eat* ponce's rubber band of stomach. (You are.) As the sociable people of Acadiana are wont to do, Dwayne Vidrine, one of Ruby's owners, noticed my hesitation and asked where I was from. I explained that boudin had brought me to the area. Did he have any suggestions? "Eunice Superette & Slaughterhouse," he answered without pausing to think. "I was just there this morning. Had boudin for breakfast."

A potentially gruesome word, *slaughterhouse* is a term of hope as far as my work is concerned, as it denotes a preservation hall for pieces and parts—the trotters and the ears, the tails and the backbones—that allow for boucherie-type meals in an era when refrigeration and meat cases have rendered the boucherie custom all but obsolete. Slaughterhouses also sell some of the region's best boudin, because the meat and the liver are so fresh, and also because the trimmings are thrown into the grinder, adding extra dimensions of porkiness. At a slaughterhouse, the bones are available for simmering, making extraordinary gravies, and thus extraordinary boudins.

That's my take on the boudin at Hebert's Slaughter House & Meat Market in Abbeville, anyway: extraordinary. I do admit to a bias, as the primary boudin maker at Hebert's today is a woman. And it doesn't hurt that she also makes boudin rouge.

## THE QUEEN OF BOUDIN

On the morning I arrived at Hebert's to observe and interview the boudin maker Beverly Giardelli, three men stood around a long steel table picking through a cooked mixture of ribs, shanks, trimmings, liver, kidneys, and heart, separating meat from bones. When they finished, Giardelli knelt on top of another production table to reach the feeding tray of a meat grinder, through which she passed whole peeled raw onions and all the cooked pieces and parts that produce Hebert's full, round pork-intensive boudin. The grinding complete, she tumbled the meat and onions in an automatic mixer, incorporating three Magnalite pots of cooked medium-grain rice, along with green onion tops and unmeasured handfuls of black pepper, red pepper, and salt. Before stuffing the sausage mixture into casings, Giardelli set a few gallons of the mixture aside for making blood sausage later.

Hebert's is only the second source of commercial blood boudin I've come across in Acadiana (the first was Babineaux Slaughter House in Breaux Bridge), but not for lack of trying. While the idea of it may be morbid, blood boudin is a delight to eat; it has a limitless depth of flavor, and yet it's somehow also mellow and smooth, a juxtaposition that calls to mind the region's impenetrably black but easy-to-drink dark roast coffee.

Fresh pig's blood maintains a beautiful deep rose hue for hours after it's spilled. Giardelli told me that she almost passed out her first time making sausage with it, but that she loved eating blood boudin as a child while growing up in Abbeville. Today, some of Hebert's best blood boudin customers are children. As for Giardelli, she's about had enough. When lunchtime rolled around, she ordered us both foot-long chili dogs from Sonic.

It took her just four hours to produce about four hundred pounds of boudin, with the help of several coworkers who wordlessly stepped in to assist at just the right moments. Meanwhile, a persistent stream of customers passed through the meat market's doors, some buying links of hot boudin to eat in the parking lot, others dropping in to inquire about the cost of purchasing a whole butchered pig. It was Monday, and I remarked on the impressive flow of business. "This is nothing," Giardelli said. "Just wait for the colder months—October and November. That's when people start bringing their animals in from pasture, and then to the slaughterhouse to be processed. Leave them out all winter long and they'll lose too much weight."

Wintertime is Hebert's busiest season, just as it was high season for the old-time boucheries. In the realm of boudin, it sometimes seems that not so much has changed after all. And why would it? Boudin is a historical food, a beloved food, a food that refuses to stale. There's no end to the oral histories I could conduct for the Boudin Trail—my interview wish list contains a few dozen folks, and every time I pass through Cajun country I add a few more. That supermarket, this convenience store, those butcher shops. More seem to open every day. If in a hundred years the Sam's Clubs and gas stations have all been replaced by online shopping kiosks and battery-charging bays, I am certain that the boudin will still be here.

*Naomi Shihab Nye's most recent books are* Transfer *(poems) and* There Is No Long Distance Now *(stories). This poem originally appeared in the collection* Fuel.

# Boy & Egg

## Naomi Shihab Nye

Every few minutes, he wants
to march the trail of flattened rye grass
back to the house of muttering
hens. He too could make
a bed in hay. Yesterday the egg so fresh
it felt hot in his hand and he pressed it
to his ear while the other children
laughed and ran with a ball, leaving him,
so little yet, too forgetful in games,
ready to cry if the ball brushed him,
riveted to the secret of birds
caught up inside his fist,
not ready to give it over
to the refrigerator
or the rest of the day.

Sarah Nagem studied journalism at West Virginia University and now lives in Raleigh, North Carolina, and works for the News & Observer.

# As ConAgra Pulls Out, Workers Face Uncertainty

## Sarah Nagem

For the past two years, Debra Pettiway has gone to work in the building where her only son died.

As she saw it, she didn't have much choice.

"I had to pay my bills," Pettiway said.

Pettiway, fifty, walked out of the ConAgra Foods Slim Jim plant for the final time last week as her thirty-two-year career with the company came to an end.

For the first time in four decades, the sprawling plant on Jones Sausage Road is no longer producing meat snacks. Twenty-three months after an explosion sparked by natural gas rocked the plant, ConAgra wrapped up Slim Jim production on Friday and is shifting its operation to a plant in Ohio.

The move is an end of an era—and a way of life—in Garner, where the plant has offered stable, decent-paying jobs for thousands of workers over the years.

Now the remaining two hundred ConAgra employees are wondering what's next as they begin a new chapter in their lives. As it has been for many people, the food plant has been the only job Pettiway has ever known.

When she graduated in 1979 from Smithfield-Selma High School, seventeen-year-old Pettiway accepted a job at the plant. The pay was good, and she worked her way up to a supervisor position overseeing production.

Pettiway's son, Lewis Junior Watson, quit Clayton High after the tenth grade and floundered for a while. So when he got on at ConAgra when he was about twenty-two, Pettiway was pleased.

"He was young," she said. "He needed to work."

They were on different shifts, but some mornings Pettiway would take grits and sausage to her son at the plant.

Pettiway was on vacation on June 9, 2009, but her son was at work. That morning, as workers were installing a new water heater, an explosion blasted through the building. A fire broke out, walls crumbled, and debris went flying.

Dozens were injured, some with severe burns. Pettiway figures her son, thirty-three, was at his meat-cutting station at the time of the blast.

Watson didn't make it out alive.

## DWINDLING NUMBERS

In the months following the blast, ConAgra's future in Garner—and the future of the plant's nine hundred workers—was murky.

At first, ConAgra executives said they wanted to rebuild the plant. Garner and Wake County rallied to persuade the company to stay.

As ConAgra scaled back production at the Garner site, many people lost their jobs. In November 2009, five months after the explosion, ConAgra laid off 250 workers. Another big layoff occurred last month [April 2011] when 243 workers were let go.

In March 2010, ConAgra gave the news some workers said they had been expecting—Slim Jim production was leaving Garner and shifting to a plant in Troy, Ohio.

The choice wasn't an easy one for ConAgra, said Greg Smith, executive vice president of supply chain.

"It's always difficult," Smith said. "Any time you make a decision that impacts communities, it's difficult for us. . . . It's especially hard when you have a good base like in Garner."

Earlier this year, ConAgra hosted a job fair at the plant in hopes of helping its workers find new employment. About twenty companies—many that offer manufacturing jobs—took part, and nearly four hundred workers showed up, said Dave Jackson, a ConAgra spokesman.

ConAgra isn't keeping track of how many workers are finding jobs and where. But as the Triangle unemployment rate hovers at 7.5 percent, some say it's a waiting game.

## LOOKING FOR WORK

Calvin Sanders, thirty-seven, spent eighteen years at the plant grinding meat. It was his only job since high school.

"I'm getting my resume out there now trying to find something," Sanders said.

He went to ConAgra's job fair and applied with several companies, including Time Warner Cable, biopharmaceutical company Talecris, and food manufacturer Northeast Foods.

So far, no word.

But Sanders said he's optimistic. He enrolled in an online college program about a year ago, and he plans to earn a bachelor's degree in health care administration in 2014. Eventually he wants to work as a medical office manager.

In the meantime, Sanders said, he'll use money he earns umpiring sporting events to help support his wife and four-year-old son.

While Sanders and others continue to look for work, Anthony Spruill, fifty-six, of Garner is just trying to get through each day.

Spruill was in the plant when the explosion rocked the building, and the experience haunts his thoughts.

"The only thing I remember is the loud explosion," Spruill said. "I haven't had a whole night's sleep since."

Doctors told him he's suffering from post-traumatic stress. The medicine they gave him helps some, Spruill said, but he still has nightmares in which he hears people screaming.

As a machine operator, Spruill said he brought home between $400 and $500 a week. Now's he getting by on $1,200 a month in disability payments.

"It's been rough, I tell you," he said. "You do the best you can, you know?"

Growing up in a small community in Halifax County, Spruill said, he didn't have many job options. So when he landed a job at the Jesse Jones Sausage Co. in the early 1980s, he was thrilled. It was a good job for someone like him, Spruill said, who hadn't finished high school.

These days, Spruill can't even bear to drive by the site of his old job.

"I don't even want to go out that way," he said. "I always go around. I don't care about that building."

## TRYING TO RESTART

Garner is making plans for the future of the ConAgra site. As a parting gift, the company is giving the 106-acre property to the town.

It's also handing over $500,000 for the town to market the site, along with $2.5 million for a community center.

The goal is to bring in a company—or multiple companies—that will replace the ConAgra jobs and offer competitive wages, said Tony Beasley, Garner's economic development director.

Two food manufacturers have already toured the site, Beasley said, and four more plan to visit. By next November or December, the town should have a clearer sense of what could take shape there, he said.

"It's still a little bit early to tell," Beasley said. "The big thing is if (companies) can pay the wages and have the tax base ConAgra had."

Pettiway, who had planned to work at ConAgra until retirement, said she'd like to see a pharmaceutical company move in. After the job fair, she applied with several companies, including Kellogg's, Butterball, and Campbell's.

"I hope somebody calls me," Pettiway said.

At the age of fifty, she said, she never dreamed she'd be looking for work.

Pettiway said she enrolled in a management-training program at Johnston Community College, and she's set to start next month. She wants to manage a restaurant.

ConAgra offered its Garner workers the chance to transfer to another plant, but Pettiway said that wasn't an option for her. It would be too expensive to move, she said.

Eleven workers from the Garner plant asked to transfer, said Jackson, the ConAgra spokesman. The company said yes to all of them.

But Pettiway doesn't plan on leaving her Johnston County home. And as she looks back on the roller coaster ride of the past couple of years, she questions the way her longtime employer handled the aftermath of the tragedy.

"They took what you can't replace," Pettiway said of her son's life. "A phone call, 'how you doing?' I ain't got a phone call yet. It's been almost two years."

She'll no longer work in the factory where her son spent his final moments, but that is little consolation. Her bosses knew to leave her alone when she had trouble coping.

"I have my good days, and I have my bad days," Pettiway said. "They understand that. I cry a little bit and then I go back to work. . . . I tell them I hope none of them have to walk in my shoes."

# Messing with Mother Nature

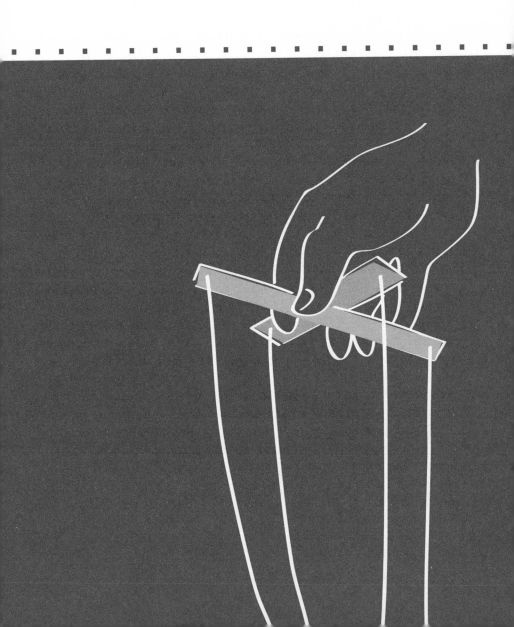

*Barry Estabrook is the author of* Tomatoland: How Modern Industrial Agriculture Destroyed Our Most Alluring Fruit. *This story originally appeared in* Gastronomica.

# Reviving Red Snapper

## Barry Estabrook

Mike Davis shoves his hand toward me. It seizes mine and latches on, as if trying to hold a fish intent on wiggling free. His grip is hard, sandpapery, and it lasts. "Morning," he drawls. "Let's get us some coffee and then we can go into my office to talk." His "office" turns out to be a chipped concrete seawall down by the docks at the A. P. Bell Fish Company in Cortez, Florida.

Cortez is a hardscrabble community of commercial fishermen who ply the Gulf of Mexico for crab, grouper, tilefish, and snapper. They live on a grid of narrow streets near Sarasota Bay in frame bungalows aging decorously into the deep-green shade of overgrown sea grapes and moss-draped live oaks. Cortez has the timeless quality of a holdover that somehow escaped the attention of the region's developers during their rush to slap up gleaming high-rises on every desirable square foot of the Sunshine State.

At a marina half a mile up the coast, yachts, sport-fishing craft, and sleek cigarette boats bob at their moorings, halyards tinkling. At the A. P. Bell Fish Company, the vessels are scuffed and stained with mildew and rust. The air is thick with the stink of fish and bottom muck. Lift trucks, top-heavy under containers of iced-down fish, rumble from dock to warehouse. Workers holler to be heard.

Like his father before him, Mike Davis is a reef fisherman. He is now forty-four years old but looks older. Since first going to sea during school breaks at the age of seven, he has been pursuing grouper and red snapper along a 120-mile swath of the Gulf of Mexico off the Florida coast. Drawing deeply on a Marlboro, he describes a hard life. Bending, hauling, and lifting on rolling boats has wrecked his back. His legs are afflicted with the stabbing pains of sciatica. Long absences at sea destroyed his seventeen-year marriage. The financial pressures of trying not to go bankrupt while catches plummeted and his income dropped by half exacerbated a drinking problem that nearly killed him. So did his job. Davis was caught in a freak storm with wind gusts over one hundred miles per hour, and a rogue wave smashed over his forty-four-foot boat, crushing the cabin where he and his crew were eating dinner, leaving them adrift all night and the next day before rescuers found them. "I thought my time had come," he says.

A few days before our conversation on the seawall, he had returned to port after a two-week trip. The fish weren't biting. All that he and his two crewmen had to show for fourteen days at sea was one thousand dollars split among them. "A fish is like a pregnant woman," he says. "They eat only what they want when they want." He exhales and looks out toward the bay. "And sometimes they can be downright miserable."

Until a couple of years ago red snapper, a commercially valuable, iconic species synonymous with warm tropical evenings, crisp white wine, and swaying palms, hovered on the brink of extinction. A decades-long cycle of misguided efforts to manage the population resulted in one failure after another as the population dropped to a mere 2 percent of what had historically swum in the Gulf.

But thanks to a recently introduced plan that turns the conventional wisdom of fisheries management on its head, the livelihoods of Davis and fishermen like him from Florida all the way over to Texas are becoming a lot less miserable. Called Individual Fishing Quotas (IFQs), the new regulations, which give a guaranteed allotment of fish to each participant instead of applying industry-wide quotas, went into effect for Gulf of Mexico Red Snapper (*Lutjanus campechanas*) in early 2007. The results were immediate and so profound that the Gulf Fishery Management Council voted earlier this year to increase the annual limit on red snapper to nearly seven million pounds from five million.

"This is the first time in a decade that I've felt comfortable with them raising the quota," says Chris Dorsett, director of fish conservation and management at the Ocean Conservancy's Austin, Texas, office. "The red snapper population's health is improving, and overfishing has ended."

Everybody should be encouraged about the results coming out of the Gulf. Most of the wild fish that we love to eat are in serious trouble, their populations in steady decline. According to the Environmental Defense Fund, fifty-four American fish stocks are already overfished, and an additional forty-five stocks are being caught at rates that will soon put them in that category. Aquaculture is not the solution because it pollutes the oceans, and carnivorous fish such as salmon must be fed fishmeal from fully exploited stocks of anchovies and other small species. The successes of the red snapper fishery show that there is a way out of this downward spiral. IFQ-style programs are being introduced in several major American fisheries. This spring the entire Northeast Coast adopted a similar approach to management. Boats that target nearly fifty types of bottom-feeding fish along the entire Pacific Coast of the lower forty-eight states are in the process of following suit.

IFQs and similar programs, variously called "sectors," "catch shares," or "limited access privilege programs," were first used in Australia, New Zealand, and Iceland in the 1970s. According to Christopher Costello, a professor of resource economics at the Bren School at the University of California, Santa Barbara, and the lead author of a groundbreaking paper in the September 2008 issue of *Science*, "Can Catch Shares Prevent Fisheries Collapse?" all of these plans give fishermen what amounts to "ownership" of a portion of the fishery. Like shareholders in a company who see the value of their holdings go up when the company prospers, the fishermen stand to benefit as the fish populations increase. In many catch-share arrangements, the participants have the right to buy, sell, or lease shares in their fishery, just like any other property. All the more reason to take good care of the resource.

Costello notes that traditional fisheries management practices fail to recognize what the ecologist Garrett Hardin called the "tragedy of the commons." In a 1968 paper Hardin contended that when individuals who share a common resource act in their own best interest, that resource will ultimately become depleted, even if the decline helps no one in the long term. Typical regulations, such as set fishing seasons, limits on the number of days that fishermen are allowed to go to sea, restrictions on equipment, and caps on the total amount of fish that can be caught by an entire fishery, lead to what the industry calls "derby fishing," a Wild-West mentality where each participant scrambles to get as much of the total as he or she can, as quickly as possible. Fishermen try not only to out-compete each other but to out-smart regulators. If the government permits only so many days at sea, it makes sense to get a bigger boat to catch more fish in the allotted time.

According to Costello, who looked at fifty-year records at more than eleven thousand fisheries for mollusks, crabs, lobsters, finfish—every type of seafood—in virtually all countries and ecosystems around the world, this "race to fish" creates "a spiral of excessive harvests, and eventual collapse." A much-cited paper published by Boris Worm of Dalhousie University in 2006 predicted that unless changes were made, all of the world's fisheries could be decimated by 2048.

Among the eleven thousand fisheries they examined, Costello and his co-authors found a tiny fragment, only 121, that used catch-share management. But in what the authors called "a marked reversal of previous predictions," those that did adopt the program stopped the decline in fish populations.

Clearly, something about catch shares worked. To look at the approach more closely, the Environmental Defense Fund assembled a team of thirty specialists to examine how ten North American catch-share fisheries were faring. Their report, "Sustaining America's Fisheries and Fishing Communities: An Evaluation of Incentive-Based Management," added weight to Costello's findings. Catch-share fisheries were twice as likely to stay within legal limits as non-catch-share operations. Over all, catch-share fisheries actually undershot their limits by 5 percent. Bycatch, the industry term for unwanted or illegal fish that have to be thrown overboard, usually dead, dropped by 40 percent.

Catch shares were good for fishermen, too. Revenues per boat actually increased by 80 percent. And the chance of getting hurt—a big issue in an industry where jobs are thirty-five times more dangerous than the average American job (much more dangerous than mining)—was cut by more than half.

This is all very well on paper, but convincing fishermen like Mike Davis that IFQs were the way to reverse the decline in red snapper took more than a decade. Pam Baker, the senior policy advisor to the Environmental Defense Fund's Gulf of Mexico Ocean Program in Austin, Texas, has been involved with attempts to rebuild the Gulf red snapper population since the late 1990s. "The old system told fishermen when to fish, how to fish, where to fish, how many fish to catch per trip, and what size of fish to catch," she says. "IFQ-based management gets rid of all that. It says to each fisherman, "Here's how much fish you can catch. You have to show us that you've stayed within that limit. The rest is pretty much up to you."

But the old highly regulated system was the devil everyone knew. Catch shares were held in such suspicion in government circles that in 1996 a federal moratorium was put on such programs as an amendment to the Sustainable Fisheries Act and wasn't lifted until 2006. By that time, a different mentality had settled upon the Gulf fishery. Every other management technique had been tried and found lacking. IFQs were adopted almost by default. "The red snapper population had dropped so low that fishermen and regulators began to realize that it was not a question of choosing between catch shares and some idealized notion of the past," Baker says. "It was a choice between catch shares and nothing." In 2004 a majority of red snapper fishermen voted to begin work on an IFQ program.

Agreeing in principle was only half the battle. "The success in any catch-share program is to clearly define your objectives up front," says

Costello, who has investigated more than two hundred catch-share fisheries. "There are lots of ways to design a program." The first step is to use hard scientific facts to determine how large the total "pie" is going to be. Before IFQs, catch limits on Gulf red snapper had everything to do with wishful thinking and politics and nothing to do with science. In the mid-1990s managers knew that the maximum sustainable yield of red snapper in the Gulf was six million pounds per year. Nonetheless, year after year fishermen were legally allowed to take nine million pounds, an amount that was 50 percent higher than the sustainable yield. You don't need a degree in resource economics to understand what that will do to a population.

Once the correct size of the red-snapper pie was determined (closer to five million pounds), it had to be divided according to an equitable formula, inevitably a contentious process. In the Gulf, the quantity of fish caught over previous seasons was the determinant, but fishermen still grumbled that it wasn't fair. Because red snapper had been all but extirpated from the Florida Gulf Coast during the lean years, Mike Davis and other captains working out of Cortez didn't fish for them, so he received minimal allotment. He contends that wasn't reasonable.

Managers decided that each fisherman would have ownership rights to his quota, which could be bought, sold, traded, and leased. "One thing that happens in catch shares," says Costello, "is that efficient fishermen tend to buy out those who are less efficient. So you can get consolidation of fleet." To prevent a handful of large companies or powerful fishermen from buying up all the quota, no one could control more than 6 percent of the total snapper catch. On January 1, 2007, the National Marine Fisheries Service gave the completed plan its official blessing.

Results came quickly. For the first time in two decades Gulf fishermen could catch and sell snappers year-round—previously they had been limited to ten days per month. With guaranteed allotments, fishermen could pick and choose when they went out. Derby fishing became a relic of the past. They fished when market prices were high and the weather was good and stayed in when the fishing was poor, the prices low, or the weather stormy. All told, they spent much less time at sea. But because landings kept pace with demand, as opposed to flooding the market during brief open periods, prices rose by 25 percent, from a little over three dollars a pound to nearly four dollars. Bycatch was reduced by 70 percent because managers were able to lower the minimum size for legal snapper. This meant that fish that were once thrown overboard as undersized (with only one in five surviving, according to the NMFS) were kept and counted toward quota. The fishermen, who were required to carefully report and monitor what they caught and often had government inspectors on board, erred on the side of caution and came in a little under their catch limit after years of regularly exceeding it by wide margins. The number of vessels chasing the limited snapper resource declined, as more serious players bought quota from dabblers, reducing pressure on the fish population and making fishing more viable for those who remained on the water. Fishermen who primarily targeted grouper, tossing unintentionally caught red snapper back as bycatch, started to lease snapper quota from those who had extra. Being able to sell the once-wasted snappers made trips more profitable for the grouper fishermen, and the weight of the snappers was figured into the total allowable catch. Under the old system, every player was losing—regulators, fishermen, and particularly the fish. Under IFQs it has been a win-win for all involved. Tellingly, when IFQs were expanded to include Gulf of Mexico grouper and tilefish early this year there was almost no opposition.

There is another group of unplanned-for winners—us, the fish-eating public. Costello found that "literally every catch-share fishery" he looked at resulted in a lengthening of the season and an increase in the quality of product sold to consumers. Before, all the fish were caught in a short period. The catch had to be frozen and often shipped all over the world because local markets were glutted. Under catch shares, supply meets demand. Fish is sold fresh and locally at premium prices.

So what's not to like? Some Gulf of Mexico fishery veterans worry that regulators are getting caught up in the exuberance, and that it is too soon to say for certain that better times lie ahead for red snapper. Jim Cowan, a professor in the Department of Oceanography and Coastal Sciences at Louisiana State University, expresses doubts about the wisdom of raising the catch limit so soon. "There were two large classes of red snapper born in 2004 and 2006," he says. "Those fish are getting big enough to be working their way into the fishery now. So the fishermen are seeing a lot of fish. But I've been at this for twenty years, and I've seen the same thing happen four times—you get a good year, and the council caves into pressure and raises the catch limit. I worry that we are repeating the same mistakes all over again."

But this time, at least, the powers that be listened to Cowan. After originally considering increasing the snapper limit to nine million pounds, they settled on a more conservative six million. If the new limit proves too high, there is a mechanism to roll it back. Chris Dorsett of the Ocean Conservancy, like most of those involved in the red snapper fishery, is comfortable with the new catch limits. "As a science-based organization, we tracked the decision-making process, and while there were some issues where we would have made a slightly different choice, it appears that the population is rebuilding, and there are adequate safeguards to ensure that the new level is safe," he says.

Pam Baker of the Environmental Defense Fund concurs. "If there are more fish there, I'm glad they are going to increase the catch and that people are going to benefit," she said. She also thinks catch-share management bodes well for the fishing industry in general. "Destroyed fish stocks, unfortunately, are common. What the IFQ did here is show that if you have the management right—and that includes fishermen—and you have the right incentives, and people are accountable, you can solve the problems in a fishery and provide the sorts of benefits we would all like to see from our natural resources."

Mike Davis is not the sort of guy who puts much stock in talk. "But there are a hell of a lot more snappers out there now, sometimes so many that you can't even get your lines down before they fill up with fish," he says. And he acknowledges one other important benefit of IFQs: "least I don't have to take a chance getting myself killed." The Gulf oil spill has added an element of uncertainty, and although it is too early to determine its long-term damage to fish populations, industry leaders say that without catch shares, the fishery's future would be even more doubtful.

*Jennifer Justus is the food culture reporter at the* Tennessean *in Nashville. She also blogs at* A Nasty Bite, *a name her grandmother gave to simple meals.*

# Flooded

## Jennifer Justus

My editor wanted a story on banana pudding.

People need a break from the flood, she said. You're helping them by giving them that.

I didn't believe her.

Sitting at my desk with stacks of cookbooks, less than a week after the flood of May 2010, I couldn't keep my eyes on the Word document where I should have been writing about tricks for perfectly peaked meringue or which wafers taste best.

No, my eyes were fixed on Facebook instead.

I read that Jeremy, the chef at Tayst, had made gumbo for a team of volunteers helping Marne Duke, a tireless supporter of the local food community who had lost her home. I saw pictures of food that Tandy and his staff at City House delivered to the Red Cross. My friend Michelle even helped a stranger named Mary clean out the Madison home she had lived in for fifty years.

My city was still underwater. Friends needed help. And I was supposed to write about banana pudding?

Then I remembered my grandfather. He ate banana pudding every chance he could get.

A tall thin man with a booming voice, I had seen him clear out half a casserole of the stuff, scooping it into a soup bowl rather than a dessert plate. He ate it at his sisters' houses. He ate it at restaurants. He made it at home. But I also saw him eat it at a makeshift table of plywood laid across two sawhorses in the middle of a flooded hardware store. It was 1990, and the family business that his father had started in the 1930s—and that he sold to my parents in 1981—had just been carried away.

The plywood table was a drop-off spot for donated food. Church ladies brought potato salad. Neighbors brought green beans and crock-pots of soup. My grandfather's sister Ruth had brought my grandfather a specially prepared gift.

So okay, I thought. A story on banana pudding it is.

My parents were inside the hardware store as it began to flood. The mayor of our small town, McCaysville, Georgia, had called early that morning to warn them that water was lapping the town bridge. My mom grabbed a broom on the way out the door thinking she might need to sweep out some water.

About two hundred yards from the store, my dad's truck flooded out. They rushed on inside to cut the power and pick things up off the floor. The little hardware store represented three generations of livelihood for our family. They weren't about it to leave it easy.

They filled a garbage bag with the accounts receivable, about $500 cash, and insurance papers ("Which didn't mean a hill of beans," Mom learned later) and started out the door. But the water against the front door was already over three feet high. They couldn't push it open using both their body weights—lucky for them, because the current would have carried them away, too.

Trapped, they called 911. Maybe we'll wait it out, they thought. But the water was thigh-high at that point. They started to look for other ways out, and my father literally shoved my mom out a back door and up a ridge behind the store, giving her momentum, yelling for her to climb with all her might. He went out a second side door, where water had begun to eddy at a slower rate. He grabbed a ladder from the lumberyard to climb to the top of the building. And as my mom watched from a rock on the ridge, he took a running leap—about fifteen feet—throwing himself onto the bank. And then she lost sight of him. "The water was so loud," she said of the driving rain and river. "I was yelling for him, and I couldn't hear a word until he showed up."

The water rose to seven and a half feet inside the store that day.

I have heard the story hundreds of times. It happened when I was sixteen. But hearing it last night, after I called Mom to quiz her about banana pudding, my grandfather, and the flood, I realized for the first time how close I truly came to losing them. The aftermath of the flood here somehow brought it home to me.

The water receded quickly at my family's store—much quicker than it has here. We started cleanup the following day, but it took us two days to clear a path to the office. It was a mess of paint cans, overturned display cases, rolls of wallpaper, and cabinetry. A chair from the office sat on top of the front counter. But my mom remembers the florescent light bulbs. "They had floated all over the store, because we sold them," she said. "They were like swords."

But when the cleanup came, so came the friends. And the food. Which brings me back to banana pudding.

My grandfather had a very particular way of assembling his banana pudding. He would make a layer of wafers with a slice of banana placed precisely on each cookie, while my grandmother stirred the custard in the pan. He whipped up a meringue and baked it just until the peaks toasted. It was often a Saturday-evening process for a Sunday lunch or potluck. He was precise about many things, even insisting that my brother and I never call him Grandfather, only J. J. That was his name.

When the store flooded, my mom told him to stay away. "Please don't come, you will be heartsick," she told him. "That was three generations of work gone in that few hours. Gone."

But then again, he could never stay away. Even after "retirement," heart surgery, and a loss of most of his hearing, he'd mosey on down on most afternoons. Customers had to shout at him to say hello.

I asked my mom if J. J. had any words of wisdom after the flood—even during cleanup.

"He just got quiet," she said. "He was always there, but you could tell he was hurt. Probably hurt for us, because when we bought the business he said, 'If you guys can work this for ten years you can retire no problem.'"

But our little mining town had gone through two employee strikes and two layoffs. The mines closed. Then came the flood.

My parents did bring the business back to life. They sold it eventually. They still work at sixty-three and sixty-five, but they're okay with that. "I have my kids, I have my health," my mom said. "Stuff is just stuff."

And thinking back on J. J., I don't remember his quiet moments during the cleanup. I can't imagine it, frankly. He had charisma that could fill the cracks of a room like floodwater. I remember him finishing his banana pudding at his sister's house, dramatically scraping his bowl with the spoon—making a racket until she offered him more.

Maybe he had been subdued during the days after the flood, but I like to think—I hope—that his sister's banana pudding brought him a bit of comfort, too.

So that's my story on banana pudding. I don't have anything to say about meringue or wafers. But tonight I think I'll make a batch. Now, who needs it?

*Paul Greenberg is the James Beard Foundation Award–winning author of* Four Fish: The Future of the Last Wild Food. *This story was reported and published around the first anniversary of the BP Gulf of Mexico oil spill.*

# Reconsidering the Oyster

## Paul Greenberg

Just off the coast of Empire, Louisiana, about forty miles north of where BP's Deepwater Horizon rig sank into the sea in April 2010, Captain Eric Buras steered an open-decked barge in a tight circle hauling a dredge along the bottom. Buras's two crew members, Raymond Sylve and his son Emmett, stood at a cleaning table, hammer-headed hatchets at the ready. After five circles Buras signaled the crew to step back and when all hands and fingers were clear he threw a lever and the dredge emerged from the deep. Up it came over the railing. *Shrakkkkh* roared the chain-link holding bag and all at once around fifty wild Louisiana oysters, each as big as a man's clenched fist, spilled out on to the table. *Choppity, chop, chop,* the Sylves worked at the clumps with their hatchets, breaking them down into individual animals. Buras grabbed one, wedged a knife into its hinge, prised it open, and severed the meat's ligaments with a sweep of the knife. The liquor and the waters of the Gulf mixed in the shell.

"You wanna eat one?" he asked.

I thought seriously about this question. I thought about the spill, about the suffering the Louisiana fishing community has endured. The stories of fishermen who had lost their boats and their oyster beds in Hurricane Katrina in 2005, who were on the verge of gaining some of it back with an anticipated bumper crop in 2010 only to lose as much as 80 percent of their oysters in the spill. I thought about the reams of government data saying the seafood is safe, the counternarratives from a few in the bayous that say it is not, and the rumors whispered in oyster country that the dispersant Corexit was still being sprayed in nighttime sorties whenever a random slick bubbled up from the mud. I remembered how hard it was to find *anyone* who would take me oystering, the complicated chain of restaurant owners, oyster bed lease holders and cousins of lease holders that led me to Captain Buras, one of the only oystermen I found who wholeheartedly said "It's just good to be working again." I weighed the fact that I was a low risk seafood consumer—neither a child nor a woman of childbearing age. Then in the way one addresses a muddy-shelled Louisiana oyster fresh from the muck I pressed my lips to the very center of the meat and inhaled the whole briny mass. Not a whiff of taint. It was delicious, if a bit warm.

■　■　■

William Thackeray wrote that eating an American oyster was "like eating a baby." Presumably Thackeray was referring to the tremendous size of the *Crassostrea virginica* he encountered when Stateside, a completely different genus from *Ostrea edulis*, the smaller European oyster eaten from Colchester to Belon. But Thackeray might also have had his gag reflex triggered by the sheer abundance of American oysters that once paved the near-shore waters not only of Louisiana, but most of the American coast. As Mark Kurlansky tells in his fine book *The Big Oyster,* nineteenth-century New Yorkers consumed on average six hundred to seven hundred locally caught oysters per year. A single oyster can filter as much as forty gallons of water a day; Kurlansky estimates that the billions of oysters that used to inhabit New York Harbor cycled through the entirety of the harbor in a matter of days.

Today the oysters of New York are gone, the beds of the famed Chesapeake are in trouble, and many lesser grounds are fading fast. In a phenomenon a 2004 *Proceedings of the National Academy of Sciences* paper described as "a moving wave of exploitation," oyster collapse has moved down the American coasts with ever more distant estuaries providing the "seed" oysters to keep collapsing fisheries further north in business. Pollution accelerates the process. This trend is not exclusive to the United States. A 2011 paper by the Nature Conservancy reported an 85 percent reduction in oyster reefs worldwide. The mouths of the Thames and the Elbe have suffered as much oyster loss as the mouth of the Hudson.

The last great Northern Hemisphere stronghold of the wild oyster is their most southerly redoubt—the Gulf of Mexico. It's one of the only places left in the world where a freelance journalist can afford to sit down at a bar, order and consume a dozen oysters, and then feel financially capable of saying "you bet" when the waiter comes by and asks "How about another dozen?"

Which is why what has unfolded in the Gulf over the last year is so critical. If we lose Louisiana oysters and the fishery built around them, we will lose the last living proof that wild oysters and humans can do business with one another, to the betterment of both.

■ ■ ■

Drive down a Louisiana thoroughfare and you will pass advertisements offering a unique array of products and services. One proposes hog skin cracklin', frog legs, and turtle meat, another offers legal help with your spill claim, still another promises work for engineers out on the rigs that can cause spill claims in the first place. But the sign that caught my attention as I headed into the town of Golden Meadow was that of an oyster man. "COLLINS OYSTER CO." it read, "Out of Business After 90 Yrs. Thanks to BP's Oil and Governor Jindal's Freshwater." Inside I met Wilbert Collins and his son Nick, lifelong watermen born of watermen who explained with the charmingly elongated vowels of Cajuns speaking English what had prompted their lawn sign.

"On TV they always showed those birds full of oil. They make a big issue with it," Wilbert Collins told me, "But they killed millions and millions and millions of oysters and nobody said nothing."

What killed the oysters was not oil but freshwater.

As oil rushed toward the coast last spring the Governor's Coastal Coordinator made the call to throw open the Mississippi's freshwater diversions—devices that had been installed, ironically, to help improve the water quality of the Delta. The emergency measure was taken in hopes that a countersurge of Mississippi River water would drive oil offshore. While it's hard to judge the efficacy of this move, what it did do was drive millions of gallons of freshwater over the oyster beds. Too much freshwater blows out an oyster's pump as it tries desperately to maintain a salinity balance. Two months of open diversions on an overfull river during an El Niño year proved too much.

"Them things pushed a lot freshwater," Wilbert's son Nick told me. "A ridiculous amount. And it didn't move the oil at all."

Representatives from the state of Louisiana see their action as a very difficult but necessary choice between short-term injury and chronic damage. But both the Collinses and the state agree on one point: how little BP has done to fix the problems they caused. "BP is now refusing to provide emergency funding to help mitigate these ongoing impacts to our oyster community," Olivia Watkins from the Louisiana Department of Wildlife and Fisheries wrote to me. "BP had actually committed to that funding late last year. However, they have since changed their mind and retracted that commitment."

As proof of the oyster apocalypse, Nick Collins took me out on his boat and surveyed his beds. As in my earlier oystering trip, the dredge dragged along the bottom, came up full, and then spilled its contents onto the cleaning table. Every single oyster was a dead empty shell. This is particularly painful post–Hurricane Katrina. Katrina destroyed a lot of oysters, but hurricanes also spread larvae or "spat" far and wide. It takes three years for an oyster to reach maturity. A plethora of Katrina-spawned oysters should have been coming to market right when the BP well blew.

■   ■   ■

But even if Nick Collins were pulling up bushels of oysters full with the plump meat of yesteryear, he might not be able to sell them at a decent price today. Food scares are typically irrational. The recent dumping of radioactive water into the seas of Japan has cast a pall over the consumption of all sushi—Japanese or not. And perhaps the place where food-cautious emotions are hitting hardest after the spill are in places that sell the most oysters—Louisiana restaurants.

Tommy Cvitanovich is the owner of a popular pair of restaurants in greater New Orleans called Drago's. After telling his chef to fire up a dozen of his famous (and delicious) charbroiled oysters for me, he tried to set me straight on what he felt was the public's glaring misconception of Louisiana seafood post-spill. "The perception of our oysters not being safe is ludicrous," Cvitanovich told me. "Right now our seafood is the most tested food product in the United States. You've got Wildlife and Fisheries, the State Board of Health, the State Department of Environmental Quality all testing the waters. And that's just at a state level. On a national level you have NOAA, FDA, and the EPA and no one is coming up with positive tests."

But in spite of all of these tests the country is not being won over. A poll of national restaurants commissioned by Greater New Orleans Inc. found only 19 percent of those restaurants' clients held a favorable view of Gulf seafood in 2010, compared with 75 percent before the spill.

A lot of this is plain irrational fear from people outside the region who are not aware of the intensity of effort being directed at verifying seafood. But some of it stems from the sheer quantity of seafood Gulf residents eat. In the brackish sluiceways and milk-tea bayous of the rural part of the state, the standard unit of measurement for local seafood is the sack. A sack is a burlap bag that can hold roughly six dozen oysters, twenty dozen crawfish, or thirty dozen biganot snails. Any of these creatures might end up in a sack at any given month of the fishing season, and it is not unheard of for a family in the bayous to go through a sack in a single day several times a week.

This has prompted some, like Wilma Subra, a Louisiana chemist who provides technical assistance to the Louisiana Environmental Action Network, to cast doubt on the way the safeness of Louisiana seafood is being framed. "When the government established levels of the concern for polycyclic aromatic hydrocarbon (PAH's), they used consumption rates that are not appropriate for the Gulf," Subra told me. The Louisiana Department of Wildlife and Fisheries has countered that this is not the case. One of their recent press releases asserts the average consumer could eat 1,575 jumbo shrimp, 130 oysters, or 9 pounds of Louisiana fish every day for up to five years "without exceeding the health risks for contamination."

I can personally attest to the overwhelming presence of local seafood in the Gulf diet. By simply eating what was available in roadside shacks, people's homes, and restaurants, my final tally for a week was 97 oysters, 36 shrimp, 26 crawfish, and a half pound each of flounder, catfish, and amberjack. Most of it was fried. All of it was delicious. To date I am asymptomatic for PAH poisoning, though my doctor did mention something about elevated cholesterol. . . .

■   ■   ■

Toward the end of my time in Louisiana I found myself thinking not only about Gulf seafood's impact on my body, but also my body's impact upon Gulf seafood. And so just before heading back to New York I decided to do a little penance, driving East along Highway 10, a road literally made out of oysters that were dragged from the bay and crushed up into roadbed. My destination was a site just outside Mobile, Alabama, a place where the nongovernmental organization the Nature Conservancy was trying to rebuild what had once been a billion-strong oyster colony in Mobile Bay.

One of the only touching things about the otherwise faceless life of an oyster is that what an oyster likes best is the nubby shell of another oyster. In Louisiana where BP payments are falling short, oystermen are standing on the sidelines, lacking enough money to put "cultch" (oyster shells) back onto the beds so that if oysters spawn this spring and release larvae or "spat," the young will have somewhere to "set" and mature three years later into an adult oyster. With cultch either lacking or covered in slime from the freshwater inundations, a terrible downward spiral could be at hand. No cultch means nowhere for young oysters to set, which in turn reduces the amount of mature oysters, which in turn leads to dirtier water, which leads to even fewer oysters. And pretty soon you find yourself in an oysterless desert of brown, murky water where fish are less abundant and sediment chokes the bottom. A place like New York Harbor or the mouth of the Thames.

The only thing to be done is to put oyster shells back in the water in hopes that baby oysters will find them and make a home for themselves. Wading into Mobile Bay, water quickly washed over the top of my boots but the enthusiasm of the several dozen volunteers was warming. A few hundred meters out from the landing I joined the brigade, passing five-kilo bags of oyster shells hand-to-hand. Slowly a reef rose from water. Previous reefs built by the Nature Conservancy have shown to attract as many as one hundred oysters per square meter. By my eye the reef we were building was starting to approach ten meters total. My own personal contribution to it was perhaps a meter or two. In a morning's work, I had possibly laid the groundwork to put back into the world all that I had taken.

But humanity through its appetites, its wastes, and its accidents has dealt the oyster a terrible blow. The Gulf has lost tens of millions of them in a single year. The world has lost hundreds of billions in the last century. If we are going to fix things, not just in the Gulf but everywhere, we're going to need a lot more oysters.

*David Grunfeld has been a photo editor and staff photographer at the New Orleans* Times-Picayune *since 1993. He grew up in upstate New York.*

# The Collins Oyster Family

**David Grunfeld**

The Collins family of Golden Meadow, Louisiana, has been harvesting oysters around Bayou Lafourche for five generations.

The Collins Oyster Co. family, from left: Wilbert Sr., Tracy, Nick, Levy III, and Levy IV

Wilbert Collins has been oystering for over sixty years.

The *Braud & Tracy* in Caminada Bay.

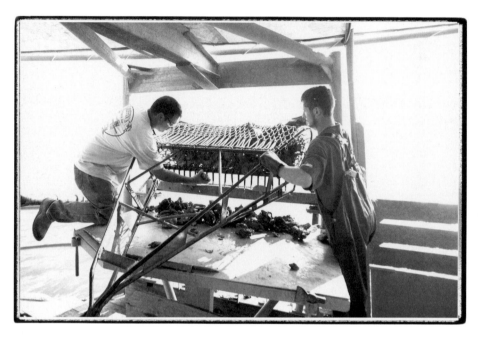

Nick Collins and his nephew, Levy IV, empty a dredge.

Levy IV

Nick Collins

The Collins Oyster Co. has been effectively out of business since the BP oil spill in 2010.

*Bob Marshall is a Pulitzer Prize–winning staff writer at the* Times-Picayune *in New Orleans. This story first appeared in August 2010, five years after Hurricane Katrina and in the midst of the BP Gulf of Mexico oil spill.*

# A Paradise Lost

## Bob Marshall

On a blustery spring day, Delacroix native Lloyd Serigne stands on the banks of Bayou Terre aux Boeufs, thirty miles south of New Orleans, talking about the village that raised him in the 1950s. Reaching into a deep well of memories, he paints an idyllic picture: a community of several hundred fishers, farmers, and trappers whose homes were surrounded by a wetlands paradise of high ridges, marshes, and swamps. The outside world—unwanted, unneeded—seemed a thousand miles away.

But the scene surrounding him only mocks that vision.

Naked slabs and raw pilings that once supported homes stand like tombstones in open, soggy ground. Bare tree trunks rise from a salt marsh that used to be a vegetable field. Battered home appliances, ice chests, and derelict boats litter the bank while a high tide moves through the remains of a hardwood forest. And a steady stream of heavy equipment heads down the road to fight the invasion of BP's oil.

None of it matches memories that seem as sharp as yesterday's news.

"Really, what we had here was a paradise—a natural paradise," says Serigne, seventy. He pauses to shake his head, a gesture half of wonder, half of despair.

"But when I try to tell the young people about this, they just stare at me like I'm crazy. They just can't imagine what was here such a short time ago.

"And now it's gone. Just gone."

Just outside the city, within earshot of the vocal crusade to save New Orleans's culture after Hurricane Katrina, communities that were the hub of a genuinely unique wetlands culture for two hundred years have quietly been slipping into history. There have been no jazz funerals or memorials for places like Delacroix, Hopedale, Pointe a la Hache, Grand Bayou, and Shell

Beach. But in the course of a few short years, place names that dotted the coastal maps for centuries have become mere ghost towns, victims of a wetlands system undercut by man, then pummeled by nature, and more recently stained by oil.

For the vast majority of city residents, these places were destinations known mostly for the seafood they shipped to local markets and the entertainment they provided sports enthusiasts on weekends. But for those who understand their history and the reasons for their demise, these communities carry an important warning for the big city.

When Serigne thinks of his childhood here, he remembers a thriving community of more than seven hundred Spanish-speaking fishers and trappers who seldom felt the need to travel to New Orleans because the ridges and wetlands of their world provided all they needed. He remembers high, dry ground covered with forests of oak, maple, and sycamore stretching from the banks of Bayou Terre aux Boeufs. He remembers wild fruit trees, citrus groves, rabbits and deer, ducks and geese, specks and reds and bass.

He remembers how children spent half of each year at distant trapping cabins with the whole family, wedging in school between seasons for shrimp, muskrat, mink, crabs, and ducks. He remembers thinking the world would always be like this.

But the most amazing memory of all: It was still mostly here just forty short years ago.

Serigne surveys the ruins surrounding him, and shrugs.

"Everything we had was based on the wetlands," he said. "When the wetlands started going, we were done for. But we just didn't realize it was happening until it was too late."

Those wetlands—the swamps and marshes of the great Mississippi River delta—were the reason Delacroix and its sister communities existed. Not only did they supply the basic sustenance for life, but for two hundred years they were as imposing an obstacle to the outward expansion of New Orleans as the Rocky Mountains were to Denver. That physical barrier allowed communities such as Delacroix to remain insulated from change despite being in the shadow of one of the nation's largest cities. Without hard-surfaced roads, without electronic communications, and without a real need to use the services and goods a city could offer, generations were raised speaking their own language and answering to a different set of social priorities.

Looking back, former residents now in their seventies realize the differences were stunning. Just forty years ago, while their contemporaries in the Crescent City were being carried along on the great cultural and economic changes of the post–World War II years—two-car garages, all-electric homes, subdivisions sprawling along interstate highways, and mandatory college educations—life in the fishing communities had changed little since the late 1800s. It was a subsistence culture revolving around fishing, trapping, hunting, and local gardens—a life divided between high land along bayou ridges and the deep marsh, between village homes and trapping cabins, where merchants from the city hawked goods from floating stores on boats, and where no one ever dreamed of leaving.

"Why would we?" asked Henry Martinez, sixty-seven, Serigne's lifelong friend. "We had meat, fish, vegetables.

"We had school, church, three dance halls. We had a community where every kid had three hundred parents. You could play in the woods, swim in the bayou, hunt, and fish.

"We had the best life anyone could think of."

And it never seemed to change. Serigne's ancestors arrived from the Canary Islands in the late 1700s, yet until the early 1960s, he and thousands of others spread across these bayou towns lived routines those ancestors would have recognized. But change was already rushing toward them. Centuries of tradition would wash away in forty years, the result of activities they witnessed—even cheered—but never fully understood.

Levees built along the river in the early 1900s shut off the spring floods that carried sediment to deltas, setting in motion a sinking of their wetlands that should have taken hundreds of years. The dredges for industry that arrived in the 1930s hastened that demise by centuries. Thousands of acres of marsh were removed in the search for oil and gas riches, and many more for shipping and development. As the delta sank and the dredges worked, small ponds grew into lakes and lakes into bays, drawing the Gulf of Mexico ever closer.

In 1965, Hurricane Betsy brought that reality home in crushing terms, basically wiping out the entire community. Within a few years, more than 80 percent of the residents had returned, but Betsy told them the end was coming. Between his teenage years in the 1950s and his thirtieth birthday in 1970, Serigne said, it became obvious that Delacroix and its unique way of life were dying. By his sixty-fifth birthday, it was gone: Hurricane Katrina was its final act.

Another of Serigne's peers, Thomas Gonzales, seventy-two, is one of the few natives still crabbing and living on the island. But to accomplish that, he resides in a house trailer resting on pilings seventeen feet above the narrow stretch of land remaining on the east bank of Bayou Terre aux Boeufs.

"When I grew up, all you saw from the front steps was woods and the bayou and other homes," he said.

"Now all I can see is water where the trees and marsh used to be.

"This ain't the Delacroix we boys was raised in. Not even close."

Today Delacroix and other fishing villages are either ghost towns, reclamation projects for sportsmen, or temporary boom towns for the BP disaster response. Some commercial fishermen still dock along the bayou, but they are commuters, driving in from communities on the protected side of the levees. Families that lived along the bayous for hundreds of years have given up, chased away not just by the violence of recent storms but by the certainty of more to come. If there's new construction, it's largely by city anglers building recreational retreats.

The newcomers seek their sport in a dying wetlands complex that is a skeleton of the vibrant ecosystem Serigne remembers from his childhood.

The landscape surrounding Serigne on his walks today is as close to his childhood memories as the Sahara is to the Amazon. The forest has been replaced by a salt marsh, the only reminder of the former woodlands a ghostly line of dead trees rising from an encroaching salt marsh that became the graveyard for homes, businesses, farm fields, and playgrounds. The community that once was home to a population estimated at seven hundred now hosts about fifteen full-time residents. The BP cleanup boom has boosted that number, but only temporarily.

"Everything changed so fast," Serigne said, surveying the empty lots and ruined boats along the bayou. "Of course, looking back with the information we have now, we can see how it all happened.

"It was the canals—the oil company canals, and the [Mississippi River–Gulf Outlet]. Back in the '50s, we could see difference in the way the tide was coming in and out. Faster. Stronger. By the '60s, we could see the marsh starting to eat out.

"Then came Betsy in '65. Then Katrina. Now it's gone. Hard to believe.

"Now when I talk to the younger people about it, they think it's a story."

It's a story worth retelling.

■   ■   ■

As children, Martinez, Serigne, and Gonzales never questioned why their home village was deep in a wetlands wilderness.

"We didn't feel isolated or anything," Serigne said. "To us, living there seemed the way life was supposed to be. It just seemed like someone made a smart decision."

History has another story, one that involves national ambitions in the age of global imperialism, royal decrees, civil wars, and traumatic social upheavals.

It turns out the wetlands community of Delacroix was never meant to be.

"The people who left the Canary Islands never intended to live in the area around what would become Delacroix," said William de Marigny Hyland, the St. Bernard Parish historian and president of Los Islenos Heritage and Cultural Society. "This is a complicated story."

It begins in late 1777, when the Canary Islands were not the vacation mecca they are today. The archipelago off the northwest coast of Africa was a strategically important staging area for Spain's colonial ambitions in the New World, but its residents had a hard life. They struggled to scratch out a living on a dry, rocky landscape, with disease and famine constant companions.

So when King Phillip III offered houses, a stipend, and—most important—free holdings on fertile land in the far-off colony of Louisiana, it was no surprise the response was overwhelming. The government had sought seven hundred volunteers; more than two thousand would eventually make the trip.

King Phillip had a specific demographic in mind, according to historian Gilbert Din: "The recruits were required to be from 17 to 36 years old, healthy, without vices, and at least 5 feet ½ inch tall. Butchers, gypsies, mulattoes, and executioners were not permitted to sign up."

The offer of new homes and land to this group was not an act of charity by the king, but a move to protect his ambitions.

"Spain had acquired New Orleans from France and knew that holding that city was the key to checking England's ideas for expanding its dominion west of the Mississippi River," Hyland said.

"Whoever controlled New Orleans controlled the Mississippi River valley from the Gulf to Canada.

"Only about four thousand people, Europeans and slaves, lived in New Orleans at the time. Spain knew it needed more residents and settlements to protect its claim."

New Orleans was vulnerable to attack via the high ground next to the river, Hyland said, so Spain wanted to develop communities to address that vulnerability.

■   ■   ■

The first Canary Islanders stepped off the *Santisimo Sacramento* in New Orleans on November 1, 1778, and by July of the next year almost sixteen hundred had made the crossing. The newcomers would start four new settlements. Two would be north of the city: Valenzuela, at the point where Bayou Lafourche left the Mississippi River, near present-day Donaldsonville, and Galveztown, on the Amite River off Lake Maurepas. Two would be south of the city: one on the west bank of the river at Barataria, and the other on the east bank south of the city at St. Bernard—San Barnardo to the Spanish newcomers.

"St. Bernard would become an area of plantations growing everything from indigo and sugar cane to rice and vegetables, and raising livestock," Hyland said. "Most of the Canary Islanders would settle in that area and work on those plantations, as well as producing some of their own crops and goods on their own properties."

The plantations occupied prime property along Bayou Terre aux Boeufs, which at that time flowed directly from the Mississippi River. Centuries of annual floods had spread rich alluvial soils and created high ground. The plantation names are carried by many current communities: Poydras, Toca, St. Bernard, Creedmore, Kenilworth, and Contreras.

"This became a very prosperous area." Hyland said. "One of the first railroads in the country would be built down there to carry goods to New Orleans markets. Many of the residents would speak Spanish at home but learned French so they could do business in the city."

And Bayou Terre aux Boeufs was the main thoroughfare. The waterway flowed south and east all the way to Chandeleur Sound, twisting through the wild wetlands on the edges of the great delta. Trappers, fishermen, and hunters had outposts there, but otherwise, the area was the domain of runaway slaves and a few Native Americans.

The Civil War would change all that.

"The war destroyed the plantation culture," said Hyland. "Many of the Canary Islanders no longer had jobs. They also didn't have property.

"So when they began looking for a place to settle—to squat—they already knew about this area down Terre aux Boeufs that was owned by a Frenchman who had never come to Louisiana."

The property was called La Isla de la Croix—the island belonging to Francois du Suau de la Croix. It was a large section of high ridges, swamps, and marsh along both sides of Bayou Terre aux Boeufs, about ten miles from the plantations.

It was known simply as La Isla—the Island—because bayous, small lakes, and swamps surrounded a large tract of high ground. Sugar had been planted in the area, but little else. It was still wild land, yet nature had plenty to offer.

Los Islenos, or the Islanders, as the new settlers would become known, could fish for shrimp, crabs, trout, and turtles. They could trap fur-bearing animals, such as mink and muskrat and otter, hunt ducks and geese and deer, and pick moss for furniture. They had plenty of high, dry land to grow vegetables and crops, raise livestock, and build their homes from the cypress and oak they also harvested. They could consume everything they took from the land, and they also could sell it to markets in the city.

"They developed a subsistence lifestyle, but they weren't poor," Hyland said. "They flourished."

■  ■  ■

Serigne was ten when his mother took the family on a trip to New Orleans to shop for items the natural bounty of their bayou home couldn't provide.

At the Woolworth's on Canal Street in the late 1950s, young Lloyd turned the faucet to wash his hands, and yanked them back, baffled.

Hot!

He turned the faucet on and off several times to see if it would happen again. It did, and he left the bathroom thoroughly confused. Only a few houses on Delacroix Island had indoor plumbing at the time, and even they had to heat water over a fire.

He asked his mother: How does the hot water get in there?

She stared at him for a few seconds before dismissing him, in Spanish—"Oh, don't bother me with things like that!"

She didn't know how the water got hot, either. The water heater, invented some sixty years earlier by Edwin Ruud, had yet to infiltrate life on the Island.

"It was a different world on the Island back then," Serigne said, recalling the story. "We did things the old ways."

The Delacroix of today resembles those childhood memories in name only. But the original name of this barren landscape provides a clue to the natural bounty that once thrived here: Terre aux Boeufs, or "land of the buffalo."

"The name was given by Bienville," said Hyland. "The wild cattle were buffalo—bison—that he saw in some numbers all over this area."

The salty Gulf was still many miles away.

In the 1950s, life—commercial as well as social—still followed nature's calendar, moving from shrimp to trapping to fishing and back to shrimping again—with crabbing throughout.

The wetlands had been healthy not just for survival, but for growth. The Delacroix of Serigne's childhood featured houses three and four deep, shaded and sheltered by oak, hackberry, maple, and sycamore trees. As many homes and businesses were constructed on the west side of Bayou Terre aux Boeufs as the east side—the only settled bank today. The community bustled, and grew.

"We had three dance halls, churches, small groceries—everything we needed," Martinez said. "It was a great place for kids. We had woods to play in, the bayou to swim in. We could go fishin', and huntin', and trappin'.

■  ■  ■

Children and teens in nearby New Orleans, like other American kids, may have been worrying about the latest TV show, what to wear to the Saturday hop or how to convince their parents to let them drive, but Delacroix kids were still connected to the land. School came only between seasons. Classes started in September, but when trapping season began in December, most of the kids moved with their parents to distant cabins in the marsh, where they helped harvest muskrat, mink, otter, and nutria. They seldom left before April. Serigne lived with his eight siblings and parents in a one-room cabin about twelve feet wide and twenty-four feet long—about the size of a FEMA trailer.

"The boys old enough would help my daddy run the traps and fish crabs, and the younger boys, the girls, and my mother, we would skin the rats, and put the skins on (frames) for drying," Serigne said. They'd pack the meat in barrels to use for crabbing, which started when they got back to Delacroix in March.

"Our camp was on a bayou with several other families," Serigne said. "And the marsh back then was solid enough to walk on, so you didn't have to spend all your time in a pirogue."

And they had other visitors. Fur buyers made the rounds to purchase pelts, and grocers steered their floating markets to the outposts so families could restock their staples.

Formal education suffered, of course, but with marsh life so successful, a lack of book knowledge wasn't considered a handicap.

"Most of us didn't speak English until we went to the first grade, and that was something we needed to learn if we traveled to the outside," said Martinez, who still crabs commercially. "But most kids became fishermen and trappers like their daddies, got married to local girls, and raised their own families there—just like it was always done."

Trapping season was followed by a spring shrimp season that was profitable, but dangerous.

Fisherman stayed out weeks at a time back then, because shrimp dealers would meet them out in the bays, buying their catch straight from the boat.

"Well, to stay out, you needed to carry plenty of extra gas," Serigne recalled. "We'd have it in barrels tied to the boat, and it was always leaking, and of course guys were smoking or engines were sparking."

One or two boats would explode every year, he said.

"You'd hear this big boom and see a red glow, and you knew someone was in trouble," Serigne said.

■　　■　　■

Summer was crabbing time, but also the season for the "chivo" migration.

"We called the sports fishermen from the city 'chivos,' which is Spanish for goat," Serigne recalled with a laugh. "They would come down on the weekends and hire our fathers to take them out fishing.

"Visitors from the city always seemed to like to stand on top of the boat cabin or on boxes, probably to see across the marsh. So they were always wobbling like goats and often fell over.

"Look at that silly chivo," one of the locals would say, or "I got some chivos coming down."

Serigne and Martinez remember the security they felt on the bayou, the confidence that life would always be that way.

But change was coming, and at a pace that would stun them. They can pinpoint now what set the demise in motion: the arrival of hard surface roads and canal dredging.

■　■　■

The end of their world did not come in the form of a cataclysm. Rather, it was like an undiagnosed disease that showed only vague and scattered symptoms until it grew terminal.

By the early 1960s, they were being tamed by hard surface roads, drowned by flood-protection levees and strangled by industries that brought canal dredging to the fragile ecosystem.

Asphalt and concrete highways were an obvious sign, and they quickly began changing the social order.

While shell and mud roads had reached Delacroix by the 1920s, getting in and out remained a difficult and time-consuming challenge, taken on mainly for commerce. The all-weather surfaces that came in the 1950s allowed more residents to get jobs at the refineries and manufacturing concerns closer to the city. As people on "The Island" got exposed to a different, more comfortable life, a slow migration began.

But a more fundamental change was under way. Serigne had always counted on being a fisherman. But as he entered his teens, his father disabused him of that notion.

"He encouraged me to move up the road, get a job in one of the towns," said Serigne, who took his father's advice and became a Teamster.

The father could see a way of life starting to slip away with the ever-higher tides, even if he didn't know exactly why at the time. "Of course, back then people didn't realize why it was happening."

In fact, for seventy years, residents mostly supported the very forces that would spell doom for their lifestyle—levees and canals dredged for oil, gas, and shipping.

If levees were all that had happened to the delta, the wetlands in place at the turn of the century would have remained largely intact for hundreds of years, coastal scientists have said. But in the 1930s, oil and gas were discovered in the coastal zone, unleashing a frenzy of canal dredging that would compress the wetlands' demise into seventy years.

■   ■   ■

"That was the shortest way to drilling sites," Martinez said. "To be honest, at the time we didn't mind those canals, because they were shortcuts across the marsh for us, too."

At first the impacts seemed incremental to residents like Serigne and Martinez. But in truth, the changes were gathering speed; as scientists now know, they are exponential. As a lagoon, canal, or lake becomes wider, wind-driven waves become larger and strike fragile shorelines with growing energy, further widening the area of open water, leading to still-larger waves and greater damage.

A total of 27,600 acres of marsh in St. Bernard Parish were converted to open water between 1930 and 2005. Today, according to federal reports, Lake Borgne's shoreline "retreat" averages between two and twenty-seven feet per year.

All those impacts were greatly exacerbated when the nation—with the support of local worthies—ordered the Army Corps of Engineers to dredge the Mississippi River–Gulf Outlet, designed as a shortcut for big ships between the Gulf of Mexico and port of New Orleans. When politicians cut the ribbons in 1963, they opened a wound seventy-six miles long, five hundred feet wide, and thirty-two feet deep into the pristine wetlands of eastern St. Bernard Parish.

The MR-GO would go down as one of the worst mistakes in Louisiana history, an economic and environmental disaster. Commercial traffic never came close to predictions, and it was a world-changing event for the local ecosystem and a culture that depended on it. The corps reports erosion rates along the north bank of the MR-GO have run fifteen to sixty-five feet per year.

Removal of the marsh wasn't the only damage canal dredging was doing. Wetlands scientists say deltas can maintain their elevation against sea level not just by the seasonal addition of new sediments from the river that builds them, but also with sediment delivered when high tides wash over the marshes, and from the detritus from the annual decay of lush plant communities.

But the canal-dredging techniques employed in coastal Louisiana deposited the removed material in a line along the canals, creating so-called spoil levees. Those levees, researchers report, form dams blocking the overbank flooding that could help maintain a delta starved of river sediment.

And the canal systems also opened highways for salty Gulf water to invade freshwater marshes in the northern end of the estuaries, removing entire plant communities, converting fresh and brackish marsh to salt, and others to open water. With plant production removed or dramatically curtailed, the wetlands lost another source of sediment.

By the 1970s, local fishermen sensed the fate of their world. The MR-GO had nearly doubled in width to a quarter mile at some points and grew monthly; much of eastern St. Bernard Parish was falling into Lake Borgne, while its southern edges were being consumed by Breton Sound and Black Bay. Land once used for vegetable gardens was now being flooded with salty water. Even small storms carried surges that could flood homes.

Even projects designed to help the decaying marsh took a toll. The Caernarvon freshwater diversion—originally designed to help oyster fishers by preventing the outer bays from becoming too salty for the crustaceans—was also hailed for its ability to strengthen marsh plants with surges of fresh water. But local fishermen said that change also pushed inshore shrimping out of business and, they believe, actually destroyed marsh rather than bolstered it.

"You can't find a brown shrimp inside no more," said Martinez. "And it's hurt that marsh. Land we used to be able to walk on is now open water. How did that help?"

A still more devastating blow came on August 29, 2005, when Hurricane Katrina basically wiped Delacroix from the map—taking as much as 120 square miles of the wetlands with it. Few natives ignored that message.

Today, fewer than fifteen families live in the community full time. Most new construction after the storm was for fishing camps. Commercial crabbing is still viable, but most crabbers commute, just like the sportsmen, the "chivos" they once ridiculed as clueless outsiders.

Thomas Gonzales knows the world surrounding his trailer now doesn't resemble the habitat where he grew up: "People talk about the 'wet lands.' The only wet lands left is in my yard when it rains. There's no land left out there."

■　■　■

In April, the few surviving remnants of the old Delacroix lifestyle became threatened when BP's Deepwater Horizon exploded and began sending a river of oil toward the surviving wetlands. Like much of the coast, most of St. Bernard Parish was closed to fishing.

Many locals began picking up paychecks as high as $1,500 a day working cleanup, and villages such as Delacroix have become boomtowns invaded by hundreds of workers. But instead of lifting spirits, the windfall has only deepened the sense of loss and anxiety among natives, the sense of a world ending.

"That money I'm getting now is good, but we all know it ain't gonna last forever, or even very long," said Martinez. "I'm worried about what we're going to have left when they leave in a few months or next year.

"If that oil messes up the crabs from laying their eggs, where are we gonna get crabs next year? And if people in other parts of the country don't want our crabs, what kind of price we gonna get here?

"If I can't crab, what am I going to do? I'm seventy years old. This is the only way I know how to make a living."

Serigne, retired several years, has been picking up an extra paycheck as a deckhand on response boats. But the financial gain comes with a price: He feels the anxiety sweeping through men and women who still want and need to live off the wetlands.

"People are really, really worried, depressed," he said. "All they talk about is, 'What's going to be left when BP leaves?' Never in my life did I think anything like this would happen. Even after all the bad stuff before—the canals, erosion, hurricanes.

"You think about what we had not long ago. You can't imagine what was there. What we already lost."

These days, when Serigne and Martinez visit the scene of their childhood adventures, they see a thin, battered strip of open land between an encroaching bayou and an expanding marsh. The hardwood forests are gone. So are the dance halls, groceries, schools, and churches. The only Spanish they hear is their own. The touchstones of their early lives have been erased.

"When you look at this—this graveyard," Serigne said, running his eyes over the empty lots and sunken boats, "it's hard to tell the young people what was here just a short time ago."

Francis Lam is features editor at Gilt Taste. A son of New Jersey, he has on good authority that he qualifies as an honorary Southerner. This story originally appeared in Gourmet.com.

# Mr. Leroy and the French Club

## Francis Lam

I just watched a table the size of a twin bed get piled with crawfish. Twice. So this is how they roll at the French Club. Outside, in the parking lot, half a dozen beer-fueled men watched propane-fueled pots, sending an eventual fifteen hundred pounds of crawfish to their hot and spicy ends.

I have to confess that I wasn't thrilled at first about showing up at the Fleur de Lis Society. This was months ago, and I was looking for stories of Cajun fishermen, but clubs kind of weird me out, with their odd little exclusivities and mutated social hierarchies. On my way over, I imagined arcane secret-society stuff: handshakes and passwords and rituals in funny hats with the window shades down. Who knows what these people are all about? I've seen movies. I don't want to end up at the bottom of the Gulf, strapped to a sack of crawfish heads.

I pulled up to their imposing meeting hall, a dead ringer for an airplane hangar, with nerves firing and walked in to find . . . a couple of guys watching SportsCenter at a bar. I met Mr. Leon, Mr. Ben, Mr. Tee, friendly men in Hawaiian shirts and pleated jeans who pulled up a chair for me and chatted the way uncles do. Leroy Duvall, the club's president, came over and shook my hand, a slight, taut man with a head of white and skin that's been in the sun his whole life. He apologized for the ruckus as I set up the recording gear. It was a big day. Three years after Katrina took their home they'd just gotten into their new building, and the first thing he did was call in a beer order, now clanging in on hand trucks and dollies.

Seventy-five years ago, Cajun fishermen looking for work moved into Biloxi from Louisiana. In a strange town far from home, they settled into a tight-knit community in East Biloxi. They founded the French Club, as everyone called it, as a place to have dinners and dances together, and occasionally raise some money for members in bad shape.

I asked whether the Club tries to preserve French culture. Mr. Leroy nodded, talking about the dances they put on, but then said, "I don't really speak very much French. I wish I did but I don't, and a lot of us don't . . . the younger people, you know." There wasn't a trace of irony in his voice when he referred to himself as one of the younger people, despite his sixty-four years.

Mr. Leroy worked on shrimp boats for most of his life. He misses it. "No traffic jams," he said to me. "No 9:00 to 5:00. You just worked. But it was just the pleasure of being out there; the freedom and the good fresh air." It's demanding work, physical work, but I imagine of the kind that makes your body still feel young at sixty-four if it didn't make you feel old at thirty-two.

But the realities of age still stand. I asked him why the club only has three hundred members now, instead of the six hundred it used to have. "The older people got older," he said. "East Biloxi started dying away. And then Katrina finished it off by taking everything out. A lot of the older people are too old to try to come back down here and start over."

I asked if he keeps in touch with his displaced members. "That's one reason we put the club back down here," he said. "After Katrina took our building away there was no consideration about going anyplace else. Our people—no matter where they're at—they know whenever they come back, the French Club is still here. A lot of our members passed away; we have a lot of older people. Every day we see them they ask when we're going to open. They want to come back and we're trying to get it back. For the people."

Behind us, men loaded the new coolers with beers and Cokes and Barq's Root Beer.

I've come back a few times since hoping to catch the Club in action, but every time I drive by, it's just Mr. Leroy's old pickup in the parking lot. I poke my head in the dark hall. It's an awfully big room for one man to be in. I say hello, he smiles warmly, counting change or taking out the trash. He tells me, every time, that I just missed everyone, that I should come by for dinner. We chat, I thank him, and leave him to his chores.

But today, I walk into the French Club and my eyes need a few minutes to adjust to the darkness from the Mississippi sun. When I can see again, the tables are crowded with people piling high the spent bodies of crawfish. The aisles are crowded with couples dancing to Cajun music played by a man with a Croatian name. I can barely make my way through the crowd, taking pictures to go with my interview, and looking for Mr. Leroy. When I finally find him, my photos all taken, he asks, "Did you get any crawfish?" I regretted saying that I had to go. "Well," he says. "You're welcome here anytime. You know that, don't you?"

I smiled back at him. "Yes I do, Mr. Leroy. Yes, I do."

# Southern Characters

*Michael Pollan is the author of six books, including* The Botany of Desire, The Omnivore's Dilemma, *and, most recently,* Food Rules. *All of them have been strongly influenced by Wendell Berry. This story originally appeared in the* Nation.

# Wendell Berry's Wisdom

## Michael Pollan

A few days after Michelle Obama broke ground on an organic vegetable garden on the South Lawn of the White House in March, the business section of the Sunday *New York Times* published a cover story bearing the headline Is a Food Revolution Now in Season? The article, written by the paper's agriculture reporter, said that "after being largely ignored for years by Washington, advocates of organic and locally grown food have found a receptive ear in the White House."

Certainly these are heady days for people who have been working to reform the way Americans grow food and feed themselves—the "food movement," as it is now often called. Markets for alternative kinds of food—local and organic and pastured—are thriving, farmers' markets are popping up like mushrooms, and for the first time in many years the number of farms tallied in the Department of Agriculture's census has gone up rather than down. The new secretary of agriculture has dedicated his department to "sustainability" and holds meetings with the sorts of farmers and activists who not many years ago stood outside the limestone walls of the USDA holding signs of protest and snarling traffic with their tractors. Cheap words, you might say; and it is true that, so far at least, there have been more words than deeds—but some of those words are astonishing. Like these: shortly before his election, Barack Obama told a reporter for *Time* that "our entire agricultural system is built on cheap oil"; he went on to connect the dots between the sprawling monocultures of industrial agriculture and, on the one side, the energy crisis and, on the other, the healthcare crisis.

Americans today are having a national conversation about food and agriculture that would have been impossible to imagine even a few short years ago. To many Americans it must sound like a brand-new conversation, with its bracing talk about the high price of cheap food, or the links between soil and health, or the impossibility of a society eating well and being in good health unless it also farms well.

But the national conversation unfolding around the subject of food and farming really began in the 1970s, with the work of writers like Wendell Berry, Frances Moore Lappé, Barry Commoner, and Joan Gussow. All four of these writers are supreme dot-connectors, deeply skeptical of reductive science and far ahead not only in their grasp of the science of ecology but in their ability to think ecologically: to draw lines of connection between a hamburger and the price of oil, or between the vibrancy of life in the soil and the health of the plants, animals, and people eating from that soil.

I would argue that the conversation got under way in earnest in 1971, when Berry published an article in *The Last Whole Earth Catalogue* introducing Americans to the work of Sir Albert Howard, the British agronomist whose thinking had deeply influenced Berry's own since he first came upon it in 1964. Indeed, much of Berry's thinking about agriculture can be read as an extended elaboration of Howard's master idea that farming should model itself on natural systems like forests and prairies, and that scientists, farmers, and medical researchers need to reconceive "the whole problem of health in soil, plant, animal, and man as one great subject." No single quotation appears more often in Berry's writing than that one, and with good reason: It is manifestly true (as even the most reductive scientists are coming to recognize) and, as a guide to thinking through so many of our problems, it is inexhaustible.

That same year, 1971, Lappé published *Diet for a Small Planet*, which linked modern meat production (and in particular the feeding of grain to cattle) to the problems of world hunger and the environment. Later in the decade, Commoner implicated industrial agriculture in the energy crisis, showing us just how much oil we were eating when we ate from the industrial food chain; and Gussow explained to her nutritionist colleagues that the problem of dietary health could not be understood without reference to the problem of agriculture.

Looking back on this remarkably fertile body of work, which told us all we needed to know about the true cost of cheap food and the value of good farming, is to register two pangs of regret, one personal, the other more political: First, that as a young writer coming to these subjects a couple of decades later, I was rather less original than I had thought; and second, that as a society we failed to heed a warning that might have averted or at least mitigated the terrible predicament in which we now find ourselves.

For what would we give today to have back the "environmental crisis" that Berry wrote about so prophetically in the 1970s, a time still innocent of the problem of climate change? Or to have back the comparatively manageable public health problems of that period, before obesity and type 2 diabetes became "epidemic"? (Most experts date the obesity epidemic to the early 1980s.)

But history will show that we failed to take up the invitation to begin thinking ecologically. As soon as oil prices subsided and Jimmy Carter was rusticated to Plains, Georgia (along with his cardigan, thermostat, and solar panels), we went back to business—and agribusiness—as usual. In the mid-1980s Ronald Reagan removed Carter's solar panels from the roof of the White House, and the issues that the early wave of ecologically conscious food writers had raised were pushed to the margins of national politics and culture.

When I began writing about agriculture in the late '80s and '90s, I quickly figured out that no editor in Manhattan thought the subject timely or worthy of his or her attention, and that I would be better off avoiding the word entirely and talking instead about food, something people then still had some use for and cared about, yet oddly never thought to connect to the soil or the work of farmers.

It was during this period that I began reading Berry's work closely—avidly, in fact, because I found in it practical answers to questions I was struggling with in my garden. I had begun growing a little of my own food, not on a farm but in the backyard of a second home in the exurbs of New York, and had found myself completely ill prepared, especially when it came to the challenges posed by critters and weeds. An obedient child of Thoreau and Emerson (both of whom mistakenly regarded weeds as emblems of wildness and gardens as declensions from nature), I honored the wild and didn't fence off my vegetables from the encroaching forest. I don't have to tell you how well that turned out. Thoreau did plant a bean field at Walden, but he couldn't square his love of nature with the need to defend his crop from weeds and birds, and eventually he gave up on agriculture. Thoreau went on to declare that "if it were proposed to me to dwell in the neighborhood of the most beautiful garden that ever human art contrived, or else of a dismal swamp, I should certainly decide for the swamp." With that slightly obnoxious declaration, American writing about nature all but turned its back on the domestic landscape. It's not at all surprising that we got better at conserving wilderness than at farming and gardening.

It was Wendell Berry who helped me solve my Thoreau problem, providing a sturdy bridge over the deep American divide between nature and culture. Using the farm rather than the wilderness as his text, Berry taught me I had a legitimate quarrel with nature—a lover's quarrel—and showed me how to conduct it without reaching for the heavy artillery. He relocated wildness from the woods "out there" (beyond the fence) to a handful of garden soil or the green shoot of a germinating pea, a necessary quality that could be not just conserved but cultivated. He marked out a path that led us back into nature, no longer as spectators but as full-fledged participants.

Obviously much more is at stake here than a garden fence. My Thoreau problem is another name for the problem of American environmentalism, which historically has had much more to say about leaving nature alone than about how we might use it well. To the extent that we're finally beginning to hear a new, more neighborly conversation between American environmentalists and American farmers, not to mention between urban eaters and rural food producers, Berry deserves much of the credit for getting it started with sentences like these:

> Why should conservationists have a positive interest in . . . farming? There are lots of reasons, but the plainest is: Conservationists eat. To be interested in food but not in food production is clearly absurd. Urban conservationists may feel entitled to be unconcerned about food production because they are not farmers. But they can't be let off so easily, for they are all farming by proxy. They can eat only if land is farmed on their behalf by somebody somewhere in some fashion. If conservationists will attempt to resume responsibility for their need to eat, they will be led back fairly directly to all their previous concerns for the welfare of nature.
>
> *"Conservationist and Agrarian," 2002*

That we are all implicated in farming—that, in Berry's now-famous formulation, "eating is an agricultural act"—is perhaps his signal contribution to the rethinking of food and farming under way today. All those taking part in that conversation, whether in the White House or at the farmers' market, are deep in his debt.

*Ben Montgomery is an enterprise reporter for the* St. Petersburg Times *writing news features. He was a finalist for the Pulitzer Prize in 2009 for the series "For Their Own Good," about abuses at a state-run reform school in North Florida.*

# Tom Pritchard, Local Culinary Rock Star and Stuff of Legend

**Ben Montgomery**

The old man looks uncomfortable.

*Tell the one about the dead baby,* everyone is saying. *Tell the one about stealing three cabs in one night.*

It's late afternoon at MJ's Martini Jazz Lounge in St. Petersburg, and Chef Tom Pritchard is holding court on the patio. The fifty or so guests here to plan his upcoming charity roast have adjourned their meeting and some are now mingling around the guest of honor, wine glasses in hand, prodding him.

Pritchard sits quietly, but he wants to please.

*Tell the one about snorting Tabasco.*

Pritchard looks up.

"Anyone can *drink* Tabasco," he mumbles.

Thus the man who has arguably had the largest impact of any chef on the local culinary scene in the past twenty years begins his story:

"I was in a hard-boiled egg eating contest against the four-hundred-pound hard-boiled egg eating champion of Aspen, Colorado, so I knew I had to cheat if I wanted to win.

"I gargled Tabasco sauce to strip the lining of my mouth and I snorted it— I drove a straw through a cheese ball and put it in my nose and snorted it—to strip the lining of my nasal cavity. You can eat faster that way."

The crowd is laughing now, and leaning closer.

"I got so far ahead of him. But by the end, he almost caught me because I ran out of hot sauce."

The crowd erupts.

This is the one about snorting Tabasco. There is one about serving Sonny Liston seven pounds of carp. One about talking Mexican tequila with Richard Nixon. One about smuggling hash into Spain in a size thirteen cowboy boot box.

One for every place, every recipe, every occasion.

Chef Tom Pritchard has lived an incredible life. So the story goes.

■   ■   ■

Pritchard, sixty-seven, lives in a modest house on a finger of land in northeast St. Petersburg. On this Monday afternoon, he stands in his driveway beside a 1981 Jeep with a stone crab cracker mounted on the rear. Something resembling a pitch fork is poking out the back.

"It's a dung fork," he says. "One thing about chefs, we're all full of s——."

He leads the way through the house—spare, classy, lots of books and original art—to a screened patio overlooking a channel on Tampa Bay. We talk while he plays fetch with his golden retriever. Pritchard is wearing his uniform: sauce-stained T-shirt (pens, papers, and a thermometer protruding from the pocket), shorts, Velcro shoes, a grungy ball cap, and his signature beard. This is how people know Tom Pritchard.

"He has his own unique dress code," says Howard Sachs, a financial planner. "If the occasion calls for a name tag, it never says Tom Pritchard. It says Gorilla Monsoon or Tom the Busboy."

Pritchard is executive chef at four independent restaurants: Salt Rock Grill in Indian Shores, Island Way Grill and Rumba Island Bar & Grill in Clearwater, and Marlin Darlin' in Belleair Bluffs.

In the mid-1990s, he partnered with Frank Chivas, a seafood broker who had experimented with a small chain called Pep's Sea Grill, to open the first, Salt Rock Grill.

There were other fine dining establishments at the time, but Salt Rock broke new ground.

"The result is so far above beach condo bland I am tempted to invoke a word rarely heard in these parts, 'hip,'" wrote restaurant critic Chris Sherman in the *St. Petersburg Times* in 1997.

Salt Rock's kitchen, under Pritchard's guidance, became a training ground for up-and-coming chefs.

"I heard about him as soon as I moved down here," says Mark Hrycko, chef at Island Way Grill. "He's a culinary legend is what he is."

"He's the reason I'm here," says Bruce Turner, manager at MJ's Martini Jazz Lounge. "It's always a pleasure to be in Tom's presence. He's either teaching you something or making a situation better."

"He supports a lot of independent restaurants," says Marty Blitz, chef at Tampa's Mise en Place. "He's kind of like an icon in the Tampa Bay area."

Tell Pritchard what people say about him and he smiles.

"That's very nice," he says. "Thank you."

Not bad for a guy who lied his way into the restaurant business.

■   ■   ■

His first restaurant job came at fourteen in Baldwin, New York.

"My dad says, 'Tommy, go down and see Guy Lombardo. He's got a job for you.'"

That Guy Lombardo. The band leader. Pritchard went to work shucking oysters at the East Point House on Long Island. He left home for college in Des Moines, Iowa, and was drafted into the Army. He was stationed in Germany for several years, then hopscotched across the region—Scotland, London, Morocco—before settling on Majorca, a Spanish island in the Mediterranean.

"The caper capital of the world," he says.

He fell in love with food in Majorca, at the fresh markets, walking past suckling pigs, fresh vegetables, and a copious caper harvest. He bought a British bar that served Watney's Red Barrel ale and had Otis Redding on the jukebox.

He moved into a house near the Spanish artist Joan Miro and had a fling with a rich American expatriate whose millionaire father had sent her to live in Spain due to her love for Johnny Walker scotch.

After three years abroad, he moved in with friends in San Diego, then went in with a partner on a company called Land and Sky Waterbeds in Denver. This was the early '70s, before waterbeds caught on, and the company scored an order for three thousand from *Playboy*'s Hugh Hefner.

"I walked into the United Bank of Denver and got a huge loan with Hugh Hefner's letter," he says. "That money went . . ."

He trails off, smiling.

"That money went where it shouldn't have gone."

The contract fell through, and the company missed its loan payments. Pritchard stole the loan paperwork from the bank, fled to Juarez, Mexico, and acquired the alias Moose Mazaraka.

Pritchard wound up in Miami and got a job as a chef at the Rusty Pelican with an embellished resume and no culinary training.

"You just say you worked at La Cote Basque in New Port, California, and trust that they won't call."

He was a quick learner, and he faked his way into knowledge. He attended a wine seminar and introduced himself to Clive Coates, the British wine writer, then stood as close to him as possible during the tastings. Everything Coates did, Tom Pritchard did.

"The secret to learning is being around people you think are smarter than you," he says.

He entered cooking contests under the name Milo Wellington ("Milo sounds sophisticated, Wellington sounds like something you eat") and worked his way into a job as executive chef for Specialty Restaurants Corp., which owned some sixty restaurants.

He found himself frequently in Tampa on business, met a woman who wouldn't move, and thought about settling down. The two bought the 94th Aero Squadron restaurant in 1991 and went into business for themselves. When the roof collapsed a few years later, Pritchard went looking for another way in. That's when he teamed up with Frank Chivas.

Pritchard is asked how much of this whole story is true.

He fetches an old, gray photo. It's Pritchard and another man, leaning on a Ford Thunderbird in front of a Spanish villa.

"The first time we met I was chained to the wall of a jail in Germany," he says.

This is the guy, he says, who can verify everything.

■　■　■

Now Pritchard is standing over four bowls in the kitchen at Salt Rock, working on his latest creation. This is where the magic happens.

He's trying to perfect a recipe for *sangrita*, a tequila chaser he first tasted in Guadalajara. Five recipes are typed in code (K sal is kosher salt) on a sheet of paper, and an assistant chef is adding pomegranate molasses and pureed peppers.

"Let's put another cup of tomato juice in this one," Pritchard says.

Pritchard doesn't cook much anymore. He's sixty-seven and has known for a year that he has Parkinson's disease. His hand shakes sometimes, and he has issues with balance.

"Grab another bowl and let's mix some of this and that and try it," he says to one chef. He calls another over for a taste test. Everyone agrees the thin sangrita is best.

"That's my original recipe I wrote years ago," he says. "The rest of these I picked out of books and off the Internet. I guess these newfangled ways of doing it aren't working." This from a guy who still uses the oldest cell phone he could find.

He orders bottles of Don Julio and Herradura brought from the bar and talks about complimenting Richard Nixon—whom he met at Miami's

Jamaica Inn—on working out a trade agreement with Mexico in 1968 that allowed the free flow of good tequila across the border.

Really?

Yeah, he says.

This is what's perhaps most interesting and hard to believe: Pritchard seems to know everybody, and he has an inventory of stories for every situation.

"He's like the godfather of chefs," says Dan Smith, owner of Pacific Wave restaurant.

"There's never been one time that I've told a story about being somewhere that Tom hasn't known something about that place, or known someone from there," says Howard Sachs. "Every story he's told me is beyond convincing. . . . He's as close to Forrest Gump as anybody I've ever met."

His wife, Jody, knows the stories by heart.

"You think they can't possibly be true," she says, "but then years later I'll run into somebody and find out that they're true.

"It's amazing."

■　■　■

Brad Dixon is the sommelier at Bern's Steak House in Tampa. He has known Tom for twenty years and has heard all his stories. He used to have a hard time believing them.

"This is what I call the confirmation story," Dixon says. "One night, I was working for him at the Island Way Grill, and I was talking to this guy named Harvey who had been in once or twice before. He was buying some fairly expensive bottles, and I was spending some time with him. That's my job.

"Anyway, we were deep in conversation about wine, and I totally lost Harvey. He was looking up. He was looking at Tom. It was 10 p.m., and Tom has just come in from a day of catering.

"He says, 'Who is that?' I say, 'That's Chef Tom. He's a partner here.' He says, 'Tom Mazaraka? Moose?'"

Uh-oh.

"I'm thinking, 'Wait a second. What if Moose stole this guy's money. Or what if Moose slept with his wife?' Those Moose Mazaraka stories were crazy. So I go over to Tom and tell him this guy is asking about Moose Mazaraka. Tom says, 'Oh s——. That's Harvey. He was vice president of the waterbed company!'"

■　■　■

The guy in the old picture—the guy who can confirm everything—is Mike Boren. I track him down in one of the most desolate places in America: the

Big Bend National Park, on the Mexican border in southwest Texas. Boren is executive director of the Big Bend Natural History Association.

"I don't know why he had you call me," he says on the phone, "because I know where all the bodies are buried."

Is it true that they met in a jail in Germany?

"That's true," says Boren. "You know what he was there for? Impersonating an officer. He had stolen a brigadier general's jacket and was bracing soldiers in bars."

Boren says he worked at the jail and, one day, heard a prisoner screaming. The guards said the prisoner was a spook, an intel guy who runs all the Army computers, and he was telling them that if they messed with him, he'd have their furniture shipped to Alaska.

Boren walked back to see.

"He starts yelling, 'Go ahead, torture me! I know you f——! You're going to torture me!' I said, 'Not really. How would you like to get out of here with no record?' He said, 'Yeah, okay.' I said, 'I've got a friend in Kampala I want to go visit. Can you get me on an embassy flight to Kampala?' He said, 'Yeah, sure.' . . . Well, I cut him loose. That sumb—— never did get me to Kampala. He couldn't get me closer than Ethiopia."

Boren laughs, then stops laughing.

"Did he tell you about the Congo? Did he tell you about Beirut?"

No, and no.

Boren says they went to work as mercenaries in the Congo—"One of the spookiest f—— places in the world"—and then fled because they thought they were being set up for the assassination of ousted prime minister Patrice Lumumba. They tried to smuggle some hash into Spain in a size thirteen cowboy boot box, but Pritchard got spooked on the ferry and dumped the hash overboard.

In Majorca, Pritchard began hosting a yearly expatriate Thanksgiving dinner.

"He said, 'You gotta help me, buddy. I don't know how to cook.' I said, 'How many people have you invited?' He said, 'About three hundred.' I said, 'What are you going to do?' He said, 'Buy some turkeys.'

"I'll be damned if that wasn't the best Thanksgiving dinner I've ever had."

■   ■   ■

It's after dark, and Pritchard is working the dining room at Salt Rock. Table to table he goes, saying hello, asking about the food. All the while he's looking for ways to improve. Is the lighting right? The sound?

When he's finished, he shuffles over and sits at a table and orders a dark import.

I tell him I talked to Mike Boren, and he smiles.

"Only a fool would've given you that number," he says.

I want to offer a last shot at coming clean. I look at his eyes.

How much of that is true?

"All of the above," he says.

*Jane Black is a freelance food writer. She is at work on a book about one West Virginia town's effort to change the way it eats. This story originally appeared in the* Washington Post *in 2010.*

# Home Grown

## Jane Black

Sean Brock can talk. He can talk all day about seed saving or pig farming or pickling. And on this particular day, a swampy, humid summer afternoon, the Charleston chef was holding forth on the rice pea.

The heirloom variety had first come to the lowcountry with Italian immigrants who arrived to build a canal system, and it soon became a South Carolina staple. Brock was just about to explain why, after the Civil War, the rice pea had disappeared from local farms and the city's cuisine when he dropped one of the tiny peas. Immediately, he fell to his knees and began combing through the grass. He searched quietly for a minute or two, the first time he had been silent all day. Then he looked up and flashed the smile of a child who has just completed a task and knows he will soon be rewarded: "There, I found it."

For Brock, the award-winning chef of McCrady's, the rice pea is not just an heirloom seed worth saving. It's the kernel of his vision to re-imagine Southern cuisine. In a 1.5-acre garden in a nearby town, he is growing dozens of disappearing varieties: Charleston Gray watermelons, African Guinea Flint corn, goose beans, and tall, white-flowered stalks of benne, the traditional Southern sesame seed that was once a cornerstone of regional cooking. His favorites end up not only on diners' plates but also in a Technicolor, full-sleeve tattoo on his arm.

Brock, who thanks to his cherubic cheeks and impish grin looks impossibly young, already has reeled in some of his industry's most prestigious awards. This past May, at thirty-two, he was named "Best Chef: Southeast" by the James Beard Foundation; it was the first year he was nominated or indeed eligible. Next year, Artisan, which has published books by Thomas Keller and Eric Ripert, will unveil his first cookbook. But to "preach the gospel of corn bread and country ham," Brock is opening a new restaurant, Husk, in November.

At McCrady's, Brock uses exotic ingredients such as tonka beans, soy powder, and liquid nitrogen. At Husk, there will be strict rules about what can be served. Every item must be grown in and have historical relevance to the South. That means no salmon, no olive oil, and no balsamic vinegar, among other things. But there will be sarsaparilla-glazed pork ribs with pickled peaches, wood-smoked chicken with Rev. Taylor butterbeans and chanterelles, and breads made with antebellum flours. "I'm not trying to prove anything. I'm trying to educate," Brock said. "But I need rules. Otherwise, I'll be reaching for the olive oil. And if they taste olive oil, they'll think that's what Southern food tastes like."

At first look, the concept of Husk might not seem so revolutionary. What contemporary chef, whether motivated by passion or public relations, doesn't espouse the righteousness of heirloom varieties and local sourcing? But Husk aims to take farm-to-table to the next level. Brock is not fixated on local but regional flavors. He'll get pigs from Virginia, bourbon from Kentucky, and South Carolina grits. For produce, he'll do more than support farmers who revive heirloom plants. He will grow them and bring them to market for other Southern restaurants.

"What separates Sean from the legion of chefs of decades past is his focus on identity preservation," said Glenn Roberts, the founder of heirloom grain company Anson Mills, who has helped Brock plan his heritage garden. "It's remarkable how multilevel his thinking is. He's a farmer and he thinks like a farmer. He's a seedsman and he thinks like a seedsman. He's a culinary historian and he thinks like one. He's always thinking about the cultural relevance."

Southern cooks have long abused their classic dishes. They made grits with the processed, instant kind and loaded their cornbread with sugar. Over the past decade, chefs such as Frank Stitt in Birmingham and Linton Hopkins and Scott Peacock in Atlanta have worked to change that, lightening and refining the food in their respective cities. But Charleston, a town that oozes and is obsessed with history, remained a kind of culinary Disney World: a commonly uttered description is "a thousand restaurants with one menu." When Brock arrived at McCrady's in 2006, he had a hard time finding good-quality ingredients. That's when he decided he needed his own farm.

Brock rented a 2.5-acre plot on Wadmalaw Island, about twenty miles from the city. There, without any help or real farming experience, he raised pigs and vegetables for McCrady's. (Silky slices of house-cured ham are now on the menu.)

The idea of Brock in the fields was a surprise to some of his regulars. In his twenties, he cooked at the Lemaire restaurant in Richmond and the Hermitage Hotel in Nashville and earned a reputation for his mastery of hydrocolloids—gelling agents such as xanthan gum and agar agar—not heirlooms. Though he was firmly rooted in the South, he ran with a crowd of rock star New York chefs: WD-50's Wylie Dufresne, who brought the world fried mayonnaise, David Chang of pork bun fame, and Jean-Georges pastry chef Johnny Iuzzini. But Brock's interest in farming and sustainability predates the fashion for eco-awareness.

Brock grew up in Wise, Virginia, a coal town with no restaurants or stoplights. His family grew, cooked, and preserved much of their food. Even as he obsessed over guar gum and methylcellulose (which he told *Food & Wine* in 2006 was his favorite ingredient), he continued to study agriculture. While working in Richmond, he would drive up to Monticello to pepper master gardener Peter Hatch with questions. "I've never known a Sean who isn't engaged in Appalachian history and his roots and any technique that suited him," said Hopkins, chef at Atlanta's Restaurant Eugene. "If he were just doing whiz-bang tricks with food, that would be hollow."

The Wadmalaw farm became too much to manage, however. In high summer, Brock says, there would be so much zucchini that it would be piled up in the entryway of the restaurant. Gary Thornhill, one of the owners of McCrady's, offered him a plot on his hundred-acre farm in nearby McClellanville. Brock, with the help of his staff and farmer Maria Baldwin of the nonprofit Our Local Foods, maintains the 1.5-acre heritage garden, where they cultivate crops of endangered heirlooms. Anson Mills' Roberts says Brock exhaustively researches every seed he saves and grows. If Roberts recommends a certain variety, for example, Brock wants to see the historical documentation on its place in Southern agriculture. "He works like a journalist. He'll come to me, turn on a tape recorder for an hour to try to understand where and how the seed fits," Roberts said.

What Brock grows in the garden is not generally for eating but for seed saving. "This," Brock says excitedly, holding out several long, pale green pods, "is what okra is supposed to look like. We got the seeds from Tennessee, but this okra is from Georgetown, just up the road. It's a return home for okra. Isn't that bad-ass?"

When Brock has collected a critical mass of seeds, he will share them with Baldwin, who will grow the heirloom crops at Thornhill Farm for McCrady's and Husk. Brock helps decide what to plant. "But when the crops are ready, they come," he said. "It's not like I say I'll take a case of this or that. When it's ready, we figure out what to do with it."

By design, that plays into the concept of Husk. When customers enter the white postbellum mansion on Queen Street, one of the first things they'll see is an oversized chalkboard divided into two sections. Under "pantry" will be a list of oils, vinegars, flours, and house-made jams, chutneys, country hams, and hot sauces. Under "fresh" will be whatever has arrived from the farm and sea that day, and who brought it. If tomatoes are in season, they'll appear in snacks, appetizers, and entrees. "We're not trying to be the French Laundry and cook different dishes without repetition. We're trying to create a sense of time and place," Brock said. "You'll know when you eat at Husk that it's summer in the South."

Although the ingredients at Husk will be strictly Southern, Brock says he won't hesitate to employ modern kitchen techniques. Take the process for making mashed potatoes. First, Brock contracts with a farmer to grow a variety called Nicola. Next, he cooks them sous-vide, sealing them in plastic and simmering them in a water bath for one hour at 71 degrees Celsius (or 160 degrees Fahrenheit), a temperature at which the potato expels its starch. The potatoes are then dunked in ice water, which gels the starch so that it can easily be discarded. The potatoes are then resealed and cooked again in a water bath, pushed through a ricer to remove the skins and blended with butter and milk. The result is a rich puree with an airy, almost marshmallowy consistency.

In short, Husk aims to create a kind of third way for restaurants. In today's culinary scene, most restaurants fall into one of two categories. There are the rustic, farm-to-table joints, which, inspired by Alice Waters and Chez Panisse, try to reconnect diners with where food comes from. There are the high temples of molecular gastronomy where chefs exploit diners' disconnection by transforming the old-fashioned meat and three into plates of smoke and foam. "You have to find the balance between simple and making them say, 'Wow, how did you do that?'" Brock said. "The whole idea is to change the idea of Southern food. It's a celebration of Southern food, not Southern cooking."

And Southern food, as Brock is discovering, is far less limited than many people think. Conventional wisdom says that a real Southern cook uses pork fat for just about everything, whether it's a stew of collard greens or a pie crust. But Brock's research shows that Thomas Jefferson brought olive trees to Charleston as early as the 18th century. For several decades, before benne oil and then lard replaced it as a fat of choice, Charleston cooks turned to it for frying. Brock is busily searching for the strain that thrived in the low-country's humid climate. If he succeeds, he might one day find himself reaching for the olive oil again. Because that will be the taste of the South.

*Kim Severson is the Atlanta bureau chief for the* New York Times. *This story is adapted from her book* Spoon Fed: How Eight Cooks Saved My Life.

# Blood and Water

## Kim Severson

I knew I would meet Edna Lewis from the moment I saw her framed photograph on the long hallway wall in Marion Cunningham's California ranch house. In it, she is sitting in the sun with Marion, looking the same as she does on the covers of her cookbooks and in nearly every other photograph I have seen of her since—her bun always loose at the nape of her neck, her head just barely tilted back, her face painted with an enigmatic smile that makes Mona Lisa look like Jim Carrey. It's an odd thing, but somehow, on a purely intuitive level, I knew she had answers—that she knew about family and cooking and life and that, somehow, our very different worlds would come together.

In many ways, Miss Lewis was the last direct link to a way of cooking and eating that began in the soft Virginia soil where she grew up. Just a generation beyond slavery, she was one of six children. She was born in a small settlement called Freetown in 1916 and had a life that was deeply rooted in a sense of place. Miss Lewis learned to cook at a time when what came out of the ground was what you had to work with. As a result, she was always a resourceful cook, believing in the purity of the ingredients and taking a lead from nature on what to eat and when to eat it. Growing, gathering and preparing food was more than just sustenance for the family; it was a form of entertainment. Without fancy cooking equipment, the family improvised, measuring baking powder on coins and cooking everything over wood.

The life she would later write about in her books centered on cooking for Baptist revivals, holidays or just because it was morning and a family breakfast on a farm in the South matters. Almost every meal was to be shared. In that way, we had something else in common. It didn't take me long to figure out that the best way to find a place in my family was to be as close to the kitchen as possible.

"Whenever I go back to visit my sisters and brothers, we relive old times, remembering the past," Miss Lewis wrote in the introduction to her second book, *The Taste of Country Cooking*. "And we share again in gathering wild strawberries, canning, rendering lard, finding walnuts, picking persimmons, making fruitcake, I realize how much the bond that held us together had to do with food."

Even though my brothers and sisters all live in different cities, we share a tight bond. And the language of that bond is often the language of food. Some of them still fight it, refusing to cook a big holiday meal or picking fast food over their own kitchen, but we are a family that will end up together at the table. And that's what attracted me to Miss Lewis. James Beard said her food represented a time when American cooking was a series of family events. To me, that's the best kind of cooking to do. You can cook when you're hungry or cook to make a living or to feel creative or even just as a distraction, but cooking for the people whom you wake up and go to sleep with is the best thing ever.

Miss Lewis's recipes, for dishes like minted peas and creamed ham and cucumber pickles and hickory nut cookies, came from a time when ice had only a cameo role and was used mostly to churn ice cream. If something couldn't be eaten right away, it went into the springhouse over the stream or it was preserved and canned for later. Recipes were developed to accommodate tender lettuces that had to be picked young before they "bolted," or became bitter when they went to seed prematurely in the hot sun. That lettuce was best, she believed, served with gently assertive young scallions and a special dressing with vinegar and sugar and a little salt and pepper. Oil would weigh down the tender leaves.

"I feel fortunate to have been raised at a time when the vegetables from the garden, the fruit from the orchard, and the meat from the smokehouse were all good and pure, unadulterated by chemicals and long-life packaging," she wrote in *The Taste of Country Cooking*. "As a result, I believe I know how food should taste. So now, whether I am experimenting with a new dish or trying to recapture the taste of a simple, old-fashioned dish, I have that memory of good flavor to go by."

In that book and in her third, *In Pursuit of Flavor*, you can learn about a kind of Southern cooking that erases all of your ideas about it. I guess I thought I knew about Southern food, but it was a cartoon version. I had eaten plenty of chicken-fried steaks and beans and barbecue in the cowboy corners of Houston when I was a kid. During the few years I spent living around Oakland, I always circled back to a handful of urban soul food spots and rib joints. But that is not what Miss Lewis would consider Southern food. She hated the term *soul food*. Inner-city restaurants that served watery greens and greasy fried chicken and dull macaroni and cheese were a bastardization of real, true Southern cooking and, to her mind, didn't represent anything good. I didn't know how much I didn't know about Southern cooking until I started reading what Miss Lewis had written. Soon it spoke to me in a way that is second only to the food of Italy.

People have come to call Miss Lewis the grande dame of Southern cooking, but the biggest piece of her cooking career was in New York. She had been drawn to the city because of its politics and culture. Politics were very important to Miss Lewis. She had been the first in her family to vote, and said her greatest honor was to work for Franklin D. Roosevelt's first presidential race. Later, she would march with Dr. Martin Luther King at the Poor People's March in Washington in 1968. Her last cooking job was at a Brooklyn restaurant called Gage and Tollner, when she was in her seventies and by all rights should have been retired. But the most glamorous restaurant job came in the late 1940s and early 1950s, when she cooked at the Café Nicholson on the ground floor of a brownstone near Second Avenue on Manhattan's East Side. Wendell Brock, the longtime writer for the *Atlanta Journal-Constitution*, talked to her once about café society as she came to see it from her vantage point in the kitchen.

"We had everybody that was anybody," Miss Lewis told him. Howard Hughes, Salvador Dalí, Marlene Dietrich, Eleanor Roosevelt, Lillian Hellman and Dashiell Hammett all visited. When William Faulkner came in, the food impressed him so much that he asked Miss Lewis if she had studied in Paris. She was flattered. She had never been out of the United States.

Tennessee Williams lived nearby, so he sometimes walked her home at night. And Greta Garbo dropped in with her two little poodles. "She came on a Monday night when we were closed," Miss Lewis told Mr. Brock. "They dined by themselves. But by the time they got ready to go, the sidewalk was lined because the word had spread that it was Garbo."

Truman Capote was a regular. "He was a big mess," Miss Lewis recalled. "He had on these little pumps. If he got something new, he would come in and say, 'How do you like my beloved pants?' He was cute."

Although she was a great cook, she also had the ability to explain, in the simplest language, the beauty of food. A couple of years ago, Ruth Reichl had the good fortune of coming upon an essay Miss Lewis had written on lined sheets of yellow paper in the 1990s, and published it in *Gourmet* magazine. The essay was Miss Lewis's attempt to describe what it means to be Southern. She wrote of the way her bare feet felt when they pushed against warm, just-plowed earth and the way a shroud of mist hangs low on a Southern spring morning. And she offered up a long and glorious list of dishes:

"Southern is a pitcher of lemonade, filled with sliced lemon and a big piece of ice from the ice house, and served with buttermilk cookies."

"Southern is a great yeast roll, the dough put down overnight to rise and the next morning shaped into rolls and baked. Served hot from the oven, they are light as a dandelion in a high wind."

"Southern is leftover pieces of boiled ham trimmed and added to a saucepan of heavy cream set on the back of the stove to mull and bring out the ham flavor, then served spooned over hot biscuits."

"Southern is a pot of boiling coffee sending its aroma out to greet you on your way in from the barn."

And, tucked among the lovely descriptions of food and her strikingly clear childhood memories, she writes about the man with whom she would make the most unlikely family: "Southern is Scott Peacock, one of the South's most creative young chefs."

■　　■　　■

At first, Scott didn't want me at that kitchen table where Miss Lewis spent her last days drinking coffee and watching TV. He wasn't about to let some reporter just parade by her like she was an exotic bird at the zoo.

I had headed to Atlanta originally to write about fried chicken. Although Scott puts out impeccable versions of sharp pimento cheese, summer squash, biscuits and catfish, it was his fried chicken that was packing his restaurant, Watershed, in nearby Decatur. (He has since bought an antebellum house to restore in his native Alabama and left the restaurant.) The mixture of music and chicken was a hard one for me to pass by.

The chicken that comes out of the cast-iron pans in that kitchen is the perfect marriage of the cultures that Miss Lewis and Scott were born into. The recipe starts with a long soak in brine and then in buttermilk, which is how they do it in the part of southern Alabama where Scott was born and raised. Next comes a toss in seasoned flour. Then the pieces get slipped into a pan filled with lard and butter seasoned with a piece of Virginia ham, which is how Miss Lewis liked it.

I had eaten a big plateful of that chicken several months earlier when I was in Atlanta visiting friends. It was so good I had to find a way to get back to write about it. After a little digging around, I figured out that the story might be bigger than just fried chicken. It was about family, really. One that a gay white man from Alabama had created with a straight African American woman forty years his senior, with a famous lesbian folk singer thrown in for good measure.

So I traveled back to Atlanta to report the story. Scott was waiting for me in a coffee shop near his restaurant. He had plenty of reasons to be wary. For one thing, I would be asking a lot of questions, and publicity had not always turned out so well for him. And he knew I wanted to meet Miss Lewis. It was important for the story, sure. But I had personal reasons. She was among the great American women whom I admired because they had cooked their way through life's ups and downs.

By the time I made it to Miss Lewis, she was almost ninety and very frail. She had dementia and spent most of her time in the apartment she shared with Scott. They didn't start out as a family. Miss Lewis was seventy-three when they met and still cooking in New York. He was twenty-six and working as a chef at the Georgia governor's mansion. Scott was one of those young, tender men who thought all of the answers could be found in a bigger city, a bigger place—anywhere else but his small town. He had seen her picture in a magazine once, struck by how lovely she was. He'd even met her a few times, but he was sure she would never remember him. Then he was asked to help Miss Lewis cook at a fund-raising dinner in Atlanta. He was to meet her at the station when she got off the train from New York.

He spotted her at the end of the platform, walking toward him dragging a cardboard box wrapped in blue nylon rope. It was filled with one hundred pounds of pie dough. "I will never forget that," he said. "Here is that regal lady dragging this big ol' box of pie dough down the road."

Miss Lewis, who always tried to perfect whatever task she had at hand, figured there would not be enough time to make good pie dough. So she brought her own. Scott was swooning. Shortly after that, he gave up trying to cook seasonal food inspired by France or Italy—it was the fashion at the time—and decided he should cook Southern. It meant getting over his notion that Southern food was poor food and that cooking it meant embracing his childhood.

"It really was a Paul-on-the-road-to-Damascus moment," he said.

Miss Lewis had shown him he did not have to run from his past, but that there was strength in embracing it. And that set them off on a lifelong relationship, one that would eventually help me understand how my past—my family—was actually my greatest strength.

Miss Lewis eventually moved to Atlanta, where they worked together to preserve Southern food. They wrote a book. Then she developed some medical problems. Scott took care of her. And it started to dawn on him how much she meant to him.

"Aside from someone I was seeing at the time, she was the person I thought about the most and related to the most," he said. "I do remember at some point being very clear that she understood me in a way that other people didn't and later feeling that I felt that way about her, too."

He began to realize they had the makings of something that looked an awful lot like a family. She was his first phone call in the morning, and they would speak throughout the day. "We became increasingly dependent on each other," he said. Miss Lewis had come to rely on Scott to record and keep alive her knowledge of Southern cooking, but she was also coming to rely on him for her health and well-being. Scott would worry if she was taking her medicine or if her refrigerator was full. And Miss Lewis liked doing small, loving things for him, like ironing his shirts or making him little gifts. It was unconditional, which is really what we all want from our families, right?

She saw him for who he could be, and she helped him accept who he was. "I was a success as a chef before Miss Lewis," he said, "but I was a failure as a human being."

His love for Miss Lewis was the power he needed to get over his fears and anxieties. And it was that love that carried him through the slow progression of days to her death, which was in the very apartment the two first moved into and in which Scott still lives.

So you can see why Scott was so wary the day I asked to meet her. "I was worried what you would think if she was having one of those days when she was asleep at the table," he told me later. "I didn't want you to see her if she was having a bad day. I hate that—when it's like walking people through there to see the panda, the icon in a wheelchair. Laying eyes on her just to lay eyes on her seemed creepy."

Besides, surprise visitors can upset a person with dementia. "People think if they can just make them remember the one right thing it will all come flooding back," Scott said. "But it doesn't work that way. It just makes them more agitated."

Scott had other reasons to feel protective. Months earlier, members of her biological family had challenged Scott's place in her life. They took him to court. The whole mess started after Alice Waters approached Scott at a wedding they had both been invited to. Alice had been good friends with Miss Lewis. Like so many women in that elite circle of cooks, Alice worried about what would happen to the generation of cooks just ahead of her when they got old. Here they were, Marion Cunningham and Edna Lewis and Julia Child and a dozen other women who were the stars of their culinary genera-tion, and they were all frail and dying. Who would take care of them?

A few chefs with big restaurants or television shows or the special fortunes of Julia Child might be rich, but that's the exception. Great cooks who mostly cook and write great books, especially ones of Miss Lewis's generation, end up much poorer than people imagine and can't provide for themselves once they can't cook or write anymore.

Miss Lewis's money came mostly from her books. In the late 1960s, she was sidelined with a broken leg after a fall on an icy New York street. To pass the time, she began writing out some recipes and it turned into her first book, *The Edna Lewis Cookbook*. Her next, *The Taste of Country Cooking*, would become a classic study of Southern cooking, and one that sits on the shelves of America's best chefs. It helped put an end to the knee-slapping, cornpone image of Southern food among many American cooks. Her last book was with Scott, called *The Gift of Southern Cooking*. It would become her best-selling work. But even lumped together, the books never made enough money to provide for her care as she aged. Scott could barely shoulder the financial burden of taking care of her alone. Alice knew this, and she told Scott that people who admired Miss Lewis wanted to help. So he agreed to set up a fund through the Georgia Community Trust to pay for some of her care. Another supporter drafted a letter appealing for help, a copy of which made its way to her relatives in Virginia. That was a turning point in what had been a distant but respectful relationship between Scott and her family.

Her younger sister, Ruth Lewis Smith, and some other family members, including a son from Africa she had adopted when he was an adult, asked a probate judge in Decatur to decide whether Miss Lewis should live in Unionville, Virginia, with her siblings, or stay with Scott. "I told him I am willing to take care of her, you need not ask for money," Mrs. Smith told me. "I think he would respect Edna by letting her come home."

She and other family members and a few friends made it clear that they were very uncomfortable having someone who was not a blood relation caring for an ailing relative. That he was a young man responsible for an elderly woman made them uncomfortable. Perhaps that he was white made them uncomfortable. Perhaps it was that he was a ho-mo-SEX-u-al, as some said when I called.

But Scott knew she wanted to stay with him. Miss Lewis had told him so. Now that I have known Scott for some years, I know that he would have taken her back to Virginia in a New York minute if she had asked him to. But that day we met, I had no idea whether to believe him and his story about the court case, about her health and about the family he said they had created, just him and Miss Lewis.

"So would it be possible to meet her?" I asked. "Just to say hello?"

"I'm sorry," he said. "Miss Lewis just isn't that well today."

After a couple hours of talk both about work and about ourselves, we said our good-byes outside the coffee shop. There was no need to play hardball.

This wasn't a corrupt government official or someone asking for money. They were just a couple of cooks. My story would be fine without laying eyes on her. I got into the rental car and started the engine. Then Scott was at the window. He had had a change of heart.

"Would you like to meet her?" he asked.

I followed him into their apartment. Miss Lewis sat at the table in their crowded kitchen. A little television sat on a corner of the table, tucked next to a sugar bowl and a glass filled with tiny violets. An episode of *The Little Rascals* flickered on the screen.

"Miss Lewis, this is Kim Severson from *The New York Times*," Scott said.

"Hello, Miss Lewis," I said and reached out.

She raised her hand to mine, and I held it. She looked at me with that enigmatic smile. I murmured something about what an honor it was to meet her. She nodded.

"Can I take your photograph with Miss Severson, Miss Lewis?" Scott asked.

She gave him a look and raised her eyebrows. I could barely hear her when she said no. Then she turned back to her show.

Scott explained later that the fade was slow at first, but that things got more difficult almost daily. As she slipped away, his despair worsened. Not much could pull her from that private fog in her last days. Nature sometimes would, but the little bit of moss or wildflowers Scott would bring in from the outdoors had become unreliable mood lifters. Even food, her beloved touchstone, wasn't doing much to stir her anymore.

As she grew increasingly feeble, Scott took precise care of her. He would tease her when the dementia propelled her out of bed at night. He'd tuck her back in and say, "I don't want to come in here and find any strange men." If that didn't get a laugh out of her, nothing would. But days would pass without even a glimmer of her old self.

One day, in a stroke of pure luck, he discovered something that could reach her. It had an almost medicinal effect on her mood and attentiveness. It was *The Little Rascals*, a series from the 1930s and '40s that featured little children running around and getting into trouble, including the controversial African American character called Buckwheat.

His first clue came when, watching television together, he noticed that Miss Lewis would perk up when children were on the screen. He tried different child-centric movies with no luck. Then he brought home *The Little Rascals* and Miss Lewis immediately brightened. She was her old self, even if just for the span of a television show.

"It was one of the happiest days," he said. They'd watch an episode together and laugh so hard they'd nearly hit the floor in tears. Sometimes at night, after he had helped her bathe, they'd walk down the hall, his arm entwined in hers.

"Let's see what the boys are doing," Scott would tell her.

Later he told me he thanked God for *The Little Rascals*.

During the trial, when her biological family was challenging Scott's care, that show became an issue. Her relatives' lawyer argued that exposing an old black woman to repeated episodes of a show that employed broad stereotypical images of African Americans was cruel and insensitive. It lacked dignity. And it proved Scott wasn't the right person to care for her. The judge didn't agree with that argument or others they made.

Miss Lewis would be allowed to die with Scott, which was, as best as outsiders could tell, what she wanted.

He knew the end was coming when her interest in food faded. One day, she poured curdled milk into her coffee and didn't know it. So Scott started making her beloved coffee for her. It was like communion for him. He would always heat the milk just so, and make sure it was all piping hot, just as she liked it. Then came the morning she had no interest in coffee at all. "That was so heartbreaking for me and so sad because all of that had been part of how we had communicated," he said.

In her last days, when she was in bed and so close to death he could feel it, he played her favorite music and coated her lips with honey and a bit of Virginia country ham so she could leave this earth with the flavors of her youth. Miss Lewis died on February 13, 2006. She was two months shy of her ninetieth birthday.

"I never fell out of awe with Edna Lewis," he told me later. "Even at the end when I was cleaning her and dressing her every day, even when she was a corpse at the funeral home, I would just look at her and connect. I would think, God, you are an incredible woman, How lucky am I? She was my family, most certainly."

It was kind of inevitable that Scott and I would later end up friends. For one thing, we share some major themes. We both don't drink. We love food. And we both knew we were big ol' homosexuals early on. He wanted an Easy Bake oven. I wanted a catcher's mitt. There's an informal social glue that sometimes forms among gays and lesbians because you are connected at a root level. In a world that expects and often demands heterosexuality, you both know the pain that can come when you just can't deliver. You share the scars from getting called a faggot or a dyke. You know what it's like to feel "other," even in your own family. Especially in your own family.

When you grow up in a family like his, where the threat of being exposed as a homosexual is used as a weapon, or like mine, where matters of sex, let alone homosexuality, aren't really discussed with anything approaching clarity, you quickly develop a secret life. And it can bring on a terrible feeling of never being good enough, of always being at risk of disappointing someone. It's something Scott and I share, and something we have both spent a lifetime trying to unlearn.

"If someone said they loved my shoes, I thought, Oh, they hate my pants," he told me during one of the long phone conversations that usually started with a recipe and ended with mutual psychoanalysis.

"If someone said something nice, of course, it was never enough," he said.

I'd counter with my own special version of the theme.

"Or how about this," I'd say. "No matter how good I am, it will never be enough to counter all the ways I just don't measure up. And if I don't measure up, I will never be seen." I always knew it was safe to talk about these things with Scott. Because, like me, he adores the family he was born into. We both know a lot of our pain comes from growing up gay in a house where there wasn't any room for it. But we also cherish the families that made us who we are.

*Andrea Weigl has been the food writer for the* News & Observer *in Raleigh, North Carolina, since 2007. This profile first appeared in the* News & Observer *in 2011.*

# A Force of Nature

## Andrea Weigl

Oyster knives and cans of Stroh's beer in hand, three chefs sneak out the back door of Poole's Diner, the funky, acclaimed seventy-five-seat restaurant on Raleigh's McDowell Street. It's 6:50 p.m. on a Sunday night in January, almost showtime. In the dark parking lot, the chefs glow in their white jackets and aprons. They stab holes in the bottom of the cans, tilt their heads back and down the beers in one long swig.

"Wow! That is ice cold," says Ashley Christensen, Poole's executive chef and owner.

"Brain freeze!" cries chef Tandy Wilson.

"Smooth!" adds chef Tyler Brown.

Once the ritual, borrowed from Wilson's Nashville restaurant kitchen, is complete, the chefs are ready to crank out dinner for almost fifty people who have paid $150 each for the privilege. On this weekend, Christensen and friends will raise $8,000 for one of the many causes she supports.

Christensen's friends describe her as a "whirling dervish" and "a bottomless pit of energy." They talk about her passion for life, cooking, and doing good. This month, she received an award at the Frankie Lemmon Foundation's annual gala for her innovative fundraising efforts. Christensen estimates that she and philanthropist Eliza Kraft Olander have raised close to $500,000 in the last eleven years for a variety of causes—Raleigh's Frankie Lemmon School, which serves children with developmental disabilities, being one of the primary beneficiaries.

At thirty-four, Christensen is a foodie phenomenon who owns Poole's outright, having paid off her sole investor in December after three years in business.

In her kitchen, Christensen, blond hair always meticulously pulled into a bun at the nape of her neck, is exacting. Before plates leave the kitchen, she wipes smears away with a damp paper towel. Waiters are expected to do the same behind her. Her obsessive tick: no kitchen towel within view is left unfolded.

In her uniform of T-shirts, slim corduroy pants, and black Birkenstock clogs, she works seventy to eighty hours a week. She is single and has a large network of friends. Sometimes she texts employees so early in the morning after a long night at the restaurant that they wonder how she manages on so little sleep.

Christensen is ambitious: in 2011 she opened three new eateries—a burger joint, a fried chicken and honey place, and an underground bar—in a four-thousand-square-foot space in downtown Raleigh. She calls the food "simple but with a lot of energy going into the details."

That could describe her entire approach to food.

Award-winning chef John Currence, who owns the City Grocery in Oxford, Mississippi, was a guest chef at a fundraiser for the Southern Foodways Alliance last year and dined at Poole's the night before. He recalls the first course of pimento cheese as "this cloud of deliciousness," curled into a perfect oval on the plate and so pure that he could taste each ingredient.

"That's the mark of a great chef, when you take something as pedestrian as pimento cheese and make it transcendent," Currence says.

Christensen's national profile is rising. She has been highlighted in *Food & Wine, Bon Appetit,* and the now-defunct *Gourmet* magazine. She has also been a semifinalist for a James Beard Foundation Best Chef in the Southeast award—one of the highest honors for an American chef.

■   ■   ■

So much of Christensen's world involves creating community: at her restaurant, bringing people together for a meal; drinking a beer with fellow chefs before buckling down in the kitchen; rallying folks behind a cause.

Community inspired her to start a series of two-day fundraisers to benefit the Southern Foodways Alliance: The first night is the dinner at Poole's to celebrate guest chefs from out of town, the second a laid-back potluck at her home that brings food industry folks together from across the Triangle.

"I really liked supporting a project that represents extended community," she says.

Her energy is a constant. At the potluck, Christensen stands in her home kitchen, with its restaurant gear, pointing out Portuguese rissoles, a breaded deep-fried pastry, that must be tasted. She dashes off to introduce someone to guest bartender Gary Crunkleton, who is making cocktails with rye, apple wine, and homemade radish bitters. Moments later, she's strolling through her patio with a garbage bag picking up trash.

The community she has created makes it seem normal to strike up a conversation with a former engineering school dean about how he ended up as a lamb farmer in Virginia or with a guest chef's girlfriend about the red Holga camera dangling around her neck.

That easy welcome is the way it's always been at Christensen's parties.

In her second year at N.C. State University, Christensen, who had a full scholarship, moved into a large old house off Hillsborough Street and started throwing dinner parties. Always with a limited budget, she cooked for four, then twelve, then thirty people.

Regardless, Christensen says, "I would challenge myself to do something I hadn't done before."

Her friend Shaun Stripling recalls: "Maybe we'd be eating on paper plates. But it was about the conversation and the music. She's really great at pulling diverse people together. Her ability to foster community is amazing."

Those parties were based on what Christensen watched her parents do back home in Kernersville. Her father was a truck driver who raised bees and grew everything from okra to asparagus in a large organic garden. Her mother was a real estate agent and an accomplished Southern cook who had learned from her grandmother. They threw large parties, serving whatever was ripe in the garden.

Those taste memories and gatherings prepared Christensen for a future as a hostess and cook, then a catering business launched while she was in college. She asked her parents to pay for culinary school, but they couldn't afford it.

Instead, she took on restaurant jobs, first at Caffé Luna, then Humble Pie, then part time under chef Andrea Reusing at Enoteca Vin and chef Scott Howell at Nana's.

Seth Kingsbury, who owns Pazzo! in Chapel Hill, was the chef de cuisine at Nana's when Christensen came to learn. She was working with culinary school graduates who had been trained to cut an onion precisely and how to fillet fish. But Kingsbury says that didn't deter Christensen; she asked questions and showed a thirst for learning. "She was very green," he says, "but you could tell there was something there."

By twenty-four, Christensen was executive chef at Enoteca Vin, a farm-to-table restaurant that was ahead of its time in Raleigh and closed in 2009. Eventually, she decided she wanted to pour her energy into her own business instead of working as hard as an owner but without the stake. That's why she opened Poole's Diner in 2007.

■ ■ ■

It's a decision she has never regretted. Not only has the restaurant been embraced by critics and diners, but it gives her a way to give back.

At Poole's on that cold Sunday night in January, the main course of Cheerwine-braised shortribs, fried catfish, collard greens, and sorghum-glazed sweet potatoes has been served and only dessert remains. The cakes—a play on that classic Southern combination of cornbread and buttermilk, four layers of cornbread cake with buttermilk pastry cream, covered with buttermilk frosting—sit on the restaurant's bar. They have been admired all night.

"Do we have the plates out there?" Christensen asks.

"Yes," someone replies.

"Let's do it," she says.

She, Wilson and Brown head out to the bar. She cuts the tall cakes into sixteen slices. Brown places each slice onto a plate. Wilson sets the plates on the double-horseshoe bar for the waiters to pick up. Wilson and Christensen high-five behind the bar. Their work is done.

Then the three clink glasses of Basil Hayden bourbon, tilt back their heads, and swig.

John Dufresne has published four novels, two story collections, and two books on writing. He lives in South Florida. This piece originally appeared in Alimentum.

# St. Francine at the Café Max

**John Dufresne**

St. Francine of Delray Beach told me she rubs pepper on her face lest she succumb to the sin of vanity. All I had said was, I'm John, I'll be your waiter this afternoon. This was at the Café Max in Boca. Pepper, she said, or a scouring pad. I told her I don't mean to be impertinent, but isn't it already vain to think it was beauty she was corrupting—if only for the moment? I said, for example, I don't rub irritants into my skin. And if I did, would I think I was a saint? The woman she was with, her Aunt Nina, told me that her niece had an appetite for suffering. I said, Might I then suggest the *Gaspachee* or the Black Bean Soup? Francine scourged herself, chewed bitter herbs, scrubbed lime into her chapped hands, fasted unmercifully, denied herself sleep, wore a hair shirt studded with thorns, and dragged a wooden cross around her daddy's garden. I wondered if we weren't calling attention to ourselves, being, perhaps, a tad melodramatic. Francine said she'd have the Mariscada en Salsa Verde. Aunty would have the *Txangurro*. Very good, I said. Francine said she was visited by the devil. I suggested a Woodward Canyon Cabernet Sauvignon. Full-bodied, I said. I may have overstepped my bounds. Aunt Nina said, Excuse me? I said, you'll enjoy the winery's full-bore oak treatment. Francine said she punished herself with a crown of nettle. She said during Lent she spends her days in a tiny room, a cell, with only the dummy of a corpse in a coffin as company. Sometimes she wears an iron girdle for mortification. I mentioned St. Agnes, breasts on a silver platter and all that. She said the Cabernet would do.

Edward Behr, publisher of the magazine the Art of Eating, is the author of The Art of Eating Cookbook. This story was originally published as part of "Acadian Food in Southwest Louisiana" in the Art of Eating, Spring 1995. Eula Mae Doré died in 2008.

# Eula Mae Doré

## Edward Behr

Eula Mae Doré lives in a modest house behind the general store on Avery Island. The 2,200-acre area, created by a salt dome that rises 150 feet or so above the surrounding marsh, lies several miles from open water in the Cajun Country of southwest Louisiana. The island, like the store, is owned by the McIlhenny Company, which began to make its famous Tabasco pepper sauce there after the Civil War. Miss Eula Mae, as she is always called, ran the store with her late husband, and she worked for the company as a highly praised cook, preparing the Cajun food she had always known. She is sixty-five years old and not long retired, with golden red hair and an uncommon sweetness. She is most at home speaking French.

A generation ago, few Cajuns had much money, but the environment they lived in was rich and they had the time to cultivate it. When Eula Mae Doré was growing up on her parents' farm, on the table there were "always homemade syrup, always a pitcher of honey, and always bread. We ate well, we ate healthy—we were healthy."

"We were four in the family, two boys and two girls," she said. "I was the oldest of the little girls, so I would help Mama, and my brother was the oldest of the boys, so he would help my father. My job was to—let's say we were having a chicken—I would go to the pen where the chickens ate corn. The hens were fat. The roosters were for the gumbos, you know. The hens were for baking or pot roasts—*étouffées dans des gros oignons*." Chicken smothered in big onions is an old Cajun dish. One of the farm's cash crops was hot peppers; her father grew about an acre each of four varieties, which he sold to the Trappey hot sauce company, a McIlhenny competitor. "My father cut the hay. We had a square by the barn and he would make four or six haystacks, way high. He would take twenty-foot sticks and stack that hay around neat. I don't know if you know the farmer's life: You didn't lose anything."

"A Cajun dish," Eula Mae said, "is *cuit doucement et bien saisonné*—slowly cooked and well seasoned. Whatever you do, you have to have that good taste. You must have the time to make preparations—to think of what you're going to cook and the time it's going to take—and not to do two or three things at once. You don't iron and cook, read and cook; you *cook*." Today when young women ask her advice, she sometimes answers: "You don't want to hear what I have to tell you." The real distinction between the cooking of the past and the present, she said, is that "they had more *quality* time in the past. Today, we live at a fast pace."

Even before she began to help her mother, she explained, "I cooked with my grandmother in a fireplace. I was a little girl. She would cook with those iron pots with those hooks." She showed me her grandmother's *petite chaudière*, from which her uncle the blacksmith had removed the three legs, to Eula Mae's present regret, so the pot could sit on a stove. The pot was also called the *ti four*, the "little oven," because, placed among the embers on the hearth with more embers shoveled on the lid, it baked excellent cornbread. Her family grew and ground the corn, and passed it through a series of three sieves. The coarsest milled corn was used for hominy, the medium made grits, and the fine made cornbread.

I wondered about all the store-bought fluffy white bread that Cajuns eat today. Had people once baked bread at home? "My mama would make it," said Eula Mae. It was called *pain levé*, as opposed to the day-old *pain français* (for which they traded a dozen eggs to an old man who came by in a wagon) or *pain de maïs*, which means cornbread. When her mother made bread, Eula Mae explained, "She would take some peach leaves and she boiled them, like you would make a tea, and she would put cornmeal in it and a little piece of dough, and let it rise. Each time she would save a little piece of that homemade dough. When you want to make bread one or two days later, you put in the little ball. You knead it all together to make a big loaf." If you don't make bread again within two or three days, you must refresh the little ball by adding more flour and water. In summer, when the weather was hot, the dough would rise quickly and sometimes overflow the bowl. In winter, the dough rose slowly; sometimes it grew sour.

The reason no one makes such bread today, Eula Mae said, is that the cornmeal for the starter is "not made the same." Maybe it contains pesticides, she guessed. The old unbleached white flour, too, was better than the bleached flour sold in Louisiana today. The flour came in a sack with a white dove on it. "That was in the '30s, okay?" At the family's midday dinner, there was corn bread or biscuits; at supper, there was *pain levé.*

The family raised *canardins*, Muscovy ducks, and *canards français*, mallards; the two kinds were put together in a cage to mate and produce big, meaty *canards mulets*. (The word means "mules," but the birds weren't barren.) The ducks and chickens ate the corn raised on the farm. "Sometimes they were so fat they could hardly walk, because they ate all the time. All our animals ate the grain."

The family made sausages and hung them on a cord to dry outdoors, choosing a day with good sun and a dry north wind. Some sausages they smoked. "My father used pecan wood; this was his favorite wood to smoke." He also used peach. Deep-frying, as well the rendering of fat and the making of *gratons*, or cracklings, took place outdoors, never indoors, because of the danger from the hot grease. It was always *graisse de cochon*, lard, kept in stoneware crocks. *Boucheries*, the cooperative neighborhood slaughterings that used to take place every week or two, are still held now and then in certain places. Eula Mae said, "It makes my heart happy to see that. It's strangers, but it's a gathering."

Her father sold most of the farm's sugar cane to a mill, but he kept some to press at home in his own small sugar mill. The juice was cooked down into three forms of syrup. The lightest was called *le sirop*, next was *la cuite*, and the darkest was molasses, which in those days was called *le Black Joe*. "We wouldn't buy nothing. We would make our own stuff—everything—even our brooms."

I asked Eula Mae whether perhaps her family had made its own beer, and she made clear that no judgment was attached to her answer. "We never did partake any liquor," she said. "We never smoked." Now at a party she may drink a very little, to be polite. Long ago, "when we would get on the *galerie*, which was a porch, my father would play the harmonica, and *could* he sing." The drinks were root beer that they made from sassafras roots and lemonade they made from lemons from their own trees. They had oranges, too. Otherwise, they drank milk, water, herb teas, and coffee. Her mother bought green coffee beans in a fifty-pound sack and roasted coffee every week.

Every morning it was Eula Mae's job to light the stove and to grind and brew coffee. Her brother got up and milked the cow, so the family would have sweet milk for breakfast. Milk was also left outdoors overnight in a screened box to form *caillé*, curd, which had to be eaten right away before it spoiled. Or her mother would drain the curd in a flour sack to make *caillé égoutté*, fresh cheese, which would keep for several days. The family made butter, preferring to use the cream while it was still sweet, but sometimes they left the cream for a week to become sour, because that helped the butter to keep. Her mother used the delicious buttermilk in her biscuits.

"Soon," Eula Mae said, "the young won't know where milk comes from, where meat comes from. It's sad." Talking about the past, she said, "blesses my heart. It brings back memories which I wouldn't trade for anything in the world."

Tim Carman is a writer for the Washington Post. He's been nominated twice for a James Beard Foundation Award, winning in 2011 for columns and commentary. He's the former food editor of the Washington City Paper, where this story first appeared.

# How *Not* to Hire a Chef

**Tim Carman**

Near the tail end of his Southern road trip, Andy Shallal had come to a horrible realization: The winner of the *Top Chef*–like contest he'd staged wasn't the right man to lead the kitchen in his new restaurant after all. At the time of his epiphany in late March, Shallal and Chris Newsome, the lone chef standing after the grueling competition, were both silently milling around the New Orleans airport, fresh off a multiday tour of the South to sample the food that would define their project. Shallal, to be fair, wasn't the only one in crisis.

Newsome had just learned that his elderly grandmother had died. Instead of catching a flight back to D.C. with Shallal, the chef was going to rent a car so he could drive to Birmingham, Alabama, and attend the funeral of the woman who had influenced his love of food. Shallal, meanwhile, was stewing over recent events. During the past few days, Shallal had been arguing with his new chef over what dishes to feature at Eatonville, the restaurant he was about to open across V Street NW from the restaurateur's first Busboys & Poets outlet in Shaw. Shallal, who was born in Iraq, wanted to limit the pork offerings. Newsome, an Alabama native, couldn't imagine a Southern restaurant without pig products.

As he stood there in the airport, Shallal simply couldn't fathom why his willful new hire thought so highly of himself. Had Newsome ever opened his own restaurant? Did he have any clue what middle-aged African American women—Eatonville's targeted palate—really wanted to eat? Hell, as far as Shallal could determine, Newsome was a nobody. Shallal even had evidence: the lack of Google hits when the restaurateur searched on Newsome's name.

At some point—Newsome says it was after he learned about his grandmother's death, and Shallal says it was before—the owner finally spouted off to his chef. "You're interested in opening Chris Newsome's restaurant," Shallal told the toque. "Who the hell do you think you are?"

And with that, Shallal fired Newsome before the chef ever had a chance to cook a single meal at Eatonville.

It was an unpredictable ending to what had, just weeks earlier, all the signs of being a classic partnership. Back in February, Newsome was one of more than two hundred people to submit résumés in hopes of landing the executive chef position at Eatonville, a gig with a $75,000 salary attached to it. Only twenty-three of those applicants, though, were called in for interviews. Newsome was one, and for good reason. He not only studied the culinary arts at Johnson & Wales University in Charleston, South Carolina, but had also worked for the James Beard award–winning Bob Kinkead, first as a sous chef at Kinkead's and later as chef de cuisine at the now-shuttered Colvin Run Tavern.

Newsome's interview, however, started out on an odd note. Before even one question was posed, the job candidate was asked to sign a release so that videographers could record every word of his interview session. Newsome signed it and proceeded to spend the next twenty minutes or so fielding questions from Shallal and Carla Hall, the Wheaton-based caterer and former *Top Chef* finalist who was helping to weed through the candidates. The interviewers felt an instant connection to Newsome. "When he walked out of the room, we both had tears in our eyes," Hall said later. In a way, they felt as if they had already found their man. "This is our chef," Hall recalled thinking.

Because he was clearly partial to Newsome, Shallal admitted right after the contest that he was "a little harder on him from the beginning." You'd have a hard time proving that, though. Shallal checked only one of Newsome's references, and the chef all but breezed through the various rounds, each tied to some Southern ingredients or Southern dishes or the Southern strains of Zora Neale Hurston's novel *Their Eyes Were Watching God*, which is partially set in Eatonville, Florida, the writer's all-black hometown.

Then again, Newsome probably could have won this contest without a biased panel, which did include both Shallal and Hall as judges for the championship round. Newsome's final menu, after all, was a clever amalgam of food and Hurston biography. His "sweet and spicy" barbecued oysters, he told the judges, were inspired by Hurston's similarly "sweet and spicy" personality. His cornmeal-crusted flounder with tasso ham was a nod to Hurston's connection to the Southern coast, with its endless bounty of fresh fish. His gingerbread-scone dessert was even inspired by the character Tea Cake in *Their Eyes Were Watching God*.

The judges ate that treacly stuff up. Mike Curtin, CEO for D.C. Central

Kitchen, felt that Newsome's approach showed the chef was putting the Eatonville concept before his own ego. "It's clear that [the chef] is cooking for this restaurant," Curtin said during the final challenge. "He's not cooking to show off."

Curtin's assessment makes you wonder how, over the course of just a few weeks in March, Newsome could have shape-shifted from a thematically sensitive chef willing to sacrifice his ego in the name of Eatonville to an egomaniac willing to undermine his boss's very vision of the restaurant. The answer perhaps requires some background first.

To begin with, executive chefs typically aren't hired by means of a Food Network–esque contest designed to drum up public interest in a restaurant. No chef or restaurateur contacted for this story had *ever* heard of an executive chef hired via a competitive cook-off—save, of course, for those winners of reality shows such as *Hell's Kitchen*. Too much is at risk, most said, to hand over your multimillion-dollar restaurant to some chef who's only proven that he can cook a great meal.

A true executive chef, says Michael Babin, co-owner of the Neighborhood Restaurant Group, requires more skills than the ability to impress a random collection of judges who may not even understand your restaurant's concept. Chefs must also manage the motley crew of cooks who work under them. It takes someone with a big ego *and* a sense of humility. A chef must have the humility to accept feedback and to dish out 101 minor criticisms every day "without wiping out the people who work for them," Babin says. But a chef must also have an iron-will ego to prevent small compromises from creeping into the kitchen systems, the recipes, or whatever else might diminish the experience out in the dining room.

To find such a person, Babin will "use every means at [his] disposal." He'll interview the chef himself, then pass the potential hire to the director of operations, the manager of the restaurant, even to the public relations person for further questioning. Babin will also call everyone and anyone who might have an opinion on the chef, venturing far beyond the candidate's provided references. Babin wants to find out, among other things, if the chef is a screamer, a plate-thrower, or a bum who shows up late and leaves early, perhaps with a few tenderloins stuffed under his whites. Babin will, of course, also conduct a tasting or two with the chef. "It can be a long process," he says.

It's also a process with little guarantee for success, particularly for young cooks moving into the executive chef position for the first time. Babin believes such newbies succeed only about 30 percent of the time. The main problem with just about any hiring process is that you can only see how a chef works once he's in your kitchen for days and weeks. No exhaustive background check or interview session can tell you whether the chef has the necessary drive. Or if he's trustworthy. Or if he's philosophically aligned with the restaurant's mission.

But of all the analytical tools available to a restaurateur, a cooking contest is likely the least effective way to suss out a chef's real personality, says R. J. Cooper, the Beard Award–winning toque. At Cooper's Vidalia, cooks are almost always promoted from within once they've learned the restaurant's system and values. Even line cooks at Vidalia aren't hired until they make it through a brutal two-day ritual in which they must perform a wide variety of tasks, often under a number of different people. Cooper's trying to assess their dedication and determination. "You're not going to find that in a contest," he says.

Andy Shallal will be the first to tell you that he doesn't kowtow to the cult of celebrity chefs—or even noncelebrity chefs. By his own recollection, he burned through three toques in three years at his last chef-driven restaurant, MiMi's American Bistro off Dupont Circle. After fighting over food costs, cleanliness, and basic kitchen management, Shallal told himself that "I'd never go down the chef route again."

And for years, he didn't. The model for his wildly successful Busboys & Poets chain doesn't include chefs. Instead, the restaurateur relies on kitchen managers to hire and train sous chefs and line cooks who, day in and day out, are content to execute a budget-minded menu of pizzas, burgers, sandwiches, salads, and a small number of entrees. In return, these kitchen drones receive a salary, benefits, health insurance, and paid vacations. "For my people, it's a job," Shallal says. "It's not about the showmanship."

But when it came time to develop Eatonville, Shallal realized he needed a fresh concept, particularly given the restaurant's proximity to the Busboys & Poets on 14th Street NW. "I can't do the same thing," Shallal notes. So he decided instead to build a chef-driven destination for "more foodie types."

It was Shallal's idea to turn his chef selection into a publicity stunt. His plan was both elaborate and sophisticated. He rented out CulinAerie, the new cooking school on 14th Street NW, to host the multiday contest. He hired a team of videographers to capture every moment, from the initial interviews to the final cook-off. He paid the nine competitors after each stage of the competition, starting at $100 per chef for the first round and culminating at $1,000 per chef for the two finalists, Newsome and Rusty Holman, a North Carolina native who last cooked for the Young Republican crowd at the exclusive Rookery in the West End.

Shallal spent nearly $25,000 to stage the competition, but he hoped to reap the benefits in terms of press coverage and public excitement. His plan was to create a series of videos, which he would release over a period of weeks on the Eatonville website, concluding with one announcing the new chef just as the restaurant was set to open.

Complications arose from the day the contest started, at least for some of the chefs. The nine contestants had to elbow for room in CulinAerie's main instructional kitchen, which had a limited number of burners and ovens. In a way, the kitchen forced these competitors to act more like colleagues as they politely negotiated for space and open stoves. But on the second day of the contest, with six chefs remaining, each one required to make fried chicken, the contestants were confronted with an even bigger issue: no deep fryers at CulinAerie.

The chefs had to fall back on pan-frying techniques or had to improvise their own deep fryers on the stove top. This may explain why the judges weren't too impressed with the birds. "I'm an African American," said E. Ethelbert Miller, a literary activist and editor of *Poet Lore* magazine, during the competition. "I've been eating chicken all my life . . . I didn't taste any chicken that I wanted to go back and eat some more."

A far more complicated problem, however, surfaced at the end of the fried-chicken round: The judges ultimately wanted to cut both of the African American chefs, leaving only four white men for the remainder of the contest. Shallal balked at the idea. "We can't allow the process to be guided by race alone," the owner said. But "when I am honest, race plays a role." And with that remark, Shallal decided that five chefs would move into the next round, including Jacques Ford, one of the previously ousted toques.

The truth be told, the best chef—or at least the one with the most experience as executive chef—didn't win the contest. Trent Conry, previously head toque at both Ardeo and 701, was asked to leave in the semifinal round, a victim of his own refined skills. Conry prepared such dishes as a beet risotto, a potato cake topped with smothered onions and shiitake mushrooms, and a "coffee and doughnuts" dessert in which the drink was a multilayered parfait-like creation with java-flavored granita in the middle.

"I'd say you're probably the most talented [chef] we had, but that's not all we're looking for," Shallal told Conry when he gave him the boot. "I'm not sure we're going to be a great fit, and that's why I think we need to move on."

Minutes before he delivered the blow, though, Shallal told Conry one other thing: He thought the chef would be "a major challenge" to work with.

Shallal's comment, perhaps, should have been a warning sign to Chris Newsome.

The Southern road trip was part of Shallal's master plan; he wanted his new chef to experience the real Eatonville, so that he could better understand the food and the culture that had shaped Hurston and, by extension, the new restaurant that pays homage to the writer. A number of people had told Shallal the trip was a bad idea.

Privately, Newsome didn't think much of the trip either. It's hard enough, he figured, traveling with friends and family, let alone traveling with three strangers—his new boss, Shallal's brother-in-law, and Brian Evans, an Eatonville manager. The chef's mood didn't improve any when Shallal allegedly told Newsome that he had never before visited the South, nor had he ever cracked open a Southern cookbook—aside, that is, from those by Vertamae Grosvenor, a culinary anthropologist who served as one of the Eatonville contest judges. (Shallal denies such remarks; he says he's visited the South repeatedly and has read a number of other cookbooks on Southern food.)

The thirty-seven-year-old Newsome, by contrast, has been steeped in Southern food and culture his entire life. He grew up on beans and corn and other crops pulled straight from his grandmother's Alabama farm; he started cooking professionally at age nineteen at the Bottega Restaurant & Café in Birmingham, where he worked under the esteemed Southern chef Frank Stitt. To Newsome, it wasn't going to be easy to swallow lectures on Deep South cooking from an amateur.

Which may have been the crux of the problem when the foursome pulled into New Orleans. It was in Crescent City that Shallal delivered his speech to Newsome about Eatonville's target eater, that mythical middle-aged African American woman. Shallal said he knew from experience what such diners wanted, and it wasn't pork. Not long after the speech, as if on cue, Shallal and Newsome came across a forty-something black woman who admired the Busboys & Poets shirt that someone in their party was wearing. Shallal introduced himself and told the stranger about his new Eatonville venture. She wondered if he had hired a chef yet.

Shallal said the chef, in fact, was standing right here, pointing to Newsome. She then turned to Newsome and asked if he will have good things on his menu.

"If I'm allowed, I will," Newsome told the woman.

Shallal wasn't at all amused by the smartass remark. To the boss, it was just another sign of his new hire's misplaced arrogance.

For his part, Newsome doesn't deny that he's confident, a character trait that he believes stops well short of arrogance. It's a self-image that would appear to jibe with Babin's earlier description of a strong kitchen leader. Shallal, however, views Newsome's personality a different way. "He just had that way about him," the owner says. "He was resistant to any kind of criticism or change. . . . To be a good chef, you got to try to listen to comments from others."

When the ax finally fell on him at the airport, Newsome felt the decision was rash, perhaps based in part on the strain of the trip as well as Shallal's inability to clearly articulate his vision for the restaurant. Shallal, the chef said, wanted his restaurant to serve Southern cuisine, authentic Southern cuisine even, but wouldn't know the real stuff "if it was staring him in the face."

Shallal admits that Newsome was "probably right," that the owner never articulated a clear vision for Eatonville. "But I really wanted a collaborative process to take shape," he adds. The owner felt like Newsome had a clear idea for Eatonville—a sort of modern take on rustic Southern cuisine—and wouldn't budge from it.

Whatever the ultimate reason for the divorce, Newsome isn't holding any grudges against Shallal, though the chef does confess that he's "thrilled that I'm not" at Eatonville. Newsome says that even though he's still without a full-time gig.

As for Shallal, well, the show must go on. He ended up hiring Rusty Holman, the second-place finisher in the chef contest. "I remember [Holman] being good, kind of hit-or-miss good" during the competition, Shallal says. "But he's come through as being very good."

If you look at Eatonville's website today, you naturally won't find a word of this dustup. Instead, you'll find an altered reality. The entire site has been designed completely around the competition; it features short descriptions of the competing chefs as well as the people who served as judges. The site, in fact, is so focused on the contest it doesn't even include a copy of Holman's opening menu.

But right there on the home page, the site boasts this bit of creative fiction, as fanciful as anything Hurston penned during her career:

"[Drum Roll] . . . The winner of our chef search is Mr. Rusty Holman!"

*Ben Westhoff is the author of* Dirty South: OutKast, Lil Wayne, Soulja Boy and the Southern Rappers Who Reinvented Hip-Hop, *where this story first appeared. His Alabama-native wife makes amazing cheese grits.*

# A Rapping Drag Queen and Her Fried Chicken

## Ben Westhoff

Ms. Peachez favors bright clown wigs, press-on nails, and pastel blouses over her beefy, middle-aged frame. In the video for her 2006 song, "Fry That Chicken," she raps in a voice deeper than my Uncle John's. The fact that she is a man is just one of many things that are odd about "Fry That Chicken."

Like many immediately catchy songs, it's so dumb it's genius. Something of a nursery rhyme crossed with a Mardi Gras march, its springy bass propels the beat along while high-register synth notes chime like Pavlov's bell. "I got a pan, and I got a plan/ I'ma fry this chicken in my pan!" she raps. "Everybody want a piece of my chicken/ Southern fried chicken/ Finger lickin'."

Its low-budget video takes place in the yard of a rural shack, surrounded by chicken coops. The scene is a good ol' country barbeque, with Ms. Peachez holding raw chickens and taunting a group of hungry grade-school children. Peachez's blue hair, and her T-shirt bearing an oversized peach, are nearly consumed by smoke from the grill, which heats a giant pan of bubbling, waiting grease. She passes thighs and legs through a bowl of flour, massaging them with her hands in time to the beat. After dropping the segments into the pan, she shakes her hips and gets the hot sauce ready.

"Fry that chicken!" the kids demand, looking half-crazed as they pound on the picnic table and wave their arms. Peachez advises the kids to wash their hands, "'Cause you're gon' be lickin' 'em!" When the food is ready the kids tear into it, eating with their fingers and then, yes, licking them.

There's something innocent and funny about the video, and the song has a way of worming its way into your head. But there's also something creepy. It vaguely recalls a nineteenth-century blackface skit, although none of the participants are white, and the production appears to have been made in earnest, rather than as an ironic joke.

The oddness of the clip has been eclipsed only by its popularity. It's been seen 3.6 million times, and still gets thousands of views per day. But as "Fry That Chicken" went viral, it somehow became one of the most politicized hip-hop documents in years. To many, it epitomized the troubling turn rap music was taking.

Even the *Washington Post* weighed in. Op-ed columnist Jabari Asim decried the antics of this "Aunt Jemima off her meds," whose video "engages—no, embraces—racial stereotypes." "Yes, it is the stuff of nightmares," he asserted. He added that it reminded him of a scene from D. W. Griffith's 1915 movie *The Birth of a Nation*, the granddaddy of American racial propaganda films, which warned of a Negro coup d'état and glorified the Ku Klux Klan.

"Maybe I've seen *Birth of a Nation* too many times, but it suddenly seemed mild when compared to 'Fry That Chicken,'" Asim wrote, adding, "How can anyone explain black performers willingly—and apparently joyfully—perpetuating such foolishness in the 21st century?"

Such criticism only seemed to spur Peachez's popularity, and she proceeded to release a series of follow-ups, each more outlandish than the last. Two and a half million more people watched her "In the Tub" video, a loose parody of 50 Cent's "In da Club." It finds her playing with rubber duckies and washing her bootie in an outdoor washbasin, her broad shoulders and flat chest exposed.

The most provocative in the series had to be "From da Country," which opens with a nearly toothless midget named Uncle Shorty, who wears a curly blond wig and chows down on some watermelon. There's a guy in a chicken suit, tractors, and Ms. Peachez showing off a plate of candied yams swarming with flies. Meanwhile, kids perform steps with names like "The Neck Bone," "The Corn Bread," and "The Collard Greens."

■　■　■

Hip-hop started in the Bronx, was dominated by New Yorkers in the 1980s, and felt its center of gravity pulled toward the West Coast the next decade, through the success of gangsta rap acts like N.W.A.

As southern rap gained popularity in the 2000s, fans of "true" hip-hop said it appealed to our most base, childish instincts. Nursery rhyme jingles, they claimed, would be the downfall of an art form that has evolved from the good-time rhymes of the Sugarhill Gang three decades ago to the enlightened compositions of Nas. By the mid-aughts this chorus reached a fever pitch.

The problem wasn't just Ms. Peachez, who was presumed to be Southern. There were plenty of other rappers to complain about, the ones responsible for the stripped-down, shucking-and-jiving ditties that were taking over the radio. These were "minstrel show" MCs, an epithet pegged to crunk artists like Lil Jon, who had a mouth full of platinum and carried around a pimp chalice.

But crunk was fading, and so the culprits became a new crop of young, blinged-out rappers whose songs often instructed listeners to do a new dance. These included Atlanta rapper Young Dro, whose hit "Shoulder Lean" told you to "bounce right to left and let your shoulder lean," and whose video features an older man dumping a bag of sugar directly into his pitcher of red Kool-Aid.

Critics argued that these artists—and their complicit record labels—were indulging in the worst black stereotypes for the entertainment of white people.

Queens-bred rapper Nas, a charter member of New York's hip-hop elite, baited southern rappers with the title of his 2006 album *Hip Hop Is Dead*. Though he denied it was aimed specifically at them, it was easy to read between the lines, considering New York rap was declining and the Southern style was ascendant. In 2009 he took a swipe at the alleged minstrel MCs, via an ostensible public service announcement known as "Eat That Watermelon."

The YouTube video begins with Nas narrating, in his most serious voice:

> There is a period of great distress in the rap universe. There was a time when hip-hop was a form of empowerment. Now the corporate world is quickly diluting our culture for nothing more than profit. With the ever mounting forces of ridiculous dances, ignorant behavior, and general buffoonery, it's only a matter of time before hip-hop's permanent annihilation. This is what the future holds if it don't stop.

The clip cuts to a pair of black-faced, blinged-out rappers called Shuck and Jive, who in their best Sambo voices set out to please "massah" with their dancin' and banjo-pickin'. Played by MTV sketch comedians Nick Cannon and Affion Crockett, the characters proceed to chow down on a giant rind of watermelon.

The clip is funny, preposterous, and slightly horrific. But it hit close to

home. Only higher production values—and a wee bit of self-awareness—
seemed to separate it from "Fry That Chicken."

■ ■ ■

Before he died, Port Arthur, Texas, rapper Pimp C offered up an expletive-
filled musical response to those who dissed his region, suggesting they put
the coastal hip-hop on one side of the store and "country rap" on the other
side, and see who sold out first.

In the early aughts hip-hop began to be dominated by southerners. Out-
Kast's 2003 album *Speakerboxxx/The Love Below* became the greatest selling
rap album of all time, and the genre's unofficial capital had relocated from
New York to Atlanta. Many pioneering New York rappers, including Nas,
followed. (Cheaper real estate and warmer weather helped.)

The mid-aughts also saw a public debate about the role of racially coded
language in popular culture. During a comedy show in West Hollywood in
2006, former *Seinfeld* star Michael Richards shouted n-bombs at black at-
tendees, and the next year radio personality Don Imus was fired for calling
members of the Rutgers women's basketball team "nappy-headed hos."

In July of 2007, thousands of folks, including the mayor of Detroit and
the governor of Michigan, gathered in Motown at the NAACP's annual convention for a symbolic funeral for the n-word. Def Jam Records cofounder
Russell Simmons, meanwhile, called on the recording and broadcasting industries to censor the n-word, as well as "bitch" and "ho," while civil rights
leaders Jesse Jackson and Al Sharpton called on rappers to regulate their own
language.

Duke University professor Mark Anthony Neal cited an "anxiety" among
middle-class blacks about hip-hop from below the Mason-Dixon line. The
*New Yorker* writer Kelefa Sanneh, meanwhile, noted the modern minstrel
rap debate largely pitted urban, mainly northern blacks against rural, mainly
Southern blacks.

Naturally, Ms. Peachez worked her way into the discussion. Sanneh insisted that understanding context was important in this debate, but that in
the case of "Fry That Chicken," that was impossible, since no one knew much
of anything about her or her intentions. Nonetheless, Sanneh was willing to
make an assumption: "I think 'Fry That Chicken,'" he said, "is very clearly a
novelty and a parody."

■ ■ ■

But is it? "Fry That Chicken" doesn't feature any winks or nods, and its
YouTube comment section is filled with racially charged name-calling.

No, I have a strange feeling that Ms. Peachez isn't of the postmodern, tongue-in-cheek set.

Having flown into New Orleans and spent a day prowling around the Hollygrove neighborhood where Lil Wayne grew up, I pilot my tiny rented Hyundai Accent five hours northwest to Shreveport.

I still haven't lined up an interview with Peachez or anyone else, but I nonetheless book the cheapest room I can find on the Internet, which just so happens to be at a casino called DiamondJacks. Seventy bucks gets me a mammoth suite with a Jacuzzi and three televisions, including one in the bathroom. Emerging from my soak I finally receive a callback from Dale Lynch, who operates a Shreveport recording studio called Millennia Music Group. Dale, whose son, the rapper Rica Da Body, sells Peachez's CD, *U Hear Me*, on his web site, says that, sadly, he can't introduce me to Ms. Peachez, as they've fallen out of touch and he doesn't have a current phone number. Still, if I want to talk to him and his son Rico, I can come by his studio tomorrow.

For a couple of hours that afternoon he and Dale unravel the story of Ms. Peachez, whose real name is Nelson Boyd. Dale originally met him before he dressed in drag, he says, back when he was a little-known MC with the downright-unoriginal rap moniker of "Hip Hop."

At the time, Boyd was more of a hard-edged rapper in the vein of Tupac Shakur, which didn't seem to fit with his personality; in real life he's a hilarious, life-of-the-party type who sometimes performs as a stand-up comedian.

And so, after Boyd began spontaneously improvising a character he called Ms. Peachez one day in the studio, Dale enlisted her to provide comic relief for his free hip-hop DVD series called *Double X-Posure*. *Double X-Posure* featured interviews with rappers—Shreveport is known for a club-oriented subgenre called "ratchet"—and subsidized itself through ads for local businesses. After outfitting himself in a dress, wig, and press-on nails, Boyd-as-Ms.-Peachez performed in funny spots for Dale's advertisers. (You can see some of them on YouTube.)

Eventually the guys decided Ms. Peachez should be a rapper, and she began performing songs Rico created. "Fry Dat Chicken" was Peachez's first song, and Rico wrote it in 2006, when he was a junior in high school. "I wasn't hungry. I wasn't thinking about chicken or nothing," he remembers. "I knew I wanted to involve children, so I was just trying to think of a chant they could say that would be catchy, that no one had done before."

They filmed the video just down the street from the studio, on the property of a local guy Dale knew. They chose the spot because, well, the man had chickens. After we finish talking, they take me over. The owner isn't around, and neither are the chickens, but Dale and Rico lead a tour of the wooded, middle-of-nowhere plot of land surrounding the pastel green shack. The grounds are littered with abandoned cars, a rusty smoker, plastic swans, and other trinkets. There's even the patio furniture on which the group of kids—whom Rico says he assembled from his neighborhood—pounded their fists.

A true, backwoods country home, Rico says, one which was perfect for their goal of shooting a different kind of rap video. "We just wanted to show what normal people do in everyday life," he says. "We fry chicken. [The video] didn't have to have no rims, no cars, no lies. Just the truth. I wanted to do something positive. Nothing violent or sexual. Just something fun that everybody can enjoy."

"We live down South, and it's country," adds Dale, telling me he grew up in the small town of Winnfield, Louisiana, located a hundred miles to the southeast and the birthplace of slain Louisiana governor Huey Long. "We're used to horses, cows, chickens."

They had no idea the track would cause an uproar, and Rico says he was surprised when the nasty YouTube comments began pouring in. "There were a lot of racist comments, a lot of crazy stuff that's off track," he says. "It wasn't supposed to be that, it was supposed to be something fun for the kids, but people took it and made it what they wanted it to be."

Neither man gives much credence to the charge that the Peachez character perpetuates stereotypes. "I can see why they would say that, but that wasn't our point," says Dale. "The video was pure innocence. It had nothing to do with coonery, no negative vibe at all. The world made it controversial. We're used to seeing stuff like that in the South. We eat fried chicken! We eat watermelon!"

After visiting the "Fry That Chicken" set, Rico, Dale and I go downtown for lunch, to a restaurant and pub called the Blind Tiger. I order a shrimp po'boy, which contains nothing but bread and fried shrimp.

Nowadays, Dale has stopped doing the *Double X-Posure* magazine and is focusing on his gospel albums, while Rico is working on various solo projects. He's got a song called "Holiday Sex," which he's pretty excited about. He believes it will be even more popular than a similarly titled hit from an artist called Jeremih, called "Birthday Sex."

■   ■   ■

A few months later Dale finally tracks down Nelson Boyd's number, and I catch up with him over the phone. Like Dale, he disagrees that Ms. Peachez is politically incorrect. "I'm from the country, that's how we do," he says. "That's our lifestyle, that's a part of our heritage. Just 'cause I'm talking about it, that don't make it a bad thing."

He's still astonished by how popular Ms. Peachez became, and says he continues to be recognized regularly in Shreveport. "I was signing autographs in Walmart the other day," he says. "This chick working behind the photo counter followed me to the mouthwash section."

But it hasn't been all fun and games. Someone nearly tried to fight him, he says, after hearing a little kid singing the lyrics to "In the Tub." "Why you got those kids talking about they booties?" the man said. Though some have suggested that Boyd is gay, he notes his wife and kids. Besides, Martin Lawrence wore a dress, so why can't he?

He adds that he is too bowlegged to do traditional work, and survives off disability benefits. He and Dale had hoped to monetize Ms. Peachez's success, but couldn't agree about how to best market her as a rapper. By the time they finally secured a ringtone deal for "Fry That Chicken" and had finished her CD, interest had mostly died down.

Though he continues to perform the character at his stand-up shows, her hip-hop career has been effectively aborted. Still, he maintains a soft spot for her. "She's a real ghetto country backwoods [person]," he explains. "She's wannabe-city, wannabe-glamorous, wannabe-rich, and she's trying to be in the entertainment business no matter what. But you can't take the ghetto out of her."

# Southern Drinkways

*Wayne Curtis is an* Atlantic *correspondent and drinks columnist. This story originally appeared in* Imbibe.

# Past and Presence

## Wayne Curtis

Chris McMillian and I are chatting over lunch at the Napoleon House in New Orleans when he glances through a window and spots a set of arched windows on a building across Chartres Street. "You ever take a look at those arches out there?" he asks me. "They were part of the St. Louis Hotel—the first thing any visitor to this city would see." McMillian, one of the city's best-known bartenders, starts explaining why the hotel was a central part of the history of drinking in New Orleans, talking slowly and deliberately. As he continues, his discourse gets louder and faster, and soon he's on his feet and striding toward the door. "Come on," he barks, motioning me outside to show me one of those New Orleans stories hidden in plain sight.

Seconds later, we're out on the sidewalk and McMillian is expounding about these sole remnants of the old hotel, built around the old city exchange in 1835. Half of the vast mezzanine was filled with a bustling, marble-topped bar, and McMillian quotes an 1854 account, which described the bartenders "behind their twinkling wilderness of decanters," the scene appearing from across the way "like a julep-o-rama, performed by dwarfs."

"Everybody talks about the golden age of the 1870s to 1920," he says in a gravelly, booming voice that drowns out a passing delivery truck. "But I've got a thing for antebellum bars." After filling my head with images of tippling in mid-nineteenth-century New Orleans, McMillian at last heads back inside to our table, where we finish our half-eaten sandwiches under the gaze of Napoleon and other long-dead luminaries. "I don't know how you can live in a place like this and not be drawn into its story," he says.

McMillian, forty-eight, is as large as a linebacker, with an outsized persona to match. As such, he's something of an implacable boulder amid the fast-moving stream of contemporary cocktail trends. In an era when the

*New York Times* can offer up a taxonomy of eight different types of modern bartenders ("the minimalist," "the neo-classicist"), McMillian remains *sui generis*, a category of one. "Chris is not just doing historical re-creations," says cocktail writer and historian David Wondrich. "Chris *is* a nineteenth-century bartender."

McMillian arrived in New Orleans by way of an itinerant childhood spent in Louisiana, Texas, Alaska, California, and Hawaii. His family had roots in north-central Louisiana, and during what was intended to be a brief visit with his mother more than a quarter-century ago, he met a woman named Laura, who was tending bar in Shreveport. Plans to return to Hawaii were put on hold; he and Laura married and, over time, had six children. McMillian only half-jokingly blames the Old Absinthe House for their eventually settling in New Orleans in 1984—on an early visit the raffish charm of the bar and the city set its hooks in him and never let go.

McMillian began his career as a banquet bartender, cranking out high-volume drinks at the Chateau Sonesta and other hotel bars. "It teaches you organization and dexterity, and you get comfortable with the mechanical side of [bartending]," he says. He also tended bar at the Superdome, gaining experience with high-volume cash transactions while mixing Bloody Marys by the gallon at Saints games. Meanwhile, he followed a desultory career trajectory through a number of the city's bars, including two years at the Richelieu Bar inside Arnaud's Restaurant, which dates to 1918 and feels as if it hasn't changed a whit since. McMillian's immersion in New Orleans history developed what would become a lifelong fascination with the city's historic cocktails. It was at the Richelieu that he gained a small measure of local renown for his version of the Ramos Gin Fizz, a drink invented in New Orleans and as revered locally as is the Sazerac (which was first popularized, he notes, a couple blocks away at the now-demolished Sazerac Coffee House).

His next big move was to the Ritz Carlton's Library Lounge, an intimate, wood-paneled parlor with stuffed furniture and just a handful of seats at the bar. If working as a banquet bartender taught him quantity and speed, his eight years at the Library helped him hone his skills on a personal level, and to work on perfecting the classics. "I always ask young bartenders: What's more meaningful to you?" he says. "Having a twenty-seven-year-old woman come in and say, 'This is the best Cosmopolitan I've ever had!' or having a fifty-year-old man come in and say, 'I've been drinking Old Fashioneds my whole life, and this is the best I've ever had.'"

At the Library Lounge, McMillian began to attract attention for another classic cocktail, his Mint Julep—"made with poem and mallet," as cocktail authority Dale DeGroff describes it. As it happens, this drink and venue were my first introduction to McMillian. During a trip to New Orleans in early 2005, I stopped by the bar with my brother-in-law and nephew. By chance, my nephew ordered a Mint Julep. McMillian started to prepare one, when, quite unexpectedly, florid words came tumbling out in his stentorian voice. "The Mint Julep," McMillian began. "Who has not tasted one has lived in vain. The honey of Hymettus brought no such solace to the soul; the nectar of the Gods is tame beside it."

I went through several stages during this surprise performance: curiosity that such delicate words could come from such a large man (the "honey of Hymettus?"), then slight discomfort as I realized he wasn't just chatting, but delivering a performance (as it turned out, a recitation of J. Soule Smith's paean to the Mint Julep, written in 1892). Next came utter enthrallment, as McMillian spent the next five minutes luring us into the story of this historic drink—punctuated by the syncopated pounding of a bag of ice with a mallet roughly the size of a Chevrolet. At the end, he gently pushed the silver julep cup wrapped in a white cloth napkin across the bar toward us and said, "Cheers."

I intercepted it before my nephew could get a sip. And I would like to state for the record that this Julep was best I'd ever tasted. It wasn't the bourbon, or the mint, or even the precise technique that made it so good. The dominant ingredient—as in any superb cocktail—was a good story, well told. McMillian delivered a drink that had all the passion and intrigue of the Old Testament, with a bit of the *Odyssey* thrown in. "For Chris, history is not some academic thing," says Wondrich. "It's not that it's nice to know the history of a drink: For him, it's essential. It's the story of his city, his life, of America."

In the contemporary cocktail renaissance, the spotlight is often turned upon the artistry of the drink itself—whether a precise re-creation of a classic tipple from Jerry Thomas, or a modern cocktail using market-fresh ingredients. McMillian sees his job more broadly, making him the sort of bartender who was once common, and is now rare. "I've always been intimidated by these young, creative bartenders doing the over-the-top stuff," he says. "I don't consider myself an artist. I consider myself a craftsman. Making drinks is only 10 percent of what I do as a bartender. I'm a host, concierge, tour guide, theater recommender—I do any number of things in addition to making drinks."

In his role as historian and storyteller, McMillian is also cofounder of the Museum of the American Cocktail, which opened in 2008 within the Southern Food and Beverage Museum on the New Orleans riverfront. There, he and his wife have been organizing monthly cocktail seminars, including recent sessions by cocktail expert Tony Abou-Ganim and tiki drink historian Jeff "Beachbum" Berry.

DeGroff says that this approach truly links McMillian with the bartenders of an earlier time. "I arrived in New York City at the end of an era," he says, "and I saw what this business is all about: the relationship between bartender and customer. The bartender is a friend, caretaker, doctor, advisor, and a whole bunch of other things rolled up in one. With all the fancy and geeky bar stuff these days, we're losing some of that tradition." DeGroff says that he's even had bar owners ask him to conduct workshops for bartenders on the proper telling of a story.

McMillian, DeGroff says, embraces these old-school traditions. He feels at home in the footsteps of the great New Orleans bartenders of the past, like Joseph Santini, who is credited with inventing the Brandy Crusta, and Nick Castrogiovanni, famous for building thirty-layer Pousse Cafés at Nick's Big Train Bar. It probably doesn't hurt that McMillian is a fourth-generation bartender—"my great-grandfather was a saloonkeeper," he says, "and my uncles were notorious saloonkeepers [in north-central Louisiana]. My grandmother tended bars."

That heritage helped him maintain the view that a bar is first and foremost a community center, an idea that can be lost in bar-as-vitrine attitude, in which cocktails are put on display like jewels in a case. "We forget that these drinks are just supposed to taste good and please average people," he says. "Right now, cocktails are in, and we're riding the crest. But that's because it's fun—and it has to stay fun. People are there for the entertainment. I've had people come in and say, 'Oh, I went to this bar in New York, and they all had their giant mustaches, but they were very aloof.' That's not how it works."

Today, McMillian plies his trade at Bar UnCommon, a modern cocktail lounge within the 1925 Renaissance Pere Marquette Hotel, a block upriver from the French Quarter. (The Library Lounge was closed to the public in 2007 when it was turned into a private cigar club.) Opened in 2008 and built during post-Katrina renovations, it lacks the historic patina of much of New Orleans, but McMillian says it suits him fine. "It's like our city—preserving the old while embracing the new," he says. "Anyway, a bar is just four walls with people in it."

Our Napoleon House lunch concluded, McMillian and I wander out to look at some old bars he wants to show me—among them, his beloved Old Absinthe House, which violated Prohibition so many times in the 1920s that the owners were ordered to auction everything off, including the elegant absinthe drip fountains. After being separated for some seventy-five years, the fountains were finally repatriated in 2005 and reinstalled in a dim back room of the building. "And you'll never see them if nobody tells you about them," McMillian concludes.

Much the same could be said of McMillian himself, who tends his bar without a lot of hype or fuss. You could come to New Orleans and never know what you missed. "Chris is a national treasure," DeGroff says. "There's nobody around like this anymore. A hundred years from now, people will be saying, 'Man, there was once this guy making juleps in New Orleans like you wouldn't believe!'"

*Charles D. Thompson Jr. is the director of the undergraduate program at Duke University's Center for Documentary Studies. This story is excerpted from his book* Spirits of Just Men: Mountaineers, Liquor Bosses, and Lawmen in the Moonshine Capital of the World.

# Whiskey and Geography

## Charles D. Thompson Jr.

Whiskey making, while rare in southern England, was highly developed in both Scotland and Ireland by the time of the Ulster immigration. We can credit the Ulster immigrants for helping introduce the tradition to America. Through their influence, whiskey making became commonplace everywhere in the new colony, particularly on the frontier. Frenchman Marquis de Chastelleaux observed that it was the only drink served in the American backcountry. In the Pennsylvania backwoods of the 1700s, everyone made and drank whiskey, no matter their standing in the community.

The newcomers built both farm-based distilleries and larger-scale commercial operations in the cities, and they had a ready market for their products. From the Philadelphia elite on down to the redemptioners who worked for them, nearly all the easterners downed alcohol with meals, though those who could afford it also purchased imported rum and wine. Men, women, and often even children drank whiskey at various times of day, and the beverage enlivened nearly every kind of gathering, from church meetings and elections to dances and prize fights. With this kind of consumption pattern among the English, they had little room to ridicule people of the western mountains as habitual drunks. But they did so, even though their words rang with hypocrisy.

In fact, it was whiskey's popularity among the English that gave the back-border farmers impetus to produce more than they could consume and haul it back East to sell. Whiskey became the first frontier cash crop and the main source of income when the supplies of animal furs dwindled as woods gave way to farm fields. Whiskey made small loads on a single packhorse profitable, whereas grain alone or most any other farm product could barely pay for the trip. On the western Pennsylvania and Virginia frontiers, whiskey sold for twenty-five cents a gallon. In the more populous areas, a gallon of rye could bring as much as a dollar. No entrepreneur would bother to transport sacks of grain by horse and wagon across mountains when it could be reduced in volume through distillation and bring in more money in the process.

As people moved into the backcountry, it was common to see settlers with copper worms and small still pots slung under their Conestoga wagons or on their packhorses. Some took with them only the knowledge of how to build a rig. Coppersmiths soon set up shop in the mountains and built and sold stills to their neighbors to supplement their farm earnings. Those who had made poteen in Ireland needed only equipment and grain to get started. Those who had no prior knowledge worked with neighbors and learned by doing. Soon nearly every community had stills and nearly all the farm families had some way of making or procuring whiskey. Eventually distillation spread to other areas of the colonies.

On plantations throughout the colonies, a still house was a common out-building in which barrels of whiskey were distilled and aged. By independence, small distilleries were everywhere. Even three of the first five U.S. presidents—George Washington, James Madison, and James Monroe—owned distilleries. Jefferson, who favored wine and beer, was the only one to frown on hard liquor. Adams had no distillery on his farm, but he wrote that he drank hard cider made on his place nearly every day of his life. For presidents and nearly all their fellow citizens, distilled whiskey became the indispensable and ubiquitous American drink. Even with other regions join-ing in the business of distilling, frontier whiskey continued to hold a good reputation in cities back East for both its taste and its price. Good water was another reason, as were the local ingredients they used to make it. The farther south the farmstead, the more likely it would have shifted from pro-ducing oats, barley, sheep, and cattle, common in the British Isles, to wheat, pigs, and corn. Corn became far and away the primary grain of the Appa-lachians as well as the main ingredient for the liquor produced there. The corn varieties—called Indian corn by most—developed by the first peoples were perfect for the climate and rich in taste and carbohydrates, which made for higher alcohol content per bushel and a sweeter product. As settlements shifted from hunting and trapping to sedentary farming, all the ingredients for stilling this new crop were present in one place. Making liquor where the corn was raised added freshness to the flavor as well.

On the frontier as well as back in the settlements, few had any moral problems with whiskey consumption. In fact, hospitality and courtesy of the day required offering liquor. Failing to serve it would have created a serious breach of etiquette. Custom was to furnish whiskey in liberal quantities at all community gatherings, particularly workings such as house-raisings and corn-shuckings, as well as to laborers at harvest time, haying, and fruit gathering. Whiskey also was one of the few medicines available. People used it for rheumatism, malaria, snakebite, and a variety of communicable diseases from colds to gonorrhea. Whiskey was good for helping work, sickness, and pain, as well as for making festivities more joyous. Many a song paid tribute to its transformative power. To most it was considered a God-given right.

■   ■   ■

In 1794, when Alexander Hamilton and other leaders proposed raising internal revenue for the struggling American government by taxing whiskey, the plan met with open revolt. Farmers who had fought against the British, specifically against taxation without representation, wanted nothing to do with the tax. The Whiskey Rebellion of 1794 ensued. The uprising was best organized in Monongahela County in southwestern Pennsylvania, where Protestants from northern Ireland had settled. The protesters made counter-resolutions, staged tax protests, and intimidated, even beat, revenue collectors. Tarring and feathering the revenuers was common. When the rebellion spread into northwestern Virginia and the rest of the mountain region, it became what historian John Alexander Williams called "one of the few expressions of 'perfect unanimity' in the mountain region's entire political history." Though President Washington sent troops to Pennsylvania and quelled the uprising before it managed to get out of hand, the insurrection caused the government to drastically redraw its tax policy. While a whiskey tax remained on the books until the 1840s, the feds stopped collecting it for decades to come. Congress could find no one desperate enough to take the job.

Resistance to the whiskey tax politicized and united many local communities in ways that no other issue had before. Even as Secretary of the Treasury Alexander Hamilton was oblivious to whiskey's centrality, the whiskey rebels showed Americans that citizens had to be involved in their own governance. Whiskey had linked farmers politically, and through protests they made it clear that whiskey was their only source of cash and their way out of debt. Taxing that main means of escape from dire poverty made people fight as if their lives depended on it. Indeed, they proved Hamilton's assertion to Congress that a whiskey tax was a luxury tax had been simply wrong. Instead, the whiskey tax had pushed people with no money too far. Had the whiskey rebels gotten something back from their taxes, say access via road to greater markets or maybe economic help, they may have seen the benefit of paying them and behaved differently when the collectors came calling. But no government services were forthcoming on the frontier. As Sherwood Anderson pointed out in *Kit Brandon*, these whiskey rebels had to wonder, "What was all this business about taxes? What had government done for us that we should pay taxes?"

Lucid Olason was the director of interwovenarts.com and is currently forming
an organization that provides a platform for artists at the intersection of film,
performance, and digital arts.

# Cheerwine

**Lucid Olason**

In my mind Cheerwine
is directly linked to
North Carolina summers,
almost as if they
figured out a way to
get grass stains and
stifling humidity into a
drink. I have a memory
of a friend's birthday,
a pizza party, brought
to you by Domino's.
Everyone pretended
they were pro-wrestlers
from the WWF, like Iron
Sheik or Hulk Hogan.
They fashioned a ring
out of bed sheets and
I watched the other
kids brawl and then
promptly got my ass
kicked by someone
half my size. I think
I cried out of embarrassment.
And that's what
Cheerwine tastes like:
the tears of a frustrated

nine year old, with a
rat-tail and a black eye,
stuffed like veal by the
tomato sauce covered
dough that Domino's
calls pizza.

*Matt and Ted Lee of Charleston, South Carolina, are the authors of two cookbooks:* The Lee Bros. Southern Cookbook, *from which this story is excerpted, and* The Lee Bros. Simple Fresh Southern.

# Corncob Wine

## Matt and Ted Lee

"I eat the tar out of this stuff," the late Gordon Huskey told us, referring to the fresh corn he'd hauled in from the acre and a half behind his home, a former gas station he operated until 1987 in Pigeon Forge, Tennessee. Until his ninetieth year, Huskey attacked this end-of-summer harvest ritual with gusto, hand-cutting the kernels from each cob and packing them in resealable plastic bags to freeze for the year to come.

But the next few steps in the process were what really got Huskey's heart racing (we'll say nothing of his collection of *Maxim* magazines, stacked by his recliner). Since it's difficult to shear all the kernels clean off the rounded cob, a fraction of sweet kernel gets left behind. Rather than send this residue to the compost pile, Huskey put it to a higher use, making wine by packing the half-naked cobs into a water-filled pail. Airborne wild yeasts did the work of extracting the remaining sugar from the cobs and converting it into alcohol. Corncob wine has a nice balance of sweet and tart and a nutty, unmistakably corny flavor.

For centuries Southern home winemakers have added granulated sugar to their wild grape, plum, berry, or peach wine preparations, to boost the alcohol level and make the wines more drinkable (few old-timers were exposed to the vinifera wines favored today, and most never developed the taste for the drier style of contemporary winemaking).

Huskey's corncob cuvee is no exception, though in some years the unpredictable yeasts did a more efficient job and the wine ended up drier and more elegant than usual. Either way, corncob wine offers a smooth sip and a pleasant buzz either before or after dinner; it is as welcome in our house as Dom Perignon when we're out of the professionally made stuff.

This wine makes a great gift and is also a useful all-purpose tonic in the kitchen, good for deglazing a pan or beginning a risotto with a mysterious and yet familiar corn flavor. We often pour a pearly-white shot of corncob wine into short glasses after a satisfying Southern dinner—because its sweetness and slight effervescence suit the occasion, but also because it's such a fun conversation piece. We've stumped 100 percent of the guests we've introduced to it.

*Todd Kliman, a James Beard Foundation Award winner, is food and wine editor of the* Washingtonian *and also the magazine's food critic. This story is adapted from his book* The Wild Vine: A Forgotten Grape and the Untold Story of American Wine.

# The Wild Vine

## Todd Kliman

Michael Marsh (not his real name) arrived early at the American Society for Enology and Viticulture conference and snagged a seat in the front row of the conference room of the Omni Hotel, right by the downtown pedestrian mall in Charlottesville, Virginia—mere miles, the thought struck him, from where Thomas Jefferson had tried to make wine.

His suit and tie were an outward denial of his inner anxiety: Killing time was killing him. The prospect that something, or someone, at this ASEV conference might open a door to a new and different future was thrilling and unsettling in equal measure, and impatience being one of his weaknesses—being, in fact, his biggest weakness, as if he had been cursed with a condition that made him unable to sit patiently and let things take their natural course—he couldn't wait for someone to step up to the podium and *begin* already.

It was July, 1995. Two weeks earlier, he and his partner had struck a huge, life-changing deal in a Wall Street boardroom and sold their company to a rival, and that had been both thrilling and unsettling, too. Thrilling, because they had made a more than $40 million fortune, which, in the spirit of the go-go 1990s, they immediately dipped into, celebrating that night at a midtown Manhattan restaurant with gargantuan slabs of beef, multiple bottles of aged Bordeaux, and long Cuban cigars. Unsettling, because now that part of his life was done and gone: The long hours, the constant complaints, the hassles with staff, but also the daily camaraderie, the ceaseless drip, drip, drip of adrenaline, the primordial chase of success. It had been his twelfth and most successful business—the business all the others had been building inevitably toward. And now he found himself in an odd and unprecedented position: He no longer needed to work.

"You've gotta slow down and smell the coffee," his mother urged him.

Exactly two weeks later and he was driving north to Jefferson country to meet his next challenge in a symposium on "alternative wine varieties."

The notion of alternative varieties appealed to him for a multitude of reasons, not the least of which was the fact that it chimed with his perception of himself as someone who could not be fit into the usual boxes. But more than that, it was the suspicion that there were more great wines in the world than the same half-dozen varietals always touted by sommeliers and wine critics. Just as people were infinitely more complex than the umbrellas of identification they often squeezed themselves under in their quest for belonging, so must there be other wines out there to cultivate and love and drink.

This was not his first fact-finding mission. Months earlier, seriously mulling the possibility of starting a winery, he had taken a couple of exploratory trips out west, touring Napa and Sonoma in California and the fertile Rogue River valley of Oregon, the last the source of some of the most interesting, exciting wines that were then beginning to come out of the West Coast.

The wines he drank were good, some of them great—no surprise there. The best wines in the country were coming from a stretch of land that extended from Northern California through Oregon and the midsection of Washington. As he had always done, whenever he had traveled, he tried hard to visualize himself living there, nestled among the moneyed elites—many of them, like himself, people who had made fortunes elsewhere—making ripe, fruit-forward wines and leading the sun-dappled good life. But he couldn't.

For one thing, he had reached the stage in his wine education where he had become a disciple of ABC—Anything But Chardonnay—and California was Chardonnay country. Lord knows, he hadn't made the safe, conventional choices in life; why should he make the safe, conventional choice now? Oregon, at least, held the prospect of being an alternative to Napa and Sonoma. There was only one problem: "It was all brown. They'd had years of drought. I'd grown up in Florida, where everything was lush and green. Where was the green, man? Everything was brown. Brown, brown, everywhere you looked. Yuck."

But more important than the surprising unlushness of Oregon or the boring sameness of the wines he drank up and down the West Coast was the realization that to plant roots in Napa or Sonoma or even Oregon was to do what had already been done by thousands of others, to be a copycat, a follower. The thought pierced him. It was a negation of self, a blotting out of his singular, hard-won identity.

He asked himself: Do I want to make the 375th best Merlot or Pinot Noir or Cabernet Sauvignon in the world? Or do I want to make the best fill-in-the-blank?

What that blank was, he did not yet know. But he knew enough, then, to know that he would not be satisfied until he had figured out what it was.

■　■　■

One does not suddenly decide to become a renegade, any more than one suddenly decides to become a genius. Filling in the blanks without prompting, coloring outside the lines, challenging and defying convention—these things were as hardwired into him as his suspicion that Michael Marsh, his vessel, the outward manifestation of the person he was, was not like other men, that he did not have the same impulses, that something was wrong, oddly wrong.

The suspicion had been there all along. Standing one day in the door of his parents' bedroom, which was empty, he saw his mother's silk pink pajamas thrown over the back of a chair. He loved them. He coveted them. The thought came to him: *Those should be my clothes.* He was four or five.

He said nothing to his mother, or to anyone, and promptly buried the thought, as all good boys with complicated, complicating ideas are supposed to do.

But the thought did not go away. It stayed. It lodged itself and would not leave, a boarder who took up residence in a back room of a house and disturbed no one but could not be uprooted, either.

Nor would the image go away: the clothes he wanted and should not have. Could not have. The strange, exhilarating feelings he should not, could not, talk about. As he moved through adolescence, another thought came to him, a related thought: *I'm in the wrong fuckin' body.*

But what could he do about it? He was a teenager. Sublimate it, and try to forget about it.

■　■　■

The featured speaker at the conference was a plainly dressed man with a plainspoken demeanor, a sly sense of humor, and the kind of passionate idealism that cannot be faked—that inclined you to trust whatever he had to say, regardless of whether or not you were prepared to believe him. Dennis Horton told his story by way of making his pitch to the fifty or sixty participants, many of them winery owners or winemakers in the state who were looking to broaden their education. The catacombs . . . the legend of the Norton . . . bringing the vines back to Virginia, to the would-be cradle of American winemaking, to replant them in the same soil from which they came. . . .

His was a kind of experimental vineyard, founded upon the brave new idea that little-known varietals that were disease-resistant and could survive the vagaries of the climate held the best possible hope for the state's winemaking future. Virginia was not California and never would be. There the weather always cooperated. Here it was something to manage, a variable that proved enormously difficult to solve for, with as many as fifty days of thunderstorms a year, up to forty inches of rain, ten tornadoes, the occasional hurricane, and even a spring frost. It was largely the weather that accounted for the great difficulty that many Virginia winemakers had long experienced in growing Chardonnay with any consistency and quality. But this same fickle weather was of little concern to the red Norton and the white Viognier, making them ideal grapes with which to begin populating a vineyard, hardy and resilient and vigorous. In fact, it would be tough to imagine grapes that were more nearly ideal for the radical enterprise he'd outlined. Add the fact that they were also capable of producing excellent and expressive wines—wines as good, as complex, as rewarding, as those made anywhere in the world. Well, hell: This is a no-brainer, folks! These grapes are the future! This is nature, telling us what to do. Why fight it?

As Marsh sat there and listened, Horton's exhortation sounded in the depths of his being, and he began to think that after all his travels and all his explorations, he had finally found what he was looking for. What he was hearing, in Dennis Horton's story, was in some measure his own story, a parallel narrative of his own wild desire to break out from convention and try something else, something new. Dennis Horton was talking his language. Even before Marsh took a sip, he felt an odd affinity for this grape, the Norton, he had never heard of before, this grape that Horton, like some shaman, had brought back from the dead. Who knew but that its rebirth was, in some strange way, a kind of parallel to his own?

■　　■　　■

What the hell? he thought, sticking his nose into a tasting glass that had been set out on a long side table.

He swirled the glass, sniffed again, then tipped it back and drank. All that he had learned about wine, all those books he had read and tastings he had attended had left him somehow ill prepared for his encounter with the Norton. It was big. As big as the Cabernets he'd tasted on his tour of Napa. And funky. It had the intense earthiness of some of the Spanish wines he liked, the rustic character that was soulfulness itself. And yet it was fundamentally unlike these European wines too, so much so that it was like comparing singers from different eras and slighting both in the process.

He took another sniff, another taste.

He would not leave the building until he had burned the precise memory of that nose and that resonant taste into his brain.

It was mysterious, haunting, alive.

It was different, and seemed to make a virtue of its difference.

It was not sophisticated; it did not strain for a refinement beyond its reach.

It was absolutely and utterly itself.

■　■　■

Heading south on the drive back to Florida, Michael Marsh's mind was ablaze. His thoughts were racing faster than his car.

Dennis Horton had only touched on the basic story in his talk, a cursory outline of the Norton's rise and fall. He had come to tout the viticultural virtues of the grape, after all, not deliver a history lesson.

Marsh wanted more. He wanted a meal, not just an appetizer. Who was this Daniel Norton? Why had he succeeded where Jefferson had failed? How could a grape that had showed so beautifully in the glass be so obscure? Why had it vanished in the first place?

Reading the wine press, it was as if no American grape was good enough to produce good wine. Could that be? And if so, how? *You mean to tell me,* he thought, *a continent as vast and varied as this, as rich in crops as this, could not lay claim to a single grape that could make a good table wine?*

Nope; couldn't be. Not only was the contrarian in him compelled to reject the notion outright on principle, but he had just tasted delicious and irrefutable evidence of a native grape's worth.

■　■　■

Many months after the Omni tasting, Horton invited Marsh to his vineyard in Orange for another tasting.

He pulled out two bottles of Norton and poured a glass of each. One was a young Norton, his current vintage; the other, an older Norton, from his first vintage.

Marsh picked up a glass, agitated the contents with a violent swirl that sent the dark, purplish liquid circling the globe like a tornado, dug his nose in, repeated the swirl, sniffed again, then drank.

Now he did the same with the other glass: swirl, sniff, swirl, sniff, sip.

All the while, Horton eyed his eager protégé, wondering what exactly he was tasting, wondering what was going through his mind, wondering whether he was getting the point he was trying to convey.

*Oh, my*, Marsh thought.

The differences were dramatic. The aged Norton was markedly softer, much less racy, and—here was the impressive thing—it had not sacrificed too much of its fruit in the process of mellowing. It reminded him of the aged Bordeaux he loved. Fruit *and* ageability.

He hadn't needed convincing that it was the right thing to come north and grow the grape and start a vineyard, at great personal cost and despite long odds. What his second tasting confirmed for him was that the Norton was even more special than he'd first suspected.

■  ■  ■

The grand vision that Marsh had glimpsed for himself in southern Florida had begun to coalesce into a distinct and terrifying possibility, the double helix of a new and uncertain existence.

All his life, he felt, had been leading him to this precipice, and now that he had arrived at its edge, he was frightened and exhilarated. He knew he would only be doing himself further injury to delay the inevitable, the decision to change himself, to radically remake his body, no longer a vague, romantic notion, but an urgent, practical need.

Michelangelo had famously written of the sculptor's art, of bringing forth what was already within, the release, through the black magic of art, of the human presence the marble contained and concealed. The surgeon Marsh had found and come to trust was not Michelangelo, nor could the clinic where the reassignment would take place be confused with the soaring, majestic cathedrals of Florence. But this exceedingly difficult, delicate process he was about to subject himself to was nothing less than a release from the block of marble that had contained him for four decades. He had spent his life in solitary confinement. Something, someone, needed to be set free.

Thus let loose, that something, or someone, could not return to what was, to the old assumptions, the old cares.

In his *Metamorphoses*, Ovid wrote,

> How many creatures walking on this earth
> Have their first being in another form?

How many creatures? How many *things*, wine among them?

A new life as a freed woman. A new life in the vineyards. It was almost indescribable. It sounded like heaven.

■  ■  ■

If making the change was anything close to as liberating as making the decision to make the change, Marsh thought, he was going to be one high and happy woman. He felt emboldened. Anything, now, seemed possible.

Even when he was feeling most fanciful and optimistic, the idea of starting a vineyard had seemed to him an enormous and daunting undertaking, a project far beyond his know-how and experience, a great and lunging reach that might exceed his grasp. Now, as 1995 turned into 1996 and he gave himself over to the first small steps in the arduous and painstaking process of radically remaking his appearance, it was as if he saw and felt things with a new eye, a new confidence. He felt newly powerful.

The great and unspoken benefit of making the change, he was beginning to understand, was that any other upheaval in his life, any other challenge, became suddenly less impossible. Set alongside his resolution to start over as a woman, his determination to establish his winery in Virginia on the forgotten promise of the great American grape was emptied of its ability to intimidate.

He was a novice at making wine, and the Norton was a leap into the great unknown. But just as the surgery would come with no guarantees or promises, so he could not expect to reap the immense satisfaction of taking a risk without also experiencing the pains along the way. He would teach himself to be a woman. He would teach himself to grow Norton. *I'm a builder; I build things.*

He had also learned the hard way that building takes time.

■　■　■

She hurt. Every day, she hurt. It was normal to hurt.

Ha, she thought: normal. Now there was a word. Was there even such a thing? Sexual reassignment surgery had left her in a kind of daze, a survivor of war. Yet, paradoxically, she had never felt better. She had ceased to be able to find meaning as a man, and the body she had found herself enclosed within at birth had left her feeling alienated and lonely. The soil and climate of Virginia, Jenni hoped, would nurture and sustain her, allow her to flower and thrive as she started over and tended the land—tending the land as a way of tending a wound. Enduring the lonely, difficult weeks of recovery, it occurred to her that, if she could get through this, then there was nothing to prevent her from doing anything else she dreamed. Even the ridiculous idea of making wine.

The name of the venture, Chrysalis, was the christening of a new existence. What could be more fitting, what could be more perfect—"the miraculous transformation of an ordinary thing." Grapes into wine. Man into woman.

■　■　■

By 1998, she was ensconced at her estate, and by 1999, she was not only running her own winery but also making her own wines.

In retrospect, she could accuse herself of indulging in hasty, impetuous thinking, of forcing things. She was so eager to master all the stages of the winemaking process, so eager to make herself expert, that she was racing through the stages of her own development as a winemaker. There was much she still needed to know, particularly about the Norton, and so the next year she brought in "the only white Trinidadian lesbian winemaker in the world" to work with her.

The Norton was a handful. Stubborn, independent, with a mind of its own. Oh, it was a marvel in the vineyard once it got going, requiring far less pesticide and fungicide than other grapes, particularly *vinifera* grapes like Chardonnay. In any given season, the Chardonnay grapes needed as many as fifteen sprayings; the Norton, just three. The problem was getting it going. It's an exceedingly difficult grape to propagate and has an unusually high mortality rate. On the other hand, if it survives its infancy and is then left too much on its own, it can become unruly and unmanageable, taking over the vineyard.

Still, the bigger challenge—the bigger mystery—was in the cellar.

The Norton was not like other grapes. It did not do what it was supposed to do, not even what its own chemistry seemed to tell it to.

A high-acid wine with a high pH doesn't compute, chemically speaking. But the Norton's acidity is offset by an alkaline component. In order to bring the pH down, the winemaker is forced to add tartaric acid to the juice as it ferments in the barrel. The result of this tinkering is, paradoxically, a liquid that is far more acidic to the palate than what they'd started with. To eliminate some of that excess acid, they have to tinker again, subjecting the liquid to a process called cold stabilization—freezing it at 24–26 degrees Fahrenheit—to correct the pH.

It was a 180 from just about every other kind of grape she'd ever heard about: a dream, once it got going, in the vineyard, a bitch in the cellar.

The fact that it wasn't easy to love, that it was different and quirky, that it had a mind of its own—these things spoke to her. And the fact that it didn't speak to everybody—that spoke to her, too.

■　■　■

She bottled her first Norton, the Norton Locksley Reserve, in 2000. The name paid homage to the name of her property, the former Locksley estate, but the reference to Robin of Locksley, more commonly known as Robin Hood, could not be ignored. If Chrysalis was an allusion to her transformation, then Locksley could be read as a statement of intent when it came to making the Norton. The benevolent outlaw. The crowd-pleasing rebel.

The Locksley Reserve was a premium wine, to be set aside for cellaring and aging, and its list price, $35, reflected this intention. It would take a decade or two before she knew whether she had succeeded and to what extent. The wines of her beloved Bordeaux needed at least that long to fully reveal their complexity and charm.

It was not possible to operate a successful winery by relying on intermittent sales of premium wines, and so she was also putting out a "junior Locksley," her Estate Bottled Norton, which listed for $16. Its returns were more immediate, as she discovered when she tasted her first vintage, the 2001. If it lacked the finesse she was seeking from the Locksley Reserve, the soft suppleness that aging would bring, it exploded in the mouth with a burst of ripe, concentrated fruit. It was fresh and alive. A good and interesting table wine, she thought, and one that would be helped only by pairing it with the right kinds of foods, with venison, with duck. This is the way Europeans have always looked at their table wines—as companions, not trophies, not ends in themselves.

Another vision took shape in her mind. Not only was she going to grow the Norton, but she was going to grow a lot of the Norton. In fact, she was going to grow the largest planting of the Norton anywhere in the world.

■　■　■

By her own high standards, this was a comparatively modest vision, paling beside her more recent, more radical reinventions. In the world of Virginia wine, however, it appeared so odd and so risky as to cause industry observers to speculate that she had overreached in putting nearly all of her chips down on one grape. One day, she would learn what they had learned. The Norton, interesting though it might be, was not a workhorse; you couldn't make money off of it. No less a champion of the grape than Dennis Horton had recently begun to doubt its potential in the marketplace. He was selling thirty thousand cases of wine annually, and Norton accounted for only a tenth of that total. It was an interesting grape, a good grape, an important grape. But how much Norton, Horton wondered now, could you grow and produce and still be considered a viable commercial winery?

From the eight acres of Norton that Horton had started with at Orange, he had expanded to twelve. A fifty percent expansion.

Jenni was thinking forty-plus acres.

There was simply no precedent for what she'd envisioned. The grape was being grown now in nearly two dozen states, including Missouri, Arkansas, Ohio, Illinois, Iowa, Oklahoma, Kansas, Louisiana, Tennessee, Florida, and Pennsylvania. In nearly every circumstance, however, it was limited to a handful of acres, one among several different red wine grapes, as though winemakers were unwilling to commit more time and attention and resources to it.

To grow and yet not invest, to try and yet not risk failing—it bespoke, she thought, a stinting vision, a pinched ambition. It was not going at things with gusto. It was proceeding with fear. If the Norton had ageability, as Horton had demonstrated to her, why not invest in it long term? Why not stake her entire reputation on it?

■ ■ ■

Her confirmation came in 2003, an unlikely year to have come to a confirmation about anything positive about wine in Virginia, unless it was to confirm that the business of making wine is a fool's errand, its practitioners captives to chance and caprice.

That was the year she had chosen to debut the wine that was to be her flagship: the Barrel Select, her in-between Norton—less premium than the Norton Locksley Reserve, more refined than the Estate Bottled Norton. The year 2003 stands as one of the worst years ever for wine in the state, with precipitation eclipsing the previous recorded high by six inches. Excessive rain is among the greatest nightmares for winemakers, because there is so little that can be done later to correct or subdue its damage. Heavy, continuous rain dilutes the fruit on the vine, resulting in thin, watery vines. The effect is not unlike that of pouring gallons upon gallons of water into a wine barrel.

What to do? Jenni gambled, deciding not to pick her Norton grapes until the last possible moment, in this way allowing the sun more time to dry them out and concentrate their juices. She waited until November 5, more than a month past the usual harvest day. This was not the eleventh hour. It was a few seconds short of midnight.

At the Wines of the World competition at the Los Angeles County Fair in 2005, the 2003 Norton Barrel Select from Chrysalis won a Gold Medal. Jenni had judged shrewdly in opting to pick the grapes late—a testament to her belief that winemaking required art as well as science, required intuition, love, patience, attention. But if not for the Norton's resilience, would she have looked so shrewd? How many grapes, after all, would have emerged from such a long and soggy season to not only produce decent fruit, but award-winning wine, too?

*What a fucking grape!* she thought, and added eleven more acres of the Norton that year.

There was something about this all-or-nothing zeal of hers that was oddly resonant with the grape's boom-or-bust fortunes, something Nortonian. It was Nortonian to flout the experts and make more Norton. Nortonian to confront long, impossible odds. Nortonian to stand alone.

# Identity in Motion

*Bill Addison is* Atlanta *magazine's food editor and restaurant critic.*

# Empire State South

## Athens Star Chef Hugh Acheson Brings Atlanta Its Latest Southern Sensation

**Bill Addison**

How do you describe Southern food? Pursuing that answer is as much the daydreamer's indulgence as the academic's conundrum. It's a workman's meal of sugarless, butter-smeared cornbread, swiped through a bowl of pot-likker and crumbled into the mouth. It's an antebellum fever dream: she-crab soup, shad stuffed with roe, and the sherry-soaked dessert called tipsy squire consumed using weighty silverware on snowy linens. And it is, of course, an unconquerable buffet of fried chicken, fried green tomatoes, baked ham, candied yams, black-eyed peas, and small plastic bowls filled with peach cobbler sweet enough to give you the sugar jitters.

Pork belly over creamed kimchi with smoked peanuts, a recent special at Midtown's new Empire State South, owns a place alongside those other dishes. It captures this moment in the evolution of Southern food, particularly in Atlanta. The pork belly isn't one of those jiggly specimens: It's a fist-sized hunk of dense, striated bacon. Southerners love creamed vegetables, and dairy tempers the kimchi's fire and ferment without extinguishing its character. All those Korean restaurants on Buford Highway and in Duluth? They're now influencing Southern flavors the way that Mediterranean and Indian spices, via coastal ports, have seasoned our foods for centuries.

Hugh Acheson, chef-owner of Empire State South, revels in this kind of commingling. He opened Five and Ten in Athens a decade ago and helped reignite enchantment with our regional cooking. But he didn't accomplish it by mastering the perfect biscuit or deifying caramel cake. A Canadian who worked in some of San Francisco's most ambitious kitchens and then moved to Georgia for love, he fuses European and Southern ideas with clever respect. Skate wing with brown butter and capers may be straight from the French lexicon, but Acheson paired it with a mound of Red Mule grits at Five and Ten, and it resonated in the soul of any local who's partial to a simple plate of fish and grits. He married sweetbreads and succotash with unexpected harmony, the union strengthened by tarragon jus that bridged their flavors.

After partnering on another restaurant, the National, and a wine shop in Athens, Acheson felt that Atlanta was ready for his brand of individualism. He announced Empire State South last year, and public expectations simmered as the opening date was pushed back from early spring to late summer. Yet when you walk into the restaurant, housed in the back of the 999 Peachtree building, all the antsy anticipation dissipates. The room has the relaxed air of a saloon—a sprawling come-hither bar, navy walls, knotty heart pine and pecky cypress that cover the floors and border the doors, light fixtures that resemble inverted woks. A wash of milk paint in the private dining area (often available for regular seating) colors the paneling an otherworldly gray, a hue that conjures the moss-covered trees that grow around dilapidated plantation houses in the Louisiana swamp. It puts one in the mind for whiskey.

All this—and an outdoor bocce court to boot—is a much more stylized atmosphere than Acheson's funkier Athens ventures, and the diverse Atlanta crowds have arrived to show their approval. On any given night, a gay couple will be comfortably holding hands while a Buckhead matriarch holds court two tables away. The twenty-somethings tend to eat at the bar. Everywhere, fingers hover over smart-phone keypads, recording each course for soon-to-be-texted bragging rights.

Like the Southern food it serves, Empire State South is in a continuous state of evolution—all for the better. Just a month after the restaurant launched, executive chef Nick Melvin bowed out, and Ryan Smith, most recently chef de cuisine at both Holeman and Finch and Restaurant Eugene, replaced him. Smith's changes, with Acheson's blessing, were swift and unflinching. Out with the sentimental, in with the ballsy. An "antipasti platter" of tea sandwiches, deviled eggs, spiced pecans, cream cheese, and pepper jelly disappeared, replaced by a cheeky collection of jarred lamb rillettes, chicken liver pâté, and boiled peanut hummus (major cool points for that last one), along with palate-reviving pickles. A roasted baby carrot salad gave way to smoked sturgeon, fanned like sashimi over herbed yogurt and flanked with fingerling potatoes and wax beans. Smith's fine-dining take on shrimp and grits—heady with roasted peppers, pickled Fresno chiles, and earthy snatches of celery—beautifully counterpoints Acheson's signature Frogmore stew, a laid-back bouillabaisse of shrimp, andouille, and summery vegetables in tomato broth.

The biggest early change comes in the approach to entrees. Acheson originally billed Empire State South as a riff on the meat-and-three: diners selected, say, sautéed okra and field-pea cakes from among eight or so sides to pair with their fried catfish or smothered pork chops. Smith, a chef who likes structure in the kitchen, made the decision to match sides with proteins on the menu. If you ask, any server is quick to say that you're welcome to sub in other sides for the printed "suggestions." But they don't advertise that option, and it's no loss, really. For pan-roasted redfish glossed with sherry buerre blanc, for example, I couldn't pick more appropriate pairings than the turnip greens and wonderfully soupy butternut squash risotto that Smith chose.

One area that succeeded from the get-go: the wine program. You'll drift away from dinner conversation while reading the detailed, impassioned footnotes that wine director Steve Grubbs wrote for the list. He and his team heed your likes and dislikes, and they seem as pleased to deliver a $32 bottle of an obscure Spanish mencia as they are a $105 Beaune premier cru—described on the menu as "meaty, meaty, big and bouncy." The staff in general has become warm and professional; if you experienced early service disappoints like I did, give the restaurant another shot.

Since ESS views itself as a work in progress, I offer a short wish list: I hope the brined Berkshire pork chop becomes less of a jaw workout. While the buttermilk chess tart dissolves liltingly on the tongue, the sweets overall lack whimsy and daring. Perhaps some fruit-driven desserts? Also, the breakfast menu needs attention. The coffee bar rocks, but while the humdrum array of chicken biscuits, hanger steak with scrambled eggs, and quick breads may quell office workers' hunger, the city is desperate for a morning meal destination. Surely two fireball talents like Acheson and Smith can grapple with these challenges. No matter how you define Southern food, these guys have already begun cooking up the future.

*Donald Link is the James Beard Foundation Award–winning chef-owner of Herbsaint, Cochon, and Cochon Butcher in New Orleans and of Cochon Lafayette. This story is adapted from his book* Real Cajun.

# Real Cajun

## Donald Link

I grew up on the back roads and bayous of southwest Louisiana, a place that I did not fully appreciate until later in life. Looking back, I realize that the things I took for granted, like making gumbo with my granny, fishing with my granddad Adams, and family feasts made with produce from the garden, seafood from local waters, and wild game from the woods, were special gifts that have done more to shape who I am as a chef than all my culinary training. As a child every occasion of my life revolved around food—holidays, festivals, funerals, or any other excuse to call the family together. Spicy crawfish boils, crab boils, fish fries, and hearty lakeside breakfasts (pan-fried in a cast-iron skillet) were everyday affairs in my family. Though I eventually struck out on my own, leaving Cajun Country and the food I grew up on behind for a time, those early meals at my grandparents' table would ultimately inspire the menus at Herbsaint and Cochon, my two restaurants in New Orleans.

Today, now happily settled in New Orleans with a family of my own, I have come to recognize the value and importance of this region's culinary heritage. But I've also realized that the food traditions I grew up with are in danger of disappearing, along with the people who created them. Hurricane Katrina was a painful reminder that my region's traditions—the characters, the culture, and the food—are vulnerable. I can't turn back the clock or bring my grandparents back, but because I grew up cooking their food, and because I paid close attention all those years, I am lucky enough to have the recipes and the stories to commemorate a very special place.

My family's food was typical of Acadia Parish (a parish is a county to the rest of y'all), which is in the heart of a region called Acadiana, or Cajun Country. This particular region is a swamp-rimmed stretch of I-10 west of the Atchafalaya Basin and east of Lake Charles. Acadiana is a mostly rural swath that runs along the Gulf Coast all the way to Texas. The landscape is incredibly diverse. There are salt marshes and freshwater bayous, brackish coastal bays and endless swamps (populated by 'gators, snakes, and countless birds and other beasts), and plains tilled and dammed for rice fields and crawfish. It's a land where any given gas station sells tasso, andouille, hogshead cheese, and smoked pig stomach.

Acadia Parish was settled by French exiles from Canada (the term Cajun actually comes from the word Cadian, a shortened form of the French word Acadien). The area also attracted Germans (like my ancestors), who brought along their traditions of sausage making and expert butchering. People in this area are also fondly referred to as "coonasses." That word applies if your family has been in the area a while—regardless of whether you're of French descent or not. The people here love to pass a good time, as they say. To this day, when I return, which I do as often as I can, I am amazed at the fun-loving nature of the people.

My first memory of Louisiana (my father was in the military, and we spent the first few years of my life overseas) is of sweltering, oppressive heat. We arrived at my father's parents' house in the tiny town of Sulphur, just outside of Lake Charles, in the dark, in the middle of summer. My sister Michelle and I had been asleep, but the sound of car wheels on the oyster-shell driveway at Granny and Paw Paw Link's woke us up. My memory of this moment is so vivid, in fact, that it could have happened yesterday. The steamy, pine-scented air hung over us as a stifling, motionless blanket. The pulsating drone of cicadas and bullfrogs was near deafening; I had never heard anything like it. I started to sweat through my shirt the minute I got out of the car.

That night marked the beginning of my life in Louisiana, my introduction to its exuberant food and culture—and finding out what my family was all about.

The next morning I experienced my first Louisiana food smells: Community Coffee (dark roast, the kind I still drink at home) boiled on the stovetop and pork smothered with onions and garlic. What an amazing smell—pork, onions, and rich gravy simmering slowly for hours. When we finally sat down to eat, I noticed that even the way the aroma of the steamed rice permeated the gravy was amazing. Food fragrances just seemed to linger in the thick Louisiana air.

My two sets of grandparents lived a quarter mile from one another, and we settled about a mile from them. Between my mother and father, I have thirty-four aunts and uncles. That's ten brothers and sisters on Mom's side and seven on Dad's, plus their spouses and an armada of cousins. To keep things fair, we had to go to both grandparents' houses for meals. Between those two families, we did a lot of eating.

The Zaunbrechers and Links, my uncles and cousins, are still farmers, cultivating thousands of acres of rice as well as crawfish, which handily share the land with rice, alternately feeding off the fallow fields and fertilizing them, making the soil richer for grain production. Needless to say, rice was a very important part of my childhood.

My granny Link moved to Sulphur from Crowley, where her parents had settled in the late 1880s, after emigrating from Germany. Granny's parents were rice farmers, so her food was born of rice married with the Cajun cooking typical of the area: deeply flavored bowls of gumbo, beef pot roasts, and pork roasts smothered with plenty of thinly sliced onions and garlic and served au jus (in its natural juices) over rice. It seems like there was always a pot of rice cooking in Granny's house. To this day, when I smell rice cooking I feel as if I'm standing in her kitchen. Just as the smell of rice will always remind me of Granny Link, the rich, earthy fragrance of pork fat simmering with collard greens transports me to Grandad and Grandma Adams' house. Their kitchen and dining room were tiny, but somehow we always managed to pack twenty-five or more people around the table. Grandad ruled the range in this house, and he cooked Southern fare at its simplest and best. The sheer bounty was always overwhelming. What amazed me was how many different things he produced at a single meal. We might have some smothered greens with ham hocks, cornbread, creamy lima beans simmered with bacon, fried eggplant, creamed corn, duck stew, and the list goes on. The memory of the aroma of all that food cooking in such a small space is a powerful one.

■　■　■

This kind of cooking may or may not sound familiar to you, so before we go any further let's get one thing straight: The overly spiced and blackened food that gained popularity in the 1970s is nothing like the authentic Cajun food that I grew up with. Real Cajun food translates to the best ingredients of the area, simply prepared. The flavors are focused and the food is highly seasoned, though not necessarily spicy. Examples include rice (steamed or dirty), roasted meats (served in their own fragrant juices), cured pork and sausage (grilled or used as a seasoning and braised with beans and/or vegetables), oysters (typically fried or baked in dressings), pan-fried fish from local waters, wild game, turtles, crawfish, and lots of shrimp that might be grilled, boiled with spices, or simmered in one-pot meals like fricassees, gumbos, or rich, buttery étouffées. By contrast, Creole cuisine is a melting pot of European influences and African and West Indian ingredients. It's considered fancier restaurant fare; you don't see Cajun food on white table-cloths.

Cajun food has come to mean different things to different people, but as far as I'm concerned it's really a very simple concept: Acadiana is populated by farmers who live off the land, and the cuisine is born of this specific location. My second cousin JW, who farms more than 2,000 acres of rice, raises his own food supply, including hogs, chicken, ducks, and pheasants. It seems as though everyone in the area has some sort of homemade smoker, outdoor cooking apparatus, and access to amazing local ingredients. At my cousin Bubba Frey's store in Mowata, you can still go around back and find cages of guinea hens, turtles, squab, and doves right alongside the garden where he grows tomatoes, peppers, and herbs, as well as a gigantic fig tree and the huge smoker where he smokes countless varieties of meat and sausage.

I got my first paying job in an Iranian-owned Mexican restaurant when I was fifteen. I started out washing dishes. Finally, the older guys in their mid-twenties (they bought me my first bottle of rum) taught me how to work the line. It went something like this: Here's the plate, you put the tortilla here, a spoon of this there, then this sauce and cheese, then into the oven, and there you go.

I was attending Louisiana State University and working at Sammy's Bar and Grill in Baton Rouge when I met my wife, Amanda Hammack. I was five years into a finance major and at the end of my rope. I wasn't sure what I wanted to do, but I knew I wanted more than the small-town life of my childhood. I wanted to be different, to redefine myself, and I was desperate to get out of Louisiana. Amanda felt the same way, and two months later we moved to Northern California.

When we arrived in San Francisco, I needed an income fast. I got a job at a breakfast dive in the lower Haight popular with aspiring rock stars, tattooed bikers, and junkies. For a twenty-three-year-old straight out of Louisiana, the scene was intimidating, but looking into the dining room at all the strange and different people, and the frenetic, exciting scene, I had a revelation: I loved cooking, and I wanted to do it forever.

The years that followed included stints at some of San Francisco's top restaurants, as well as a degree from the California Culinary Academy. In 1995, Amanda was accepted at Tulane, and we returned to New Orleans, where I got a job at Bayona, Susan Spicer's widely respected restaurant in the French Quarter. After Amanda graduated, we returned to San Francisco for one more West Coast adventure before relocating to Louisiana, this time for good, in 1999.

That was the year our daughter Cassidy was born, and my perspective on a lot of things changed. The word family took on a new meaning, and for the first time I had to be responsible for someone other than myself. Amanda and I wanted to buy a house, and I knew I wanted to open my own restaurant—a bistro that would meld the fresh, ingredient-driven food that I'd come to love in California with the deepest Louisiana flavors. I brainstormed with Susan Spicer, who was also looking to open a bistro-style restaurant. We joined forces with partner Ken Jackson and my in-laws, Bill Hammack and Janice Parmelee. We found a sunny space in the warehouse district, on a corner of St. Charles with a streetcar running past out front, and Herbsaint was born. We opened the doors in October 2000, and we hit the ground running. I'm proud to say the restaurant has been a roaring success ever since.

Herbsaint is named after a locally made anise-flavored liqueur, but its roots are in Acadia Parish. The menu is a sort of modern Creole: seafood from local waters and hearty meat and pork dishes, along with the game and sausages of Cajun cuisine, crossed with classical French and Italian influences. Susan and I collaborated on the inaugural menu, and after that she was gracious enough to let me do my own thing.

Proud as I was of the menu at Herbsaint, I felt strongly that authentic Cajun and home-style Southern cooking were seriously underrepresented in our city. Increasingly interested in the rustic foods I'd grown up with, I started ordering whole pigs and breaking them down. I got excited about making my own boudin sausage and house-cured bacon. It dawned on me that I had the inspiration, and the kitchen talent, to do another restaurant. I partnered with Stephen Stryjewski, and the concept for Cochon (French for "pig"), a restaurant that would celebrate authentic Cajun, was born.

Then Hurricane Katrina blew through town and changed just about everything. Amanda and I lost our house and all of our possessions in the storm and we had to relocate. Herbsaint was closed for several weeks, and Cochon's opening was delayed for several months. The storm was a painful reminder that nothing can be taken for granted.

When Katrina forced us to evacuate the city, we stayed with my dad in Lake Charles. The period of exile that followed led to some powerful emotions and realizations. For the first time, I was spending all day in the kitchen, cooking for my extended family just as my grandparents used to do. Watching me make the gumbo, my sister said how much I looked like Grandad Adams (talking to myself and all), and I relished the comparison. I knew that the food of my region at the new restaurant was simply the right thing to do.

With Cochon's unabashedly home-style menu, its commitment to local products, the in-house boucherie (butcher shop), and the photos of my family on the walls, I have really come full circle. We serve boudin balls, crawfish pies, eggplant with shrimp dressing, and rabbit stew topped with dumplings. Desserts like blueberry cobbler and German chocolate cake are equally rustic.

The emotional confluence of the past years—Hurricane Katrina, my consequent decision to commit to New Orleans, the success of Cochon, and the birth of my son Nico—made my desire even stronger to document a time when food mattered.

It took me a while to figure out just how lucky I was to have been able to enjoy the food my grandparents dished up with such ease. Like most kids, I assumed that everyone ate as we did. But to this day I have not experienced home cooking that can even come close.

*Calvin Trillin is a staff writer at the* New Yorker. *This story first appeared in the magazine in 2010. John Mosca died in July 2011.*

# No Daily Specials

## Calvin Trillin

John Mosca, whose family opened a roadhouse outside New Orleans in 1946, doesn't like change. Actually, New Orleans itself resists change—an attitude that is widely thought of as both part of its glory and one of its problems. When people talk about change in New Orleans, it's often to explain how they're doing their best to avoid it. A headline in the New Orleans *Times-Picayune* not long ago about the sale of a bar known for its po' boy sandwiches read "NEW PARASOL'S OWNERS PROMISE MINIMAL CHANGES FOR THE LEGENDARY BAR AND RESTAURANT."

I'm not much on change myself, particularly when I'm in New Orleans. The city has some remarkable restaurants of recent vintage, for instance, but when I'm back in town I gravitate toward places like Casamento's, a seafood café on Magazine Street that has been around since 1919. It's comforting to find Casamento's virtually unchanged from when I first walked in, decades ago—two simple rooms all done in tiles, so that sitting down to eat one of the renowned oyster loaves is sometimes compared to having lunch in a drained swimming pool. The Napoleon House bar, at St. Louis and Chartres, looks pretty much the way it looked when I visited New Orleans back in high school. So does Galatoire's, whose interior resembles a large and unusually elegant barbershop. Yes, Galatoire's now has an additional dining room and a bar on the second floor, but I make it a point not to go up there.

From Highway 90, which runs through what people in New Orleans call the West Bank (the side of the Mississippi River that someone studying a map would be tempted to call south of the city), Mosca's looks roughly the same as it did in 1946, around the time John Mosca came back from the war in Europe—a small white clapboard building on a deserted stretch of a double-lane highway thirty or forty minutes from the center of the city.

When John's father, Provino Mosca, who had previously operated a restaurant in Chicago Heights, Illinois, opened for business that year, he moved his family into a few rooms in the back. The area around Mosca's is still deserted. My friend James Edmunds, who lives in New Iberia, Louisiana, about a hundred and thirty miles to the west, says, "It always had the feel of a neighborhood restaurant, except there was no neighborhood."

The double-lane, though, has seen some changes. Development has stretched from the Mississippi River into what I remember as a vast darkness. When I began going to Mosca's, in the early sixties, we used to interrupt our conversation in the car—a conversation that was likely to be about, say, the possibility that Mosca's Chicken a la Grande was even better than the baked-oysters-and-bread-crumbs dish identified on the menu as Oysters Mosca—so we could concentrate on peering into the blackness for Mosca's Budweiser sign. It was illuminated, as I remember, by one bulb. When we spotted the sign, we could warn whoever was driving that in a moment he'd have to cut across the break in the median strip into Mosca's parking lot, which was and is made of gravel. Ten or twelve years ago, a storm destroyed the Budweiser sign. The Moscas tried to get another one exactly like it, but Anheuser-Busch wasn't distributing signs like that anymore. I learned about the fate of the sign only recently, when I spent some time at Mosca's—partly to see how a place reluctant to change had fared through the disasters that have brought involuntary change to New Orleans in the past five years and partly to catch up a bit on Mosca family history and partly to see if eating there a few nights in a row would finally, after all these years, give me my fill of Chicken a la Grande.

As my mention of the Budweiser sign indicates, I am not one of the people who claim that they were guided off the double-lane in those days by the smell of garlic. It is true that Mosca's devotion to garlic has remained unchanged since the days when Provino Mosca was at the stove, and almost the same can be said of the menu; it's not the sort of place that surprises you with its daily specials. I could give my order before I get out of the car. I should say "our order," since the family-style portions served at Mosca's make it not the place to go for that contemplative dinner alone. We've always wanted Italian Crab Salad, Oysters Mosca, Spaghetti Bordelaise, Chicken a la Grande, Shrimp Mosca, and Mosca's Sausage. At times, we have ordered the Chicken Cacciatore as well as the Chicken a la Grande. I consider that a permissible variation. (A local restaurant critic who can be called Andrew Ashley considers ordering both chicken dishes a necessity rather than a variation, since he remains ambivalent about which one he prefers.) We have never ordered Chicken Cacciatore instead of Chicken a la Grande. I do not consider that a permissible variation. While waiting for the food to arrive—

Mosca's cooks everything to order—I have often been in discussions about how interesting it would be sometime to try the quail or the Cornish hen or even the steak. We have never ordered any of those things.

The dining area of Mosca's always seemed the same: One room, as you entered, had a bar and a few tables and a jukebox, heavy on Louis Prima. A larger dining room was off to the right. The late Allan Jaffe, the co-founder of Preservation Hall and a storied New Orleans trencherman, once told me about a conversation he'd had in the bar dining room one autumn when he came in to repair the deprivation he'd suffered during Mosca's annual August closing. Jaffe mentioned to John Mosca, who by then was running the front of the house, that something seemed different. John explained that, some years before, he had permitted a slight extension of the bar and it had never looked right to him. It looked changed. So during the August closing he had come in and sawed it off.

The proprietorship of Mosca's has changed only with the generations, and there has always been a Mosca in the kitchen. When Provino died, in 1962, the cooking was taken over by his daughter, Mary, and, eventually, her husband, a former Louisiana oysterman named Vincent Marconi. His family was originally from the town in Italy where Provino Mosca was born—San Benedetto del Tronto, on the Adriatic. Provino's widow, Lisa, also known as Mama Mosca, became the proprietor of Mosca's. (I have always treasured her for having said to a reporter from the New Orleans States-Item, in 1977, "You can write all that you want, it won't bother me because I cannot read or write.") By the time Mary retired, John's wife, the former Mary Jo Angellotti, some of whose forebears had also made the journey from San Benedetto del Tronto to Chicago Heights, had been helping with the cooking for nearly twenty years, and she took over as chef. At Mosca's, the chef does not oversee the cooking; she cooks. When Mosca's was given a James Beard award, in 1999, Mary Jo apologized for not being able to come to the ceremony in New York to accept it. She said, "We'd have to close the restaurant."

Mary Jo cooks pretty much the same dishes that Provino did in the days when Mosca's, struggling for customers, was open for lunch to feed employees of the Avondale shipyards and remained open late at night to catch some of the customers from the gambling joints that were then prevalent in the area. The dishes aren't complicated. For instance, Chicken a la Grande—which, John Mosca informed me, was named after a horse trainer named Charles Grande—has in it, in addition to the chicken, only salt and pepper, rosemary, oregano, white wine, and, of course, ten cloves (or is it heads?) of garlic. Still, James Edmunds, who takes great pride in being able to reverse-engineer dishes from the restaurants he likes, has never been able to replicate Chicken a la Grande. "I've made any number of tasty chicken dishes in the attempt," he told me. "But no Chicken a la Grande." Since the recipe calls for the chicken to be cooked in a skillet, James suspects that his failure has something to do with his not being able to match the heat of a restaurant burner-plus the fact that, as he puts it, "they know how to do something that I don't know how to do." James's analysis reminded me again that what I was once told by Charles Reynolds, a scholar of magic, about magic tricks has wider application: by reading enough books in enough libraries, you could learn how any trick is done, but that doesn't mean you could do it.

The tales told about the Mosca family in New Orleans have also remained unchanged over the years, although it turns out that not all of them are true. Until a few years ago, I wasn't even pronouncing the family name correctly. (The Moscas pronounce it with a long "o," as in "Joe," while everyone in New Orleans has always pronounced the first syllable to rhyme with "ma" or "pa.") On my recent visit, I learned that, contrary to what I'd heard and read and repeated, Provino Mosca was never Al Capone's chef. It's true that Chicago Heights was a suburb that, like Capone's headquarters of Cicero, had a number of citizens whose funerals were likely to be observed from across the street by the F.B.I. And Mary Jo Mosca told me that her maternal grandmother, Pasqua Frattura, once catered a baptismal party at which Al Capone was the godfather. Not the godfather like Marlon Brando; the baby's godfather. (According to the story, Capone came back to the kitchen and gave each of the caterers a hundred-dollar bill. Pasqua Frattura bought a stove.) But Provino Mosca apparently never laid eyes on Al Capone. I'm not someone who finds the Mob romantic—real mobsters are less punctilious than the Corleones, who in three blood-spattered movies managed not to harm anyone who wasn't a criminal himself—but I always enjoyed imagining what it might have been like to be Al Capone's chef. Just consider the potential consequences of, say, bringing out a plate of slightly overdone fish. I suppose I'll have to quit telling the Capone story, although I do so reluctantly. I'm not much for change.

It turns out that another Mosca's story about what people in Chicago used to call The Outfit is true: Carlos Marcello, widely referred to as the crime boss of New Orleans, was indeed a regular. In fact, he was the Moscas' landlord. When the family decided to move to New Orleans, John told me, an acquaintance found them a corner bar for sale on the New Orleans side of the river, just over the Jefferson Parish line, but the deal fell through. So Marcello, whom they knew through mutual friends in Chicago Heights, rented them the white building on Highway 90. They speak of him as not only their landlord but their friend, and they say that in their dealings with him he was always a gentleman. (When John's older brother, Nick, who died in 1997, left the business, in 1960, it was to operate a restaurant in partnership with

Marcello's brother.) Eventually, Marcello sold the Moscas a lot a hundred yards or so from the restaurant, where they built a neat brick house; John and Mary Jo brought up their daughter, Lisa, there. But Marcello never got around to selling the restaurant itself; his son is now the landlord.

Particularly on slow weekday nights (Saturday night, even in the worst economy, is never slow), the Moscas are likely to wonder what it might have been like to run a restaurant that didn't require most of its customers to take a thirty- or forty-minute drive that included the Huey P. Long Bridge—a 1935 structure that used to be known for its terrifying narrowness and is now known for being clogged by a construction project aimed at widening it. About twenty years ago, according to Mary Jo, she suggested to John that they move Mosca's to premises somewhere on the New Orleans side of the river: "And he said, 'No. The house is next door. This is where my father started. This is where I'm staying until I die.'" Mary Jo later polled the customers, eighty per cent of whom are locals, on how they would feel if Mosca's were moved somewhere else—presumably somewhere more convenient. "Well, they said they didn't know about that," she told me. "So that made me stop and think."

It had been the Moscas' custom to ride out storms in order to keep an eye on the restaurant—they'd done that during Hurricane Camille and Hurricane Betsy—but, as Hurricane Katrina approached, the entire family joined the exodus, heading for Jackson, Mississippi, by car in a trip that took ten hours instead of the normal three and a half. As it turned out, they were away for a month—first with a relative in Jackson, who found himself with eighteen people in his house, and then with relatives back in Chicago Heights. Katrina left the restaurant's dining rooms essentially untouched, but there was extensive wind damage to the back of the building; among other things, the kitchen was destroyed. For the Moscas, it was time to take stock. John Mosca was then eighty—a poker-faced man with a sly wit who had married relatively late in life. Mary Jo was only fifty-five. Their daughter, Lisa, was in college. "John said, 'I've had it,'" Mary Jo told me. "He said, 'I'm going to step away. If you want this restaurant to continue, you are going to have to do it on your own.' Although he still does make oysters, and I do consult him on various things."

Rebuilding took ten months, and there were times, Mary Jo told me, when she felt like throwing in the towel. In the aftermath of Katrina, there were problems finding skilled workers. There were problems obtaining permits. When Mary Jo talks about the experience, she says she tried to keep in mind something Provino Mosca used to say: "Without trouble, there is no life." The kitchen was rebuilt—and, for the first time, it was air-conditioned. New rest rooms were installed. The dining rooms were spiffed up a bit, although not to the point of exchanging the wall units for central air-conditioning. In June of 2006, Mosca's reopened. A story in the *New York Times* was headlined "THE AROMA OF GARLIC IS BACK ON THE BAYOU." Had there been an A.T.M. machine in the bar dining room before? Had the walls in the other dining room always been painted that color? I, for one, couldn't remember. To the regulars, Mosca's looked more or less unchanged—which was, of course, the way they liked it.

Four years later, BP's well began gushing oil into the Gulf of Mexico, presenting a much more serious long-term threat to restaurants like Mosca's than Katrina had. This fall, Gulf oysters were in relatively short supply. When I dropped into Casamento's for my ritualistic oyster loaf—this was against the advice of friends, who told me that anyone eating as often as I intended to eat at Mosca's should endeavor to make a lunch out of dry toast and unsweetened tea—the waitress told me that they had ordered twenty-five sacks of oysters from their supplier and been given ten. Drago's, which is known for what it calls char-grilled oysters, had sought to ease the pressure on its oyster supply by offering char-grilled mussels as well. At Cochon, a breezy post-Katrina restaurant that serves inventive Cajun food, I ordered wood-fired oyster roast and the waitress said, "The oysters aren't in yet. They're supposed to come this afternoon, if at all." I had to settle for chicken-and-andouille gumbo and fried alligator with chili-garlic aioli. Andrew Ashley told me that at a recent meal at Galatoire's his waiter, in the spirit of full disclosure, had informed him that the Oysters Rockefeller were from the Gulf but that the Oysters en Brochette were from Oregon.

Some New Orleanians won't eat oysters that aren't from the Gulf, and these days some visitors to New Orleans are wary of eating oysters at all. (The seafood and restaurant industries have been in the position of trying to reassure customers that the seafood is fine at the same time as they complain to BP and the government that it has been disastrously compromised.) Mary Jo Mosca actually made a few test dishes of Oysters Mosca with Pacific oysters, to see what that would taste like, and she was disappointed with the results. For a while, Mosca's, which uses different suppliers from most New Orleans restaurants, was able to get enough Gulf oysters, but then came two evenings when customers were not able to order one of the restaurant's best-known dishes, Oysters Mosca; there simply weren't any. Mary Jo is as concerned with the price as she is with the supply. She had been accustomed to paying thirty-six or thirty-eight dollars a gallon for shucked oysters. Lately, she has been paying as much as sixty-eight, and she expects the price to go up.

Mosca's weeknight business has been off, but it's difficult to know how much of that is from the oil spill and how much from the soft economy.

Mary Jo told me that she had obtained a claim number, which is the first step in trying to get compensation from the BP fund, but she has yet to do the paperwork necessary to file a claim. She has considered joining a class-action lawsuit against BP and others led by Susan Spicer, a prominent New Orleans chef whose complaint says, "Simply put, the oil slick and continuing discharge of crude oil is an ecological and economic disaster for Plaintiff." Lately, Mary Jo has been thinking more and more about another saying of John's father's. "He used to say, 'If you have a person who did you wrong, talk him into going into the restaurant business: he'll make a living, but you'll get even with him for the rest of his life,'" she told me one evening. "I didn't quite understand all that until now."

On the first night of my visit, I was joined at Mosca's by James Edmunds and his wife, Susan Hester, and a friend of theirs who had moved from New Iberia to New Orleans. Some improvements in Highway 90 several years ago cut more than an hour off the driving time between New Iberia and Mosca's, meaning that James and Susan can now get there in two hours flat, have an early dinner, and be back home in time for the ten-o'clock news. James has not completely come to terms with his failure to replicate Chicken a la Grande, but he acknowledges that his new proximity to the real article has sort of taken the sting out of the defeat. The next night, there were five of us at the table, and the night after that I was joined only by one old friend. It later occurred to me that, without any consideration of how many of us were present, I might have ordered the same amount of food for the table three nights in a row, including what I have come to think of as the Cacciatore Variation. I recalled a conversation I'd had with Allan Jaffe in the seventies, after we'd eaten at Mosca's with a large group on the evening before JazzFest:

"I was looking at the check, and I think we had the same number of dishes we had when three of us came here last month," Allan said.

"But that's impossible, Allan," I said. "There were sixteen people at the table tonight."

"I don't know," he said. "I'm not too full."

On the second night, I met John and Mary Jo's daughter, Lisa. At Mosca's, the presence of assorted family members has always been assumed, whether they're in the restaurant to work or not. When John's sister, Mary, and Mary Jo's mother were sharing the nearby brick house in their declining years—John and Mary Jo and Lisa had moved to a house in Harahan, about fifteen minutes away—they would walk over every night to sit at a family table, between the bar dining room and the kitchen, in order to survey the scene. Lisa, who has put in some time in Mosca's kitchen, recently got a master's degree from Tulane—a double degree in social work and public health. Since

Mary had no children and Nick's children did not follow their father into the restaurant business ("They're smart," Mary Jo says), Lisa Mosca, who carries the name of the matriarch, is the last of the line. Aware that a family business is no respecter of degrees, I asked her if someday she might take over Mosca's. She smiled and said, "I'm not sure I have a choice."

John T. Edge, director of the Southern Foodways Alliance at the University of Mississippi, has written or edited more than a dozen books and writes for a variety of publications, including the Oxford American *magazine,* Garden & Gun, *and the* New York Times.

# Pie + Design = Change

## John T. Edge

On a sun-splashed afternoon in August, blueberry pies and peach pies cooled on wire racks inside PieLab, a white brick cafe with floor-to-ceiling windows on Main Street in Greensboro, Ala. Behind a counter made of planks salvaged from abandoned sharecropper shacks, two young women slid pie tins into a double oven stack. At trestle tables, beneath industrial pendant lights, four young men, on lunch break from their G.E.D. classes, dug into slices of taco pie and made weekend plans.

If there was any thought that this was just a typical small-town cafe, the blue flag above the front door dispelled the notion. As the fabric rippled in the breeze, the words inscribed at the edges came into view: "Pie & Conversation, Optimism & Design." Pie might be served inside, but this cafe aspired to something more.

Founded by a design collective known as Project M, PieLab came to life last year as a combination pop-up cafe, design studio and civic clubhouse. Greensboro, the 2,700-person seat of Hale County, might seem an odd place for a group of well-intentioned young graphic-designers to set up a cafe. Situated in the Black Belt, a former cotton-producing region where the soil is dark and rich, Hale County appeared to be a lost cause. About one-third of the children there live in poverty. In 2002, The Birmingham News called the Black Belt "Alabama's Third World." How could the baking and serving of pie help tackle entrenched social and economic ills?

Project M aimed to answer just such questions. Part of what has become known as the "design for good" movement, Project M was established by a designer named John Bielenberg in 2003. Based in Belfast, Me., it functions as a kind of idea incubator, where young designers are invited to two-week programs to generate solutions to social problems and enhance public life. Since 2007, Project M has been operating regularly in Greensboro. One of Project M's most successful projects in the area, Buy-a-Meter, was built around a series of pamphlets that helped raise money to hook up area residents to running water. Bielenberg, a contrarian who likes to challenge participants to "reject linear thought pathways," had turned to food before to promote social change. In Connecticut, Project M and a design group named Winterhouse held an event called Pizza Farm, inviting local farmers to an area park and using their produce to make pizza for residents, while educating them about where their food could come from.

PieLab first began to take shape in March 2009 at a bar in Belfast, where 14 members of Project M gathered over burgers and beer. "We realized that we couldn't solve global warming," recalled Megan Deal, a native of suburban Detroit, who, like most of the other Project M members, was a recent college graduate. "And we couldn't fix the plummeting economy. Before pie came to us, we were kind of paralyzed."

They started out small. Their first foray was Free Pie Day, during which Project M members stood on a Belfast street corner and handed out slices of pecan pie, pumpkin pie and apple pie to passers-by. The idea was to spur community and conversation, one slice at a time. Free Pie Day inspired similar efforts in Washington, Brooklyn and elsewhere. Most important, it inspired PieLab.

■　■　■

"When I saw them out front, I walked over," Charles Johnson, a beauty-shop owner, said. "I saw the sign"—the one that spelled out LAB with stainless-steel pegs and washers—"and I asked, 'Is this some kind of radio technology or space-center stuff?'"

PieLab opened in a makeshift space on a Greensboro side street in May of last year. Five of the original Project M team members in Maine had come south at the invitation of the Hale Empowerment and Revitalization Organization (HERO), a housing-advocacy nonprofit, which also sponsored community-minded local initiatives. The Project M team conceived of their pie shop as a pop-up—a temporary cafe—describing it as a "negative-energy inverter, fueled by pie."

The term "pop-up" implies that a concept may be too cutting-edge to sustain. And so it was with PieLab. No one expected this pop-up to last, least of all the designers who transformed the original space in a breakneck three-week stretch and managed it with gusto for the rest of the spring and summer.

But that first day at the PieLab was a success. There was music, courtesy of a customer with an acoustic guitar. The crowd was diverse. Ideas were exchanged. Intergenerational friendships were forged. The take, at two bucks per apple-pie slice, was something like $400.

PieLab had visual style. And PieLab had a formula, a back-of-the-bar-napkin equation, sketched in Maine and refined on the ground in Greensboro:

> PieLab = a neutral place + a slice of pie.
> A neutral place + a slice of pie = conversation.
> Conversation = ideas + design.
> Ideas + design = positive change.

Yet for all its ambition, PieLab never had a business plan or a firm grasp on what sort of change was sought. This was intentional. Bielenberg wasn't much interested in long-term goals; he believed in setting something in motion and letting the momentum guide the effort.

The plan was simply to open PieLab's doors, begin conversations with the people of Greensboro and encourage them to create progressive initiatives of their own. "We had an idea," said Brian W. Jones, a collaborator from Virginia. "That was it. We opened without a business license or the complete approval of the health inspector."

PieLab's logo—two crimp-crusted pie slices, positioned tip to tip to form a double beaker, an hourglass or some other old-school scientific apparatus—said it all. Here food wasn't just fuel. And design wasn't merely a way to arrange your living room furniture. Design, when applied to food, could be a catalytic force for good, even if the good wasn't specified.

PieLab operated out of temporary quarters for four months. HERO, under the direction of Pam Dorr, served as host and landlord. Six years earlier, Dorr left a job as a production manager for the Gap in California to join the social-service efforts in Hale County. Dorr collaborated with Project M on earlier projects, finding practical applications for their ideas. To support PieLab, she secured government grants, helped build ties in the community and served as a hands-off adviser.

That first PieLab space, in a tin-roofed clapboard home behind the HERO offices, was spare and studied, with glossy white walls, high ceilings and open shelving. A hand-cranked cash register sat on the front counter, alongside a silverware tray and a decommissioned library card catalog. Inscribed with the names and check-out histories of old books, the cards served as sketch pads and, on occasion, order pads for $3 slice-and-coffee combos.

The earnestness was palpable. The Project M crew baked pie and brewed coffee. They crimped crusts with forks and piled on pears and pecans gathered and delivered by neighbors. They designed Web sites for the Hale County Humane Society and created logos for the nearby city of Northport.

For the socially engaged members of Project M, PieLab was a clubhouse. For small-town characters, it was a magnet. College students from Sewanee, Tenn., ate through all the pecan pie one afternoon. A film director just back from Thailand came in for coffee and talked about his next project, a Big Foot horror movie.

Over time, the Project M folk befriended Scott Hamilton, an aspiring artist. They designed a Web site on which he posted his paintings of cities of the future, shaped like skyscraping minarets. When Charles Johnson, a regular, was in a good mood, he performed on the pine floors, moving to a line-dance routine called the Cupid Shuffle.

Within a few months of opening, following a spate of positive design-industry press, PieLab-inspired efforts popped up in cities like Portland, Ore. In Greenville, Ala., southwest of Montgomery, Nancy Rhodes recently opened Polka Dots Café, cater-corner from the town's Confederate memorial. She serves kolaches, a Czech pastry popular in Texas. Inspired by PieLab, she plans to operate a "neutral space," where people of all races and classes can gather.

■   ■   ■

"That first space was really grass roots," Megan Deal recalled. "It was so easy to build, so easy to run. There was an honesty about it, a purity. It was all about pie and conversation. All about what we intended. It worked."

More significant, it seemed to work in the Black Belt, a region that a *New York Times* writer, in the days before the cotton economy went bust, described as a "garden of slavery." Poverty rates may register higher in other counties in the region, and racial disparities have proved wider, but Hale County has long been the Black Belt's front porch. Hale was where James Agee and Walker Evans drew their famed portrait of Depression-era tenant farmer life, *Let Us Now Praise Famous Men*, a book that has served as a primary text for students of rural America in the decades since. And Hale was where Samuel Mockbee and D. K. Ruth established the Rural Studio, a design-and-build program for Auburn University architecture students, focused on creating high-concept, low-cost homes for indigent residents. Don't be "house pets to the rich," Mockbee told his charges, sounding a clarion that inspired, among others, John Bielenberg.

All this attention to social ills did not come without social costs. Almost 75 years have passed since Agee and Evans traveled the county to document the lives of poor white folk, but their work still has the power to inflame residents. If outsiders see Evans's photos and Agee's text as a candid examination of an ailing region, insiders often see the book as the product of crusading interlopers, the sort of people who parachute into the region today with little understanding of local concerns.

Amanda Buck is not the only Project M collaborator who has walked into the Hale County Library on Main Street to check out *Let Us Now Praise Famous Men* and learned that lesson. "Everybody who comes down here wants to read that book," Buck recalled a librarian saying as she handed her a copy. "You know this doesn't paint the whole picture. There are other perspectives."

■ ■ ■

Buck, a native of Brunswick, Ohio, who was a member of the original 2009 Project M program and later traveled south to work at PieLab, showed up thinking that she was to be a "change agent." But when she talked about change, many Hale County residents heard condemnation. No matter, she thought. "What are we doing here if we're not working for change?"

In the Black Belt, Project M collaborators could afford to be idealists. They worked hard, but their lives unspooled like summer-camp deferments. "On weekends we swam in the river," Brian Jones recalled. "We wandered down Main Street at sunset and admired the way the light bounced off the buildings."

They ate lunches of fried whiting and fried okra at Flava, a soul-food cafe set in a brick compound one block off Main Street. And they listened as Eugene Lyles, who built the restaurant in the 1960s, told them that, back when the black-power movement was ascendant, he was an idealist, too. Weekday afternoons, they walked the town, past shuttered storefronts. At night, they sometimes played four-square games on Main Street, sidestepping pulpwood trucks as they downshifted from the highway. They measured success in modest exchanges. Buck and Robin Mooty, another early PieLab worker, designed and painted a new sign for Charles Johnson's salon. In return, Johnson took Buck and Deal golfing.

PieLab efforts played well to the news media. Here was hope, and apple pie, and a seemingly robust new economic engine in the Black Belt, a seemingly hopeless American place. And here was an effort that aligned nicely with the national trend toward food activism. "PieLab provides a neutral environment in a traditionally segregated town where people from every race and class are welcome to sit together and talk candidly about whatever is on their mind," Brian Jones told *Fast Company* magazine.

PieLab, along with projects like Mission Pie in San Francisco (which employs at-risk youth and uses local ingredients for its pies), is part of an American movement to deploy food-focused initiatives, including restaurant operation and artisanal food production, to foster social change. The culinary establishment embraced PieLab. The magazine *Southern Living*, the prevailing arbiter of middle-class regional taste, dubbed its apple pie one of the South's best. The James Beard Foundation named the Main Street PieLab space one of three 2010 finalists for its restaurant design award.

All the attention buoyed the PieLab collaborators. But it also created problems. When Project M first arrived in Greensboro, some folk bristled at the language it employed. The conflicts began with the 2007 Buy-a-Meter project. To get the initiative under way, Project M used stark black-and-white photos (and starker messages) to draw attention to area families who lacked access to the municipal water supply. The pamphlet campaign raised about $50,000. HERO, working in conjunction with Project M, used this money to purchase and install more than 100 water meters. Beyond Alabama, Buy-a-Meter was celebrated as a financial and critical success. But back home, the slogan—"In Hale County, Alabama, Water Is Not a Right," splayed across a gatefold photograph of Greensboro's Main Street—did not always play so well. Tensions increased when a group of designers proposed a National Design Center for Rural Poverty Programs in Greensboro. To make clear the need, they described Hale County as a place where an "impoverished population suffers from substandard housing, education, health care and job opportunities."

In Greensboro, such sweeping generalizations, no matter their accuracy, stung. "What does some guy in Maine know about my life in Alabama?" asked Ann Langford, chief clerk of the Hale County Probate Court and one-time Rural Studio administrator. "Who gave him the right to speak for us?"

By that point, a number of new voices were speaking for the Black Belt. At least seven windmill-tilting organizations were doing good works in Hale County, including Project Horseshoe Farm, a residential mental-health facility. Those programs brought youthful energy to Greensboro. They also brought trouble.

"You have the same town-and-gown tensions here that you would find in a small Massachusetts college town," said Winnie Cobbs, a retired college professor who operates a local bed-and-breakfast. As she talked, two young women, wearing jogging bras and college mascot tank tops, race-walked through downtown. Inside PieLab, a Horseshoe Farm fellow hunched over her laptop, filling out medical-school application forms.

"It's universal," Cobbs said. "You hear the same talk about the loose morals of young kids. And you hear the same suspicion of the motives of outsiders."

■　■　■

"I was naïve," Buck said. "I knew nothing about baking pies and running a business."

As Buck talked, she squirmed in her chair in what was the original pop-up PieLab space and is now used by AmeriCorps Vista volunteers who run

BikeLab, a bicycle-repair and reclamation project also initiated by Project M and HERO. "We came with preconceived notions about what we would find in Alabama," she said.

In October 2009, as the PieLab crew worked to refurbish their new brick-fronted space on Main Street—the one with polished wood floors and a balloon-whisk bathroom light fixture—tensions reached a pitch in what came to be known as the "cake thing" or the "poster incident."

Designed by a couple of the PieLab workers, the poster was printed in an array of colors, the most arresting of which was bright red. Rendered in a bold, black font and capped by an exclamation point, were the words: "Eat pie." Stacked beneath, in far smaller type, was a command that began with a sexually explicit four-letter word and ended with the word "cake."

To the PieLab crew, the poster was an over-the-top exercise in sloganeering. To members of the Greensboro community, who followed the workings of PieLab on various Web sites, the document was a totem of the group's cultural insensitivities.

"The humor might have played well in Brooklyn," Buck said, taking pains to explain that the posters were never intended for local distribution. "But here it wasn't funny at all."

Posters quickly found their way into the hands of city and county power-brokers. Things came to a head during a heated conversation in the street, which Pam Dorr, of HERO, playfully described as a "near riot."

"I understand what they intended," Winnie Cobbs said. "It was playful and frivolous. I got the Marie Antoinette reference. It takes us back to the time of the French Revolution. But you have to pick your place to use that word. And posters, plastered around this town, would not have been that place."

Ann Langford still keeps a rolled copy beneath her desk at the courthouse. "I can't take a poster with that word on it home," she said. Langford understands youthful indiscretion. Yet she still gets agitated when she talks about the incident.

"So is that the best that you can come up with after going off to college?" she asked a group of PieLab workers who came to apologize. "Is that what your parents sent you to school to learn? I thought y'all were supposed to set examples."

■　■　■

Three months have now passed since "the takeover." That's the term that Pam Dorr uses to describe the process by which she jettisoned the design side of the PieLab equation. Her technique was simple: Rather than renew some of the governmental programs under which the original crew was employed, Dorr allowed certain sources of financing to lapse. One by one, the founders departed.

Under Dorr's leadership, PieLab may still realize some of the transformative goals imagined by the original crew. Early in the process, PieLab began working with YouthBuild, a job-training-and-remedial-education program, affiliated with the U.S. Department of Labor. At first, 20-somethings from programs like that were ancillary to the PieLab effort. Now job training appears to be primary. Some of the changes have been more pragmatic. PieLab no longer opens at 9 in the morning, as it did when the Project M crew ran the show. Gone are the stacks of take-one, leave-one cards with recipes for graduate-student fodder like tofu stroganoff. Gone, too, is the pie-only menu. PieLab now serves homemade biscuits at 7 in the morning to farmers and construction workers. In the afternoon, it sells butter-crusted quiches, piled with precut nubs of ham, to lunchtime tourists, drawn by glossy photos in magazines like Bon Appétit.

One recent morning, Melvin Webster, who is studying construction skills through YouthBuild while working on his G.E.D., drank coffee and talked of how he learned to blend pecan butter from cracked nuts for a HERO-sponsored initiative called Pecans! It was a task in which he seemed to take great pride. Across the counter, Sam Heartsill, a mother of two whose work at PieLab is financed in part by a federally subsidized employment program, drained a bottle of lemon-juice concentrate into homemade custard. At PieLab, both the food and the focus are still works in progress. Dorr leads the progress. As executive director of HERO, she has helped dozens of Hale County families move from busted trailers to tidy bungalows. Now, in her work with PieLab, she has proposed courses for young cooks to learn about the virtues of local produce and traditional techniques. And she holds hospitality classes for those aspiring to careers in the food industry.

When Dorr talks about PieLab, she typically drops the word "lab" and the baggage associated with it. As in, "Let's go down to Pie and get a slice." Or, "Modern Woodmen of America are having their lunch meeting at Pie." Or, "Let's go see what the girls are up to down at Pie."

"It began as cool place to drink coffee and eat pie," she said between bites of a blueberry-and-cream-cheese pastry cup. "Now it has the chance to be more than that. It may not be as cool, but it's a life-full place."

*Lolis Eric Elie, a New Orleans–based writer, is story editor of the HBO series
Treme. This story originally appeared in the* Oxford American.

# The Origin Myth of New Orleans Cuisine

## Lolis Eric Elie

Part of the difficulty in defining Louisiana Creole cuisine, and in determin-
ing the race of its inventors, is the difficulty in defining the word Creole
itself. There is a consensus that, in the case of Louisiana, Creole means a mix
of French people with folks from other cultures. But there is a dispute about
precisely which other cultures were involved in the mix.

If definitions of Creole cuisine can be considered a genre unto themselves,
then Dorothy Dix's work would be a minor masterpiece, embodying as it
does all of the elements that flummox me most in such prose: a flirtation
with, but not embrace of, historical fact; an absolute certainty about the sem-
inal role of the French in the development of Creole cuisine; an insistence
that every group of white people ever to settle in Louisiana made invaluable contributions to the cookery of the state; a lack of specificity about the
contributions made by each of these groups; and the recognition that
the natural rhythm of black people is as evident in the kitchen as it is on the
bandstand.

"Many things have contributed to make New Orleans a shrine to which
gourmets make reverent pilgrimages," Dix observes in her introduction to
Elaine Douglass Jones's *Gourmet's Guide to New Orleans Creole Cookbook*,
which was originally published in 1933.

"One is that it has what an old colored cook once described as the 'in-
grejuns' necessary to good cooking, for you cannot make omelets without
making eggs."

Though I was born and raised in New Orleans, I spent most of my adult life wholly unaware of the influence of the hot breads of Virginia on the cuisine of my hometown. This fact was but one of the "gems" revealed to me by Dix:

> Founded originally on the French cuisine, it was pepped up, so to speak, by the Spanish, given body and strength by the New England influence, a bit of warmth by the hot breads of Virginia, and finally glorified by the touch of the old Negro mammies who boasted that they had only to pass their hands over a pot to give it a flavor that would make your mouth water.

In those few words, Dix sounded the major themes of Louisiana Creole food, as defined by many if not most Creole cookbooks. Most of these definitions were written long before food studies had become the serious academic discipline that it is today. Still, there is a consistency to the definitions—and the mistakes within them—that can tell us much about history, class, and race.

■   ■   ■

Louisiana Creole cooking is said to have been started by a chorus of small bangs: the beating of pots by dissatisfied housewives seeking to get the attention of the governor.

In the introduction to Justin Wilson's 1990 book, *Home Grown Louisiana Cookin'*, Jeannine Meeds Wilson reports:

> Madame Langlois, the housekeeper for Governor Jean Baptist Le Moyne, was the first great cook in Louisiana. It seems the few women who inhabited the settlement of New Orleans in 1722 were upset over the lack of familiar cooking ingredients so far away from France. The new colony experienced chronic supply problems with frequent shortages of wheat, flour, garden vegetables, and herbs. The women marched on the governor's mansion clanging pots and spoons. Le Moyne wasn't able to do much about the supply problem, so he asked Madame Langlois to show the settlers how to cook with the foods that were so plentiful in their new home.

Wilson continued:

> Madame Langlois learned her skills from the Indians, the first inhabitants of Louisiana. . . . The Indians were masters at using

all the resources available to them. . . . The Indians gave us filé powder for flavoring and made hominy. They taught the early settlers many valuable tricks about survival in the wilderness and about the plants and animals unknown to the Europeans who were slowly moving into the area.

Honey Naylor's contribution to the 1998 book *The Food of New Orleans: Authentic Recipes from the Big Easy* adds one detail to Wilson's narrative.

It was she [Langlois] who calmed the angry wives by teaching them how to use powdered sassafras for flavor in the gumbo they'd already tasted from the hands of African slaves (gumbo being derived from the west African word for okra).

Naylor goes on to add, "It is not an error to say Creole cooking is French, even though that is a gross oversimplification."

Like many others who have sought to define Creole cuisine, Wilson's argument is self-contradictory. She refers to Langlois as "the first great cook in Louisiana" before going on to state that "Madame Langlois learned her skills from the Indians," and "the Indians were masters at using all the resources available to them." Similarly, Naylor notes that historians said this so-called "Petticoat Rebellion" was the "beginning of New Orleans Creole cuisine." But her own evidence indicates that gumbo, the emblematic dish of this cuisine, predated Mme. Langlois's contribution.

Naylor and Wilson seem to reach their conclusions about the origins of this food based on the reputations of the peoples involved. France has been renowned for the greatness of its food at least since 1533, when Catherine de Medici arrived from Florence to revolutionize French cuisine (and to wed King Henry II). By comparison, neither the myriad tribes of Louisiana Indians nor the various peoples of West Africa have enjoyed such widespread praise.

So it's no surprise that gumbo, the signature dish of Louisiana cuisine, is often considered to be a Creolized version of the bouillabaisse of Southern France. The misconception has expanded beyond cookbooks to the Internet. For example, on the website In Mama's Kitchen, David Adams writes:

The word Gumbo MAY have been derived from the African word Gombo that means "Okra." This is a derivation that is apropos since okra should probably be designated as the "Official Flower" of every state in the South. The origin of the word "gumbo" is disputed, however. Some sources say it derives from the Choctaw word "kombo" which means sassafras. Whatever the source, gumbo is based on the French soup Bouillabaisse, a soup which many believe cannot be translated from one place to another due to the seafood in local waters.

Though Adams acknowledges the assertion that bouillabaisse cannot be "translated," he then ignores his own evidence that gumbo has a source other than this French soup. As for the relationship between gumbo and bouillabaisse, I can find very little. In his book *The Food of France*, Waverley Root devotes several pages to bouillabaisse. While lobster can be included, he states that fin fish, not shellfish, dominate the dish. Seafood gumbo, by contrast, never contains fin fish. Moreover, gumbo in Cajun Louisiana often consists of sausage and fowl and no seafood. That dish lacks any connection at all to the seafood soup of Marseilles.

Gumbo does, however, have much in common with the okra soups and stews that are commonly found in Western Africa and throughout the African diaspora, where the ancestors of most Afro-Creoles came from.

The first known printed mention of gumbo was made in reference to food eaten not by French immigrants but by African maroons who had escaped slavery in Louisiana. The following passage, from a 1764 court document, was uncovered by Gwendolyn Midlo Hall, author of *Africans in Colonial Louisiana*:

> Comba and Louison, both Mandingo women in their 50's, were vendors selling cakes and other goods along the streets of New Orleans. They maintained an active social life, organized feasts where they ate and drank very well, cooked gumbo filé and rice, roasted turkeys and chickens, barbecued pigs and fish, smoked tobacco and drank rum.

The word *gumbo* is derived from the word for *okra* in many Bantu languages. It seems highly unlikely that French Creoles would apply a Bantu term to a French dish. In fact, if you are shopping for okra in France, you must use the African word *gombo*, as the French language hasn't its own term.

But because the French aristocracy was famous for its love of elegant cuisine, it was necessary to claim that French elites created the food of the Louisiana swamps.

"Among the people of New Orleans were a group of exiled aristocrats who were accustomed to the fine foods and wines in France," Wilson imparts.

The French Revolution brought displaced royal chefs to New Orleans, where they found many appreciative customers. They brought a finesse to their cooking through the rich sauces that have made many of their recipes treasures. They were also accustomed to having house servants and trained many blacks to cook for them, bringing the heritage of another whole continent into the mix.

Making a parallel point, Raymond J. Martinez writes in his 1954 book, *Louisiana Cookery*, "In the beginning, gentlemen of high rank who came to Louisiana from France demanded the excellent cooking to which they were accustomed."

*The Original Picayune Creole Cookbook* begins its definition of Creole cuisine in the interrogatory and thus raises doomed hopes that the authors will truly examine the evidence. The authors ask: How did Creole cooking come about?

From France came the chefs of that day to make their fortunes in the New World—and established themselves here with the young colony. From Spain came the best cooks of that sunny clime— and settled down beside the French artists. After a still longer while the people of the New World, who learned from them, adapted what they learned to their needs and to the materials they had at hand. The result was beyond speech.

In an interview with the New Orleans Restaurants website, cookbook author John DeMers said:

Creole cooking is based on elegant French cooking—a time-honored pampering of royalty and rich people. The glorious sauces of the Creole kitchen are at least built upon the glorious sauces of the French kitchen.

Similarly, comparing Creole and Cajun cuisines, Emeril Lagasse writes, "The Creole cuisine is a more refined one, due to the aristocratic influences of the French and Spanish settlers who lived in New Orleans."

What these authors seem to forget is that in the early days of the Louisiana colony, France had difficulty finding willing settlers, much less aristocrats, eager to risk death by yellow fever and malaria to come to an uncertain future in the heat and humidity of New Orleans. Moreover, by the time of the French Revolution, in 1789, the Louisiana colony had already been well established.

Another point these authors ignore is that the shortage of women in the French colony led to the importation of prostitutes released from prison in France and shipped to the New World. While these women may have been wonderful human beings, it is unlikely that they were expert in the cuisine of the French aristocracy.

"Creole cuisine is an art in itself, reflecting the same happy combination of opposites found in Creole people who developed it," describes the anonymous author of *Creole Cuisine*, a book published in 1951 by the utility company New Orleans Public Service Inc. "New Orleans was settled by the French and the Spanish, and the children of marriages between these races were called Creole."

According to the 1990 book *Creole Cooking (Step by Step)*, "To be considered a Creole in the strictest sense, you would have to have descended from a French or Spanish family who came to the area before 1803."

Expressing a similar view, Virginia Cooper shares the following in the 1941 book *The Creole Kitchen Cookbook*, "'Creole' is a name applied to the descendants of the French and Spaniards who explored Louisiana and settled in the state."

Lafcadio Hearn, the nineteenth-century writer who did much to create the popular notion of New Orleans and its culture, extended the ethnicity of Creoles to many other European immigrants.

In their book, *French Cooking in the New World*, Frances D. and Peter J. Robotti quote Lafcadio Hearn as defining a Creole as "a white descendant of an original Louisiana settler, who may be either French, Spanish, or German, or English, or even American."

But in this panoply of potential Creoles, only one group of people is specifically barred: Americans of African descent. Cooper makes this abundantly clear in *The Creole Kitchen Cookbook*:

> Many of the leading citizens of Louisiana are proud they are Creoles, but they would be surprised to know that there has been in existence and still lingers the belief that the word Creole is associated with "mixed-bloods," or mulattoes, as they are more generally called.

Hearn echoes Cooper's point and in the process seems unnaturally surprised to learn that some people thought native-born New Orleanians of African descent might also be considered Creole. In the essay entitled "Los Criollos," Hearn suggests:

It only remains to observe that the Creoles of New Orleans and of Louisiana (whatever right any save Spaniards may originally have had to the name), are all those native-born who can trace their ancestry to European immigrants or to European colonists of the State, whether those were English, Dutch, German, French, Spanish, Italian, Greek, Portuguese, Russian, or Sicilian.

He continues, "But the term is generally understood here as applying to French residents, especially those belonging to old French families, and few others care to claim the name."

It, therefore, seems odd, indeed, that even among the most ignorant portion of the population of this city, there should be found any person of the opinion that a Creole may be a quadroon or an octoroon. . . .

Hearn continues:

But when one considers that the light-tinted, French speaking colored element of the New Orleans,—the relatives and the children of true Creoles,—call themselves Creoles, and desire to be so called, the existence of the fallacy does not appear so extraordinary after all.

The debate about whether Africans or Europeans are the true Creoles goes back centuries. In her book *Beyond Gumbo: Creole Fusion Food From the Atlantic Rim*, Jessica B. Harris indicates that the term "may ultimately have been of African origin." She quotes Garcilaso el Inca, who wrote in 1602 that:

It's a name that the negroes invented . . . it means negroes "born in the Indies," they invented it to distinguish those . . . born in Guinea from those born in America, because they consider themselves more honorable and of better status than their children because they are from the fatherland. . . .

■   ■   ■

While the cookbook authors are resolute in their conviction that the lion's share of the credit for American Creole cuisine belongs to white people, they are a bit vague in specifically defining what these white people contributed. Exactly what does Dorothy Dix mean when she writes about how the Spanish "pepped up" Creole cuisine? What does it mean to say that the New England influence gave the cuisine "body and strength"?

At times, it seems that the writers of these cookbooks are better versed in genealogy than in food studies. "The cooking here, to speak sententiously, is grandchild to France, descendant to Spain, cousin to Italy, and also it is full fledged Southern," relates Mary Moore Bremer in *New Orleans Recipes.*

Or consider a similar passage written by the Junior League of New Orleans in their *Plantation Cookbook,* "Recipes handed down through Creole families represent the fusion of European, West Indian, and domestic influences."

The Junior Leaguers elaborate:

> French colonists brought a wealth of recipes that were to form
> the basis of Creole cooking. Robust Spanish colonials followed
> and imposed their own spicy touches to established dishes; the
> Mexicans later made similar contributions. German immigrants
> who farmed near the mouth of the river became the largest pro-
> ducers of local rice. Like corn in the uplands, rice was the staple
> of lowland tables. Italian colonists increased the use of garlic
> and hot peppers; curries and delicate spices were imported from
> far off India. Even a few Chinese epicureans made their pres-
> ence felt.

The Junior Leaguers fail to say which recipes the French brought with them. And what was the distinction between the hot peppers of the Italians and the "spicy touches" of the Spanish? In which Creole recipes does one find evidence of the debt the cuisine owes to India and China?

Hot peppers are New World spices. So when these authors refer to the spiciness of Spanish food, they are probably referring to the cuisine of the Spanish colonies in the New World. But, with few notable exceptions, the authors credit the Spanish with this culinary influence, and not the indigenous peoples of the countries Spain colonized.

"The Creoles of Louisiana learned a little from the French, Spanish, and Indians, and by a skillful blending and the use of native foods and high seasoning created Creole cooking," Martinez tells us in *Louisiana Cookery.* He then conveys:

> There was also the Italian influence upon Louisiana or Creole
> cooking which helped to give it flavor. The Italians made excel-
> lent sauces and improved the gravy for meat and fish dishes. But

it seems that the Italians, believing in their own style of cooking, refused to be influenced by the French and Spanish.

But Martinez failed to describe even one of the sauces or gravies that the Italians contributed to Creole cooking.

Although Louisiana has had residents of Italian descent even before 1870, the majority of the state's Italian immigrants came after that date. By then, Creole cuisine had already been well established as a major culinary achievement.

In 1887, William Makepeace Thackeray wrote:

[The] Old Franco Spanish city on the banks of the Mississippi, where, of all the cities of the world, you can eat the most and suffer the least, where the claret is as good as in Bordeaux, and where a ragout and bouillabaisse can be had the like of which was never eaten in Marseilles or Paris.

It is unlikely that the Italians could have greatly impacted Creole cuisine by the time of Thackeray's writing.

(It is also curious that the "bouillabaisse" Thackeray tasted was apparently different from that available in France. Perhaps, dear William, it wasn't bouillabaisse at all.)

It's also noteworthy that none of these authors mention the Haitian influence on Creole cuisine. During the decade of the Haitian Revolution, 1793–1803, black, white, free, and enslaved refugees came to New Orleans. In 1812, many of the Haitians who had fled to Cuba during the revolution were forced to leave that island and settle in Louisiana. The population of New Orleans doubled during this period.

Those Haitians, many of whom were probably born in Africa, provided the last great infusion of both French and West African culture since, owing to the Louisiana Purchase in 1803, the former French colony of New Orleans was probably a less attractive destination for Franco settlers than the French colony it had once been. Given the time these settlers had spent in Cuba, they were apt to have been well versed in the cuisine of that Spanish colony. But by defining Haitians out of Creole cuisine, these authors are able to maintain the fiction that the food of New Orleans is derived from the French aristocracy rather than from descendants of a country that is often classified as the poorest in the Western hemisphere.

The definition of Creole as it relates to American cuisine is crucial because the food itself is the most widely celebrated American culinary achievement.

Consider the effusive praise of Count Hermann Alexander Graf von Keyserling in his 1930 book, *America Set Free*:

Nowhere did the absolute superiority of real culture strike me
so forcibly as there. . . . New Orleans is the one place in America
where cooking is considered an art.

Any people acknowledged to have contributed significantly to the development of this cuisine would automatically be considered major players
on the international culinary stage. And, given the fact that people of West
African descent have always formed a substantial percentage of the population of New Orleans, it is particularly suspicious that their influence—if the
cookbook authors are to be believed—has been so miniscule.

Rudy Lombard gives voice to this suspicion in the 1978 book *Creole Feast*:

It is difficult to arrive at a universally satisfying definition of Creole cuisine. All such attempts in the past have failed to achieve a
consensus, and have seldom been used twice; several key influences or individuals are always left out or changed.

"The one feature, however, that all previous definitions have in common
is a curious effort to ascribe a secondary, lowly or nonexistent role to the
black hand in the pot," Lombard continued.

Most portrayals of the black contributions to Creole cooking assume that
black people had a mysterious talent for cooking and that, unlike the Europeans, they didn't include any of the techniques from their homeland in
their cooking in the Americas.

According to the Junior Leaguers of Baton Rouge in their 1959 book,
*River Road Recipes*, "The French enhanced their own outstanding cuisine
with the great abundance found in Louisiana—the herbs, seafood, game,
meat, vegetables and fruits."

They go on to write, "The Spanish added zest and the old Negro mammy
a touch of magic with her knowledge and use of herbs."

Virginia Cooper also finds something in the talent of black cooks:

Even the Negresses, through some unknown mystery or through
instinct, have grasped the art; they have discovered many valuable strong-flavored herbs and roots that are used for seasonings.

But in his book *Roll Jordan, Roll: The World the Slaves Made*, Eugene D.
Genovese contends that the African influence on Southern foodways was
central to the development of that cuisine. In a widely quoted passage, he
refers to this influence as "the culinary despotism of the [slave] quarters
over the big house." Considering the similarities between the Creole food of

New Orleans, the cuisine of West Africa, and the recipes of Afro-Caribbean countries such as Haiti, it would seem difficult to exclude these people from definitions of Creole cooking when such culturally distant people as New Englanders and Virginians are credited with helping to shape it.

If the sentiments expressed in these older books were purely things of the past, our discussion of them would be of no more moment than the discussion of any long buried cultural relic of the days gone by. But, more often than not, contemporary cookbooks repeat the tired sentiments about Creole cuisine being primarily the product of European cooks.

In the 1998 book *The Food of New Orleans*, Paul Greenberg posits that the "West Indians" were third-class citizens in the development of Creole cuisine. It's clear from his reference to their bare feet that the West Indians to whom he was referring were black:

> If the French represented the epitome of refinement in cooking and the lusty West Indians the barefoot contributors of seasoning, someone had to take the middle ground. Fleeing from famine, pestilence, and government upheavals came the Germans, the Italians, and the long-suffering Irish.

Yet later in that essay, Greenberg states that the Germans and Italians who immigrated to this country were poor people, hardly more prosperous than the West Indian contributors to Creole cuisine. If Greenberg is to be believed, black people invariably rank lower than even the most wretched of white people.

In order to maintain the elaborate fiction that black people contributed little or nothing to the development of New Orleans Creole cuisine, cookbook authors of previous generations had to invent an array of white enrichments that was sufficiently broad to account for the multicultural nature of this food. Acknowledging the obvious importance of the French was not enough unless it was also made clear that the non-French elements of the cuisine came almost exclusively from other Europeans. Modern food writers have tended to accept this myth without even taking the time to examine its internal contradictions. Some cookbook authors have given significant credit to black cooks, but their work has been insufficient to counterbalance the common misconception that black people were just bit players in the development of this food. But imagine what could have happened to the black image in the white mind, or the black image in the black mind (let alone the white image in the white mind), if the contributions of black Creoles to New Orleans cuisine had been fully acknowledged. Imagine, for example, if "black" or "West African" or "Haitian" were substituted for "French" in Count Keyserling's *America Set Free*:

> Owing to the French influence Americanism acquires a halo of beauty in New Orleans. . . . A time may come,—and I hope it will come—when New Orleans will wield a more attractive power in the eyes of Americans that New York. Should it come to this, then Americans would prefer the former in the same sense as every cultured German thinks more of Munich, not to mention Vienna, than Berlin.

John Kessler, a former chef, writes about food for the Atlanta Journal-Constitution. This story originally appeared in the Oxford American.

# Where Are All the Black Chefs?

## John Kessler

In 1997, I began eating my way through Atlanta in my capacity as restaurant critic for the daily paper. I enjoyed the variety: soul-food cafés and country-cooking warhorses that served meat-and-threes in compartmentalized trays, and the white-owned, white-tablecloth restaurants that sold customers on fried green tomatoes capped with swirls of creamed Alabama chèvre.

Atlanta was going through the first of several Southern cooking revivals I would witness—this one marked by savory riffs on grits and the crusting of Gulf seafood with andouille sausage and such. But where, among the practitioners of the new Southern cuisine, were the ambitious black chefs?

In place of restaurants run by famous black chefs, Atlanta had famous black restaurant owners—Sean "Diddy" Combs and Gladys Knight among them—who lent their names to concepts. There was also a growing cadre of talented black chefs who worked exclusively for rich individuals: rappers, basketball players, and entrepreneurs.

The scene changed in 2000, when Spice Restaurant announced its debut with a billboard depicting a red-hot chili spread across a woman's nude torso. Opening in a refurbished nineteenth-century bungalow in Atlanta's Midtown neighborhood, Spice was one of many new, swank dining destinations to debut that year, but it was unique.

The enterprising African American chef/co-owner, Darryl Evans, created Spice with two business partners and more than two million dollars for the lavish renovation. The menu showcased his vision against a backdrop of world cuisine—an approach that translated on the plate into dishes such as seared foie gras with a green apple and bacon compote. But Evans did not forsake his native victuals. He prepared white shrimp from Georgia coastal waters and paired venison with a sweet potato and red onion chutney.

A native of Columbus, Georgia, Evans came to Atlanta in the early 1980s to attend junior college. His first gig was as a kitchen assistant in a suburban airport hotel. He had no cooking background but worked hard. Evans's break came one morning in the form of a pancake emergency. The head chef had neglected to place the day's order and panic ensued—the kitchen had no pancake mix for the morning buffet. Looking around, Evans saw eggs, milk, oil, and flour, and offered to save the day. "I had seen my mother make pancakes every weekend," he recalls. "It didn't seem to be that hard." When Evans served a batch of flawlessly fluffy pancakes, the manager promoted him to top chef on the spot.

Evans hadn't come looking for a career as a chef. His interest in food was latent—developed while watching his mother cook and while attending family reunions, which centered around food. Based on the promise he showed while working at the hotel, though, Evans was offered an apprenticeship with the American Culinary Federation, the largest professional chefs' association in North America. As part of the program, he interned at the Cherokee Town and Country Club in Atlanta's tony Buckhead neighborhood.

"He was always asking to stay and help, even after his forty hours," recalls Tom Catherall, who was the club's chef at the time. "He used to duplicate everything I did. You'd show him once, and then he'd execute it exactly the same. I could see that Darryl had the drive to be an executive chef."

Catherall hired Evans full-time. Working toward Master Chef certification, which involved rigorous testing and far-flung competitions, Evans accompanied Catherall to events throughout the country and in Europe. Evans, often the only black face visible in a kitchen of white toques, absorbed knowledge and technique at these events. "I watched everything Chef Catherall did," Evans says, "how he made his food and how he ran his kitchen."

When Catherall left Cherokee to start Azalea, one of Atlanta's first chef-driven restaurants, he invited Evans to be his sous. Azalea served as a daring-for-its-time fusion of Asian cookery and Southern ingredients. Its trademark dish was a whole, sizzling catfish, its backbone removed and sides scored deeply so that diners could pry nuggets of flesh loose with chopsticks and dip them in soy sauce.

Like many chefs, Evans advanced at Azalea by leapfrogging from job to job, with each move demanding greater responsibility. Before he was thirty, Evans left Azalea to lead the kitchen at the Athens Country Club. The next year, he became the first African American to represent the United States Culinary Olympic Team in Germany.

On his return from overseas, Evans was recruited to lead the kitchen at Anthony's, an antebellum mansion located on three plush acres in Buckhead. Anthony's played the moonlight-and-magnolia card big time, employing hoopskirted hostesses and touting a reputation that referenced the "War of Northern Aggression." (To this day, the restaurant pledges to serve those who want "to experience the 'Old South.'")

Given carte blanche to devise a menu, Evans grafted New South and Old South, white and black. He prepared chicken livers in the style of foie gras and molded Hoppin' John into croquettes. He sourced the best regional ingredients, pairing striped bass and ravioli stuffed with goat cheese and Georgia caviar.

It was a menu that reflected the times, but also one that defined Evans's coming of age style—with a lengthy roster of dishes, each dish more elaborately garnished than the last. Yet it was built on a foundation of ingredients that any Georgian, black or white, would recognize.

After only a few months at Anthony's, Evans joined one of Atlanta's top hotels, the Occidental Grand, as executive chef. He says the reception from his new kitchen staff was less than cordial.

Some people walked out on his first day, Evans claims. "They didn't want to work for a young black chef," he suspects.

■  ■  ■

For up-and-coming black chefs, however, Evans was a beacon. "I was tracking all this from Seattle when I was in high school," recalls one admirer, Duane Nutter, who, as a boy, obsessed over magazines like *Restaurants & Institutions* the way other kids do with *Vibe* or *Sports Illustrated*.

Despite the paucity of black role models in those pages, Nutter wanted to become a chef. He loved cooking. He loved eating. He loved the idea that he could make a living this way.

Fresh from culinary school in Seattle, Nutter wrote to the three most prominent and frequently profiled African American chefs of the time.

There was Patrick Clark, then at the Hay-Adams Hotel in Washington, D.C., who had turned down the Clintons when they were looking for a White House chef. There was Johnny Rivers, the photogenic executive chef at Walt Disney World, who leveraged his time in Orlando to build a food and beverage consultancy. And there was Evans.

Evans was the only chef who wrote back. He didn't promise Nutter a job but invited him to try out.

Nutter arrived in Atlanta to find that a number of black chefs were already working the kitchen line with Evans, looking for mentorship, among them a young Chicagoan named Todd Richards. Evans had Nutter prepare a meal from a mystery basket of various goods, a typical test for a nabe cook, and was impressed enough to give him a job.

Nutter and Richards stayed together under Evans, even as the Occidental Grand hotel changed ownership. Eventually, Evans left to run the kitchen at Villa Christina, a truffles-and-pasta Italian restaurant. Nutter and Richards followed.

Taking into account the continental expectations of both the restaurant owners and their clientele, the men abandoned notions of incorporating African American vernacular into the cuisine. "Being African American didn't matter anymore at Villa Christina," Evans says.

Villa Christina was just another way station, but it was a perch from which Evans could recruit the investors who would finance him in a chef-driven restaurant—one with an urbane, glamorous setting—where he could showcase a refined take on American cookery, rooted in the South but not restrained by geography.

It wasn't easy. Evans perceived a tacit racism in the reluctance of both white and black investors, who didn't deem black cooking worthy of white-tablecloth trappings. "I could run the kitchen in a fourteen-million-dollar hotel," he recalls, "but I had to prove I was responsible enough to manage a two-million-dollar investment."

Evans persevered and did find two white investors who believed in him. Spice opened, he says, with "one of the most creative menus I've ever done." Creative, as interpreted by Evans in the Spice era, meant lobster-lacquered prawns with baby-vegetable ratatouille and a bouillabaisse infused with sassafras.

The joy was short-lived. Four months into his tenure, Evans was sickened by autoimmune cirrhosis of the liver, a chronic condition he had long battled. Deathly ill and awaiting a transplant, he left Spice behind. So advanced was his disease that he moved to the top of the transplant list, and Catherall and former colleagues rallied behind him. The American Culinary Federation held a fundraiser to pay for the expensive procedure.

■　■　■

After Spice closed, Nutter and Richards moved as a team through upscale hotel kitchens, including the Oakroom in Louisville, Kentucky, where they won a national reputation, and where Richards, the executive chef, crafted comparatively stripped-down dishes like a "pork and beans" of pork belly and white beans, glazed with a bourbon-molasses sauce he learned from his grandfather.

Last year, Nutter and Richards purchased Rolling Bones, a traditional barbecue joint, to which they introduced smoked-duck plates and pulled-pork tacos. That development came quickly on the heels of a consulting gig they shared, working to conceive and open a new restaurant, One Flew South, in Atlanta's Hartsfield-Jackson International Airport.

That operation is ambitious, with salads fashioned from Georgia goat cheese and Tennessee bacon, and sandwiches piled with duck confit and peanut relish. A casual observer would recognize a familiar, modern, farm-to-table sensibility of the menu. A closer observer would see, in the elaborate garnishing of dishes and the use of Southern ingredients, Evans's leitmotif.

No matter the recent successes, Nutter and Richards long to build, from the ground up, a restaurant that is entirely their own. They are now looking for the right location and the right investors, the sort of investors who will warm to a concept that Richards, in a tip of the hat to Evans, has taken to calling "global soul food."

■　■　■

Nine years after his liver transplant, Evans has forged a career on the periphery of the restaurant scene. He runs the kitchen at his suburban church, consults on kitchen staffing and menu design for small cafés and clubs, and caters private dinners for celebrities who recall his heyday.

Recently, I had dinner with Evans, Richards, Nutter, and their mutual friend Reggie Washington, who designed the menu for Gladys Knight and Ron Winan's Chicken & Waffles. At Shaun's, a white-owned, chef-driven bistro housed in the space that was long Deacon Burton's—the most beloved soul-food restaurant in Atlanta—I ask why, nearly ten years after Evans left Spice, there still are no African American chef-owners directing the restaurant culture in Atlanta.

"The good chefs are ashamed of soul food," Evans says. "We don't go to the farms. We've abandoned our roots." Traditional recipes, he says, are perhaps too far from the modern experience, too time-consuming. His grandmother, for instance, made the best collard greens he had ever tasted, but he explains that was largely due to her laborious method for cleaning them—a process that involved a thorough rinse with laundry detergent.

In a 2006 *New York Times* article, Michael Ruhlman argued that black families often view cooking as menial labor and stigmatize restaurant work. What's more, Ruhlman wrote, white chefs and kitchen managers sometimes harbor racist attitudes and discourage blacks from advancing within the workplace.

Nutter recognizes that, for blacks, cookery is burdened. For his part, he detests the term "soul food"—while it might suggest lesser cuts of meat and poorer ingredients that enterprising homemakers had to render edible, Nutter feels it mostly perpetuates an inaccurate marketing gimmick.

"African Americans don't like history," Richards adds. For a long time, black chefs were disinclined to use their family traditions as jumping-off points for culinary creation.

"The fact is, we don't go out to restaurants to celebrate," says Washington. "The best soul food we'll ever try is at family get-togethers where we're eating from huge pots. You know what that special flavor is in your auntie's collard greens? It's love."

This prompts me to wonder aloud what has motivated Richards and Nutter to hone a culturally rooted, historically relevant cuisine.

Richards answers obliquely, talking instead of his days in Darryl Evans's kitchen. Chefs need strong mentoring relationships early in their careers. To get that, black chefs either find an African American versed in the rigors and pedagogy of the professional kitchen or cross racial lines.

Richards and Nutter aim to make good on the vision of their mentor. Recently, they turned their dreams to Atlanta's Old Fourth Ward—a traditionally black neighborhood in the throes of revitalization.

It is here that many of Atlanta's new breed of white chef-auteurs have opened restaurants among renovated condos and studios. They already have their beachhead in the area, Rolling Bones, the barbecue joint.

But for now, Richards and Nutter are captivated by their concept for the ideal restaurant. The menu, says Richards, will "reflect African American culture, but also Chinese culture in some dishes, and other cultures as well."

They already have a name for the place—Revival.

Hanna Raskin is the food critic for the Seattle Weekly. She previously served as food critic for the Dallas Observer.

# Homesick Restaurants
## How Dallas Became a Dining Nowhereville

**Hanna Raskin**

Thousands of television sets had been sold in Dallas by 1951, but most of the time the machines weren't good for much. The city's biggest station aired a test pattern fifteen hours a day. In homes across the county, hulking Philcos and Zeniths sat stone-faced in their mahogany veneer cases until 2:30 p.m., when WFAA's musical matinee came on.

The CBS affiliate, KRLD, perked up earlier, arresting the geometric doldrums for housewives and convalescents who craved better company than their radios. Its programming opened with a fifteen-minute news segment, followed at 10:30 a.m. by Martha McDonald's cooking show.

No footage survives from McDonald's show, which ran for five years before her declining health forced her to retire, but the recipes included in her cookbook suggest she was a militantly plain cook. "She keeps her dishes simple and sensible," her coworker Louis Gibbons wrote in an introduction to *Recipes from Martha McDonald's TV Kitchen.* "One of her male viewers, an elderly gentleman, once said to me: 'I don't approve of television, but I do approve of Martha McDonald.'"

McDonald, the second of four daughters born to an Ellis County tenant farmer, was no bumpkin. She baked elaborate wedding cakes that were flanked with elegant rosettes. She could make a frilly prune whip. But Dallasites who tuned into her show, whether out of interest or desperation, found she concerned herself primarily with the food regular folks ate. Homemakers who counted their change before they wrote up their grocery lists had an ally in McDonald, whose distinctly North Texas dishes were hearty and frugal. While they weren't spicy, they had a certain roughness that, by midcentury, had come to define the region's cuisine.

There are the expected recipes for chicken fricassee and chop suey in

McDonald's cookbook, along with the usual array of hashes and fruit salads suspended in gelatin. Often, though, the author skews crude, marshaling such ingredients as onions, bacon drippings, pimentos, mustard, and chicken gizzards to whack her readers' palates. She beat eggs with massive amounts of olives and cheese, added swatches of bacon to the bowl, poured it in a pastry shell and called it a pie.

McDonald's uncouth kitchen stylings were very much in keeping with Dallas's edible sensibilities. Community cookbooks from the era strain with recipes for chili-sauced tongue, pickled peaches, horseradish-smothered tomatoes, and pickle surprise, a hostess's standby of nickel-sized dill pickles, cored and stuffed with deviled ham and mayonnaise.

Local cooks had a knack for rendering innocuous foods rather rude, spicing and seasoning with a frontiersman's disregard for refinement: Mrs. T. L. Jaggers in 1946 published the recipe for her Texas beans in the Dallas College Club's cookbook. The preparation starts with a can of beans and gets gruffer from there. The reader is instructed to add bacon grease, mustard, ketchup, and onion and warned, "If there are men present, there had better be plenty." Even hoity-toity Junior Leaguers got cheeky in the kitchen, serving up hot tamale loaves garnished with creamed beets and spiced onion pickles and broiling bacon bundles crammed with mustard sardines.

At that golden hour between Dallas reaching the population density it needed to cultivate a culture of its own and achieving the wealth it required to import the same, the city's culinary character was clear. Dallas food was nervy and brash. In an age when mothers coddled their children with milquetoast, Dallas cooks were adding two tablespoons of chili powder to one pound of pinto beans. That's a ratio a chili powder manufacturer could—and possibly did—endorse. Today, celebrity chef Paula Deen, hardly a paragon of reticence, recommends a single teaspoon for the same-sized serving.

For decades, Dallas proudly upheld a gospel of bold flavors. And then, somehow, the city forgot all about it.

The quintessential dish of Dallas's current dining scene doesn't have anything to do with peppers or mustard or pickles. It doesn't speak of the people who settled here, or the land they found. None of which has stopped almost every local restaurant with double-digit check averages from serving mussels, a seaborne mollusk that's impervious to direct seasoning. By latching onto steamed mussels, Dallas isn't just snubbing its culinary heritage—it's sacrificing its claim to being a serious and significant food city.

What counts in cookery today is a regionally specific food culture. Serving day-boat scallops two thousand miles from Nantucket Sound no longer allows a town to call its culinary scene "world class"—a status cities covet because of the bragging rights, economic advantages, and intellectual stimulation that come with it. Communities now are building their reputations on boudin and boiled whitefish, plates that plant an eater's feet firmly in the native soil.

The hyperlocal approach may have reached its apex this year with the opening of Husk, chef Sean Brock's Charleston, South Carolina, paean to the South: "If it doesn't come from the South, it's not coming through the door," Brock, a James Beard award winner, decreed.

For years, Dallas has pursued a very different course, voraciously importing ingredients, chefs, and culinary philosophies in the name of cosmopolitanism. Corporate interests have helped sculpt the city in Las Vegas's image, pasting big names on restaurants and leaching the odd and offbeat from local menus. They've garroted the development of neighborhood restaurants that innovate and thrive in places with enviable culinary reputations. It all adds up to a sensation of nowhereness that doesn't track with the contemporary food climate.

Dallas has done such a good job of disguising its edible traditions that few eaters—here or elsewhere—can confidently describe the city's cuisine. Atlanta has grits, Chicago has pizza, Memphis has barbecue and Dallas has— well, mussels. Dallas's untethered cuisine is so thoroughly out of step with how most epicureans are now thinking that the city's begun to exist in a sort of self-imposed isolation, a decidedly unhealthy position for a city with culinary ambitions.

The Dallas dining scene is broken, as anyone who's eaten out lately can attest. It's slipped from being a city that drew international attention for its renegade restaurants to a town where corporations serve as tastemakers, chefs aren't taking chances, and customers are so stingy with their food dollars that restaurants can't engage in the type of fine-dining play that distinguishes cities such as Chicago and San Francisco.

For every optimist who insists the situation's improving, there's another setback: In the past year alone, Sharon Hage shuttered York Street, a celebrated shrine to locavorism; Avner Samuel replaced his flamboyantly excessive Aurora with a sensibly priced bistro; and Go Fish Ocean Club closed almost as soon as Top Chef made executive chef Tiffany Derry a nationally known star. Industry insiders say they can imagine what a flourishing dining scene in Dallas might look like, but aren't entirely confident the city has the goods to get there.

"I don't know a single chef in Dallas," Bryan Caswell, the force behind REEF in Houston, admits. "I know chefs in every other town."

Caswell is leery of denigrating Dallas, an activity he maintains isn't an automatic corollary to his constant Houston boosterism. "There are very few things I'll debate with a customer," he says. "My gumbo and how much I love Houston." He protests he barely knows Dallas.

"Every time I go to Dallas, I get lost, go to jail, or get the shit kicked out of me," he says.

Still, it looks to Caswell like Houston, San Antonio, and Austin have eclipsed the state's biggest metro area.

"You guys are almost playing fourth fiddle," he says.

Caswell's assessment wouldn't surprise chef Stephan Pyles, who's stuck by Dallas as it's wandered off the national stage.

"I know we're not a great dining city," he says. "It's hard to accept that. I thought we'd be further along, but we're not. We're in the second tier. I think we're right up there, but there's a big gap from tier one to tier two."

Pyles, of course, was a member of the "Texas Mafia," a group of four under-forty chefs who blended the regional fervor spawned by the Bicentennial with a reverence for Diana Kennedy's take on classic Mexican cookery and came up with what *San Francisco Chronicle* restaurant critic Michael Bauer in 1983 christened the "New Southwestern Cuisine." The style didn't have any obvious antecedents, which was exactly the point: emboldened by the ascent of nouvelle cuisine and the flow of oil money coursing through the city, Pyles, Dean Fearing, Anne Greer, and Robert Del Grande mished and mashed French techniques with blue corn, poblanos, jicama, and cilantro, an herb few groceries stocked before Dallas chefs showed eaters what they could do with it.

"Whatever the ingredients, these talented young chefs are cooking the food of the '80s—light, vibrant, sparkling," *New York Times* food writer Marian Burros reported in 1986.

Southwestern cuisine—as much a product of a particular time as a specific place—hastily made the national rounds, with chefs from San Francisco to New York City adding chiles and tomatillos to their pantries. Pyles opened Tejas in Minnesota in 1987: "Talk about a bland palate—Scandinavian," he says. "But once they tasted it, that's what people expected. Big, bold flavors."

When Fearing returned to The Mansion as executive chef in 1985, he told his bosses, "The only way I was going to go back was if we marketed The Mansion as Southwestern cuisine."

"When we first started, I didn't know if it had legs, all of us being young chefs," Fearing recalls. "There was definitely a rebel side. We were all in our midtwenties and wanted to take on the world. We wanted to change Dallas from French restaurants."

Chefs working in the Southwestern idiom were pleased their experiments were attracting national press, but weren't sure they could count on brewpubs in Ann Arbor, Michigan, to keep serving mole sauce, a menu addition *Texas Monthly*'s Patricia Sharpe documented in her 1996 story "Texas Food Conquers the World!" But they were confident their concoctions would remain mainstays of Dallas menus. As Burros concluded her story, "They are certain it will always have a permanent home in the Southwest."

Yet that's not exactly what happened. Suddenly, Fearing and Pyles were the only guys in town making a serious go at a cooking style that was primed to be as regionally influential and transformative as the farm-to-table philosophy Alice Waters popularized in Northern California or the scrubbed-up Southern cuisine set forth by Frank Stitt in Alabama.

Southwestern-leaning eateries predicated on trendiness instead of talent shut down. The Mansion rekindled its Francophilia, eventually hiring a Loire Valley native to helm its dining room. And even chefs who trained under the patriarchs—Nick Badovinus, Casey Thompson, and Marc Cassel are a few of Fearing's kitchen alums who've opened their own area restaurants—gravitated away from the Southwestern genre.

While the scarcity of imitators has surely helped boost traffic at their eponymous restaurants, Fearing and Pyles are mystified why their ideas didn't catch.

"It's an interesting question," Fearing says. "Stephan and I have talked about it. Both of our trees of life are huge. But it's not like other cuisines, where people left Charlie Trotter and kind of did Charlie Trotter in their own style. It's funny that people would love me and wouldn't do Southwestern cuisine."

Perhaps Fearing's ego is an element of the equation: Famed for his outsized personality and multicolored cowboy boots, Fearing is so firmly linked with Southwestern cuisine that it's a struggle to separate the man from the masa. A young chef who lards his menu with quail tacos and ancho shrimp soup is at risk of putting on a culinary drag show, aping Fearing's signature moves.

"Stephan and I took it to unbelievable heights," theorizes Fearing, who wonders whether young chefs are paralyzed by their unspoken answer to the question: "Would I ever get it like Dean and Stephan got it?"

"What's always been disappointing to me is when people ask who are the heirs apparent, the fact is, the chefs we've trained don't do any unabashed Texas," says Pyles, a fifth-generation Texan. "It's interesting, because I have this struggle. I have to continually remind them to bring things back to this style of place."

Speaking of executive chef Matt McAllister, who's since left Pyles's restaurant, Pyles says, "He's out there wanting to do molecular, and I say 'Remember our deal here. Where are we from? Texas.' So he'll add some chiles."

McAllister confirms he's not under the sway of Southwestern cooking: "I don't really do Southwestern food," he says. "It's not my style. Mine's just kind of simple American. I'll use whatever ingredients are freshest and most in season."

It doesn't matter much to McAllister whether his dishes reflect Dallas. That's a more pressing concern for Pyles: Although Pyles's newest restaurant is a compilation of global cookery, he's smitten with his home state's foodways.

"I would like to do an in-your-face Texas concept," he says. "Maybe it's a little Disneyland-like. Ambiance is pure Texas. It would really pull from four influences: Southern, Hispanic, and the cowboy steaks and the chicken-fried steak. We do a chicken-fried steak at lunch [at Stephan Pyles] that sells like crazy."

What the Dallas dining scene really needs, the most vocal lamenters say, are more meats, grains, fruits, and vegetables grown by local farmers. Won't happen, the skeptics respond: North Texas is hot and the soil's lousy.

"That's ridiculous," says Erin Flynn, who farms near Austin. "That's absolutely ridiculous. People have been eating in Dallas for millennia."

Cranky weather conditions haven't impeded the local food scenes in Portland, Maine, where the average winter temperature is about twenty degrees, or Portland, Oregon, where farmers have to contend with almost forty inches of annual rainfall. Coaxing pigs and plants to grow isn't the problem, Flynn says: It's getting product to market.

"Just because you can grow it doesn't mean you can get to it," says Flynn, who recently moved back from Georgia to launch Green Gate Farms.

Compared with Georgia, Texas's local food scene is badly stunted, Flynn says. That's partly a result of the state consistently favoring large-scale commercial farms, and partly a result of grassroots activists failing to organize on small farms' behalf.

"In other states, the nonprofit communities and academic communities have come together to create infrastructure," Flynn says. "Texas has a different tradition."

Flynn starts to make a point about the primitive state of farm-to-table networks statewide by referencing an "Eat Local Week" meeting she attended that morning, pausing to ask the dates of Dallas's "Eat Local Week." Told no such thing exists here, she shifts her conversational course.

"Man, things are bad there," she says.

In Dallas, the local food distribution system consists primarily of Tom Spicer processing orders for arugula and squash blossoms at his ramshackle market in East Dallas.

Spicer spends a fair amount of time explaining market economics to growers and buyers. He coaches farmers on which greens to grow and teaches chefs how to use new ingredients. But a one-man show can't double as a revolution: While most leading Dallas restaurants are sufficiently savvy to tack the words "local" and "seasonal" on their menus, Spicer claims very few exercise the integrity real locavorism demands: they make exceptions for asparagus in January and substitute commercially produced ingredients for the locally grown stuff when it runs out.

"It's symbol over substance," Spicer rails. "That's Dallas."

But even chefs who aren't trying to wriggle out of their ethical obligations often find it's hard to uphold the most basic tenets of the local-food movement in Dallas, where the supply chain's twisted and tangled. Ed Lowe, whom chef Sharon Hage calls the "Godfather of the Dallas farm-to-table movement," made buying from local farmers a cornerstone of Celebration Restaurant—and then he gave up.

"In the early years, I went to Farmers Market a lot, and then it faded as a common practice for us," he says. "It's certainly easier to pick up a phone than take a van at 4 in the morning. You can pick up the phone and say, 'I want two cases of squash' or you can get into a vehicle that will support a substantial load of produce."

If you're after cantaloupe from Pecos or tomatoes from Canton, he adds, "You have to get to the Farmers Market at 10 p.m. the previous night. If you're not there, you're not going to get anything."

Lowe has recommitted his restaurant to buying local, but acknowledges the logistical hurdles remain very real. Without a coalition of growers and eaters to forge a healthy distribution network, most restaurants are stuck doing what makes financial sense.

Dallasites would do well to remember local food is about money, Flynn says.

"It's an entrepreneurial opportunity," she says. "And Dallas is known for business."

It's tempting to believe Dallas could build a vital food community solely with local spinach. But locally grown ingredients are a means, not an end. "That should be a given," Pyles says. What might matter more is the provenance of the city's chefs. If Dallas is to reclaim its former edible glory, it needs more chefs like Pyles, who have a deep connection to the region and the flavors that once exemplified it.

The mischievously audacious seasoning that once distinguished Dallas cookery is slightly at odds with the delicate nature of farm-to-table cuisine. Many chefs who chant the organic, local, seasonal mantra advocate a hands-off approach to cooking. "Chefs need to let ingredients speak for themselves," *Dallas Morning News* critic Leslie Brenner wrote in her prescription for the city's restaurants, published last summer.

The spell of minimalism is strong. The latest season of *The Next Iron Chef* featured a challenge in which the competing chefs were supposed to create a dish that "respected the potato," leading to much discussion of whether multiple layers of flavor are consistent with vegetable respect. Bryan Caswell made a tater tot, which his fellow judges decided didn't respect the potato.

"That's not my style," Pyles says of the current vogue for unadorned plates. "I'm happier to taste something intense and have it keep going in my palate."

Pyles's characteristically Texan attitude shows up at Samar, where he's corralled the intense cuisines of India, Spain, and the eastern Mediterranean. The influence of a local chef, who understands and loves North Texas, is apparent—no chicken-fried steak required. The flavors are strident and dense, just like Martha McDonald liked them.

So where are the local chefs? More than ten thousand students have passed through the culinary program at El Centro College since it debuted in 1966, but it's a long way from the classroom to restaurant ownership, especially in a dining climate Jessie Taylor-Yearwood, a professor at El Centro's Food & Hospitality Services Institute, describes as "brutal."

There's a cost to assembling the type of résumé needed to open a restaurant these days, and most El Centro students can't afford it. That's why many of them end up designing menus for nursing homes and working as prep cooks at massive hotels.

"I think to make a name for oneself is much harder than it might appear," Taylor-Yearwood says.

Prospective chefs are expected to be circuit riders, logging hours in kitchens across the country.

"A lot of people in our program can't do that," Taylor-Yearwood says. "They're not willing to move out of Dallas. These resources are not available to us. These experiences are not available to everyone."

Pyles and Fearing agree the economy's partly to blame for inhibiting a resurgence of the youthful, creative spirit that invigorated the Southwestern movement.

"I don't know if it's as easy to open up a restaurant as it used to be," Fearing says, sighing. "Back when I was doing it, people didn't know you couldn't make any money with restaurants. I worked for a group of guys who wanted a five-star restaurant in North Dallas, and they lost their shirt. We had three unbelievable years, but we never made a dime."

Toying with people's palates is far more appealing when the rent's already paid. Fearing attributes the timidity and conservatism that's made the Dallas dining scene so dreary to financial fears.

"I don't know if they can be as brave as we were, because we really didn't care," Fearing says. "I wasn't married. I had a car and an apartment."

"Dallas has become so commercialized," says Ngoc Trinh, an El Centro student who dropped out of a predental program at Baylor because, "I said, 'You know what, I love to cook.'"

Trinh, now a research chef consultant for Frito-Lay, has hopscotched through the city's top kitchens, collecting the credentials she needs to make it as an independent chef-owner.

"I've spent the last six years developing my career," she says. "I have a great concept of what I want to do. I'm building a foundation for myself. My young rebellious attitude will last until I'm thirty-five."

There are glimmers of hope for the Dallas dining scene. There are a few passionate young chefs like Trinh, who's too astute to reveal her grand plan. There's the burgeoning cocktail community, which so far hasn't shied away from the swagger that once made Dallas restaurants important destinations. And there's the State Fair of Texas's Big Tex competition, which annually commands as much attention as Southwestern cuisine ever did.

Fried beer—and all the other questionable edibles that fair vendors dunk in hot oil and impale on sticks—is carrying on the regional traditions that Dallas chefs have largely ignored. Deeply reflective of place, fried beer is simple and strange and willfully offensive to delicate palates. McDonald, who showed her television audience how to make corny dogs, would have loved it.

Reclaiming the distinctive flavors of Dallas would surely energize the local dining scene. But a food culture that enriches a city hinges on community, not any particular seasoning. When asked to share their visions for dining in Dallas, young chefs don't cite dishes or cuisines. They stress the relationship between restaurants and customers. They describe a place where restaurants don't cynically foist fads upon their guests. "Dallas food is like the mink coat that comes out in November when it's 65 degrees," Taylor-Yearwood grumbles. They speak of diners who are eager to try new foods and enthusiastically patronize independent eateries.

"I don't think people want to drop $150 in this city," Matt McAllister says. "A lot of other cities seem to support more freestanding fine-dining restaurants."

Reminded that he successfully charged $125 for the prix-fixe meal at Fuego, the molecular experience he helped create at Stephan Pyles, McAllister says, "Yeah, but it's four seats. As an enterprise, that makes no sense."

Tim Byres, a former executive chef for Stephan Pyles who's now exploring smoking and pickling at Smoke, currently the city's most interesting restaurant, shares McAllister's belief that Dallas has plenty of talent and a number of young chefs itching to innovate. What they need, he says, is customer support.

"We're a very 'it's hot or it's not' kind of city," he says. "One of the hardest things on Dallas restaurants is it's a very critical environment, and it's critical early. You can't plant a seed and expect it to be a tree. It's a gradual growth."

And, in the meantime, there's always fried beer.

Besha Rodell is the food and drink editor of Creative Loafing Atlanta, Atlanta's alternative newsweekly.

# An Open Letter to Kim Severson

## Besha Rodell

Dear Kim,

I detect in your recent demeanor, which I admit I only have access to through your Twitter feed, a certain melancholy. Not a downright sadness, but a mixture of homesickness and confusion, a kind of bewilderment about ending up here in Atlanta and what you ought to do with your newfound life. In fact, your oft-used hashtag, #mynewlife, is employed most frequently alongside Tweets that exhibit ambivalence about this town, this region. On Saturday morning, an almost woeful Tweet showed up in your feed: "Gotta get back to NYC soon for a food romp. Dyin' down here! #dontknowwhatyouvegottilitsgone."

To many Atlantans and Southerners, that Tweet seemed a little harsh — not the longing for NYC, but the "Dyin' down here!" line, which sounded a whole lot like you were saying that there's nothing worth eating "down here." I know it might not be how you meant it. But that's how it sounded.

I'll get to that part a little later, but first I wanted to share a bit. To commiserate. Because I, too, am an ex–New Yorker who left to come to the South. And I had very hard time with the change. In fact, for years I vowed to go back to New York at my first chance.

But not anymore.

Of course, I didn't leave New York to become a bureau chief for the *New York Times*. Nor did I hold any particular position of esteem in the city before I left it. Nope—I was a twenty-six-year-old waitress, and I left because I got knocked up. I couldn't imagine trying to raise a kid in New York—not as a waitress, not as a $12-an-hour assistant to literary agents (my sometimes daytime gig), not living in a charming but scummy apartment a block and a half from the Gowanus Canal. So I left, moving to North Carolina where my husband's family lives.

And it was hard. Oh God, it was hard. I missed the city, its tempo, its constant hum, the friends, the art, the fun. But mainly, I missed the food. When I left, I wrote a long essay—an ode to what I was leaving behind. Not for anyone in particular, because I wasn't writing for anyone in particular at that point, but just because my anxiety and sorrow was so great, I felt a need to put it down somewhere, to chronicle it. It was like a love letter to the food of New York. It's one of the most heartfelt things I've ever written.

In North Carolina, despite having quite a few friends and some family there, I was miserable. There were some concrete reasons for this—having come from an existence of Brooklyn and parties and music and never ending NYC life, I found myself living in a tiny house off a secondary highway outside Chapel Hill with a newborn baby, no real career prospects, and no heat apart from a woodstove. But more than that I missed New York with a ferocity I hadn't anticipated. My heart broke for the life I'd left behind, and because my heart primarily speaks in hunger, much of that ache came in the form of longing for food.

I missed out on a lot in those two years I spent in N.C. And I pushed a lot of very nice people away with my incessant moaning about how much I wished I wasn't there.

Eventually, I pulled myself up by the bootstraps, grew out of my homesickness and depression enough to make something of myself, and got this here job in Atlanta.

It took me a while to warm to Atlanta as well though. At first, I compared every restaurant here to New York restaurants. So believe me, I get it. I get how many of the places we count as favorites serve food you could easily find in some random Brooklyn café no one really cares about. How the car culture here seemingly removes the food from the street and life of the city. How—yes, the clichés are true! You can't get a good bagel! What I'd give some days for a decent turkey hero. There really isn't any restaurant in town that might possibly be in the running for four stars from your publication. Pizza? Forget it! (OK, don't. New Yorkers ought to be jealous of Antico. But I digress . . .)

But here's the thing. And it only dawned on me after you had a Twitter exchange with John T. Edge regarding your "Dyin' down here" comment (do I seem like enough of a stalker yet?) where he implored you to "look closer." And you said, "Ah, but even you must admit that despite the deliciousness of Southern food, there some itches only NYC can scratch." The thing is: I think you may be looking for the wrong thing here, food-wise.

It's your use of the words "Southern food" in your response that got me. And it reminded me of something that's been bothering me for a while, something to do with the current trendiness of Southern food. People come here from New York, Portland, California, and get all excited about how Southern we are, about our fried chicken and our biscuits, and our cute accents and how authentic our love of bacon and bourbon is, and blah blah blah. Don't get me wrong. I love these things. They're a huge part of what makes the South the place I love and am proud to call home. But there's a lot of bad fried chicken out there, and worse biscuits, and I think the barbecue in this town kinda blows. I'm just saying—to find the good stuff, you need to go beyond the obvious.

There are folks in Atlanta making teeny little tacos out of fresh tortillas that would make you cry. Our samgyupsal houses rival any anywhere in the country. There's this guy in Marietta I could introduce you to who makes his own tofu, and to hear him describe it, and then to taste it, is like seeing something you've always taken for granted as brand new, revelatory. There's this dude who illegally smokes ribs in a gas station parking lot up the street from my house, and some days he's only wearing one shoe, but GODDAMN those are some good ribs.

I went to a supper club a few weeks back, these guys who call themselves Dinner Party, who do a one-night restaurant type thing, and the night I went it was with Dashboard Co-op, an arts collective that had a pop-up gallery in a vacant retail space. They set up tables and served cocktails among all the art, and the Dinner Party folks served a bunch of food, and there was a dance performance in the midst of it all, and I looked around the room at these young, amazing people who are really some of the most interesting people in arts and food in the city right now, and I just thought "That's it. I'm in love with this town." There was so little pretension there, so little artifice, and yet there were all these people talking about food and wine and art and life and I just kind of swooned. It's like when I went to see Big Boi's collaboration with the Atlanta Ballet at the Fox Theater. The performance wasn't perfect, but man it was cool. It was something that would never happen in New York. You think the New York City Ballet is going to collaborate with KRS One? Um, no.

This is Atlanta. We're scrappy. Some of what we do lacks precision, but we're passionate and we try and we're not held to this unrealistic expectation of CUISINE, big type. There's a comfort in even our high-end restaurants, a sense of community, a sense of personality that's hard to find in the high-stakes, big money world of larger cities. This is the South, where you're most likely to find God (or whatever you want to call it) in a strip mall. The best of what we do, the best of what we are, is hidden in the nooks. It isn't easily found. That's what makes it so much fun. There are places in this town, to eat, to drink, to live, that make my heart ache with pride. I haven't felt that way since . . . well, since Brooklyn.

I sincerely, truly, really hope you get to that with Atlanta. We don't want you to die down here.

*Besha*

*Martha Foose, a Mississippi Delta native, is the author of the award-winning*
Screen Doors and Sweet Tea. *This story is adapted from her most recent book,*
A Southerly Course.

# Family Pieces

## Martha Foose

Her grandmother, like many who married right before World War I, would have been horrified to see Minter carrying the Haviland china soup tureen out of the house to a diner across town. Reasons for the cringing agitation include the possibility the lid would be broken and a lidded dish with no lid would just linger around the breakfront. But Minter, since her mother's passing, has taken to actually using the "good china" every opportunity that arises.

When she was a child spending the summers and holidays with her Atlanta side of the family, the dishes lived in a special closet blended discreetly into the wall of the dining room and came out weekly for Sunday dinner. Over the years since, the Nabob pattern service for twelve, including serving dishes, has relocated several times, spending years boxed beneath a bed and stored in attics and back rooms. Six years ago, when Minter built her home, she conceived open-door cabinets from here to kingdom come to house the dishes and all her other inherited dinnerware. For Minter, who is anything but a sentimental sap, these plates and chargers of porcelain bound her modern home to people and homes long gone. Her family has left her with these and she aims to see them used, and to be reminded on each occasion of times and events she will never be able to ask about now.

For my cousin LeAnne, who has had three houses burn thus far, the china is what always survives. When all the photographs of birthdays and anniversaries are destroyed, the soot can be washed away, the ashes cleared, and the table set. For her these pieces of bone china are the few tangible remains of her past home life. These dishes are memories vitrified.

The sterling silver kitchen spoon with the worn edge gives my aunt Caroline comfort. This spoon has cooked many of the same recipes for more than a hundred years. Slowly, over the decades, the left side curve of the bowl has straightened with the clockwise stirrings of right-handed cooks going through the same motions as Caroline. Feeling the heat or cold conduction to the tip of her tongue is a visceral connection to her personal history. Every time she raises it to her lips to taste for seasonings, she blows a cooling kiss across the spoon and across time.

Inevitably death, occasionally divorce, and unfortunately fall of fortune find family pieces dispersed, divided, and sold off piece by piece. For Katherine and Jamie, estate sales are their line. For more than a decade they have worked the intersection where family pieces are handed off to their next family and go to new homes. They try to remain as sympathetic and professional as possible in what is almost always a time of emotional upheaval for a family. There are the lingering feelings of guilt when a move to assisted living comes, and Katherine and Jamie help ease the transfer by taking care of things. Recently more sales are being held for baby-boomers wishing to downsize; many learned from dealing with their parents' possessions that even the most beloved of family pieces can become a burden if there is simply no place to keep them. At times the two are called upon to run interference for the family, sparing them the prying questions and accusations: "How could she part with Ethelen's cut glass punch bowl!" It's no one's business but their clients' why they are selling. Jamie and Katherine are nothing if not discreet. These ladies are well versed in the pecuniary value of silver services and fine china. But perhaps the most important service they provide is being knowledgeable, experienced friends in trying times.

In Sara Anne's elegant antiques shop, glass-front cases hold all manner of sterling silver tableware. Dainty asparagus tongs lie beside ice-cream knives, cold-soup spoons, fish forks, and odd servers. Sara Anne does wish the younger generation had a taste for what she considers the finer things. She is encouraged by small trends like giving an engraved cake server as a baby gift, to be used each birthday and then for the distant wedding cake. Silver water goblets have come around in vogue again and she can hardly keep the canapé servers in the shop. As Sara Anne says, "Everybody can use a canapé server." She is right, of course. She is also right when she explains how the newly wed will not remember who gave them a setting of their china pattern but will always remember who gave them the lovely hand-engraved serving piece and think of the giver each time they use it. It will become a family piece. As for me, the Haviland has been stored up in the closet above the stairs for fifteen years, each stack of china salad plates, dinner plates, and dessert plates zipped inside quilted covers. Fiestaware is what graces my table most days. My mother keeps the silver at her house. She knows all the rules, not letting it come in contact with anything rubber and protecting it from the sullying effects of salt, eggs, and fruits. The one piece of silver I keep out is the gravy boat. For me it's enough for most holiday tables. As much as I wish it were more in my nature to take the time to pull out all the stops and set out the finery, it's just not. My son will recognize a few items as family pieces—the small chocolate pots from my grandmother, the gravy boat with the copper showing through at the edges, and the stout little pig that stirs the mustard pot. My maiden aunt Lina instructed in her will that we were all to gather at her home after the service and draw straws for her worldly possessions. The short straw got the mustard pot. The stories will be handed down as well. Joe will come to see as family pieces, too, the ceramic work of potter friends from across the state. The McCardy tumblers and the deviled-egg plate Jamie Mae Collier made are what he will see when he looks back through photos of holidays when he grows up. The same cake stand turns up in volumes of photo albums all the way back to the sepia-toned. I think these will be the pieces he values the most.

Jack Hitt is a contributing writer for the New York Times Magazine and the public radio program This American Life. His work also appears in Harper's, Rolling Stone, and Wired. He is the author of Off the Road: A Modern-Day Walk Down the Pilgrim's Route into Spain, which has been made into The Way, a motion picture starring Martin Sheen. This story first appeared in the collection Man with a Pan.

# Putting Food on the Family

**Jack Hitt**

*"You're working hard to put food on your family."*
Presidential candidate George W. Bush, Nashua,
New Hampshire, January 27, 2000

I became a man, one might argue, the night I was completely unmanned by a cup of celery leaves. On a frigid night, Lisa, the woman who had just agreed to be my wife, and I were trying out our first house in New Haven. She'd recently been admitted to medical school and had hit the books on a cold afternoon for a six-hour study jag. I had built a fire and snapped open the paper to stumble upon one of those overwrought *New York Times* food columns: "Curried Red Snapper Chowder." Every one of those words suddenly read delicious.

The writer extolled the virtues of this midwinter dish with the romantic-etymology move: "Chaudière refers to the heavy pots Breton fishermen traditionally used to simmer their soup." Doesn't that sound all big wool sweatery and crackling fire-y and maybe even tasty? I thought so, too.

Chowder, the writer elaborated, was "a state of heart and mind more than a specific culinary technique." There was an existential howl in every bowl, something only Herman Melville and a few lobstermen might understand: "It's a brace against the whistling winds and quiet nights of the soul ..." Maybe I should wear a scarf while I cook?

The writer really knew how to sell it. Chowder was also a "balm to the free-floating desire for cuddle and comfort." This was not just a savory dinner; it was a full-blooded narrative, a French movie of a meal that would begin in a kitchen made aromatic by artisanal broths and spiced carrots and end upstairs in a pile of quilts.

Lisa stepped down momentarily to find me clambering into the house with bags of supplies—fresh snapper bought at the best seafood market and colorful veggies from the local grocer. She glanced down at the newspaper recipe.

"Hmmm," she said cautiously, "this violates my old home-ec teacher's rule: never cook anything with more than one column of ingredients." Please, I indicated, speaking in the language of my right eyebrow.

I stood at the counter of that kitchen, a long, roomy work space that ran the length of one wall and opened entirely onto the dining room. It was essentially my stage, and I had set out my props. There were lots of pots and pans and bowls and blenders. I had the ingredients set up in a conga line, my spices preselected. I had bought a plain apron (no dopey slogans, please) of a dark testosterone shade. I was a man in the kitchen, looking for love, confident of a meal.

In the medieval period of the current culinary renascence—that is, pre–Food Network—you often heard people say, "I love to cook." The phrase was merely part of the mating prattle of those long-ago dark ages. It was a signifier of a grand future ahead, but also of a lived life—a life already so packed with experience that other similar convictions could easily be flicked off: "I hate disco" or "I love *Casablanca*" or "I never watch television, except *The Larry Sanders Show*." These were things that one said but didn't necessarily have to believe or ever act upon.

But suddenly, there I was one night, no longer in the pretend world of scrambled eggs and toast. I was in the very muck of a recipe, dealing with the world of hurt and confusion that can come from only three or four words such as "Puree until liquefied. Strain."

How is it that straining a quart of my pureed goop only produces four red drops in my five gallon chaudière? Can that be right?

Then there was this other simple instruction. I read it over and over again:

Heat the remaining olive oil in a skillet. Fry the celery leaves until crisp.

Crisp? It's moments like these when you realize that what you are reading is not really English but rather half a lifetime of kitchen experience compressed into a pearl of culinary haiku. You try it anyway—because you have always considered yourself someone who "loves to cook," i.e., how hard can it be? As you lay the leaves in the oil, they instantly wilt, curl, and tighten into inch-long chlorophyll threads like the kind you might pop out of a buttonhole in a green cotton shirt. You look back at the words in the newspaper and then stare into your frying pan swimming with thread. What the—?

You refuse to be defeated, and jump in the car. A few minutes later, you return with two new bunches of celery boasting audacious nosegays of fresh green leaves. Maybe the trick is that you have to lay them carefully in the oil, nice and flat. That makes sense. Of course that's what it is. You're a little annoyed that the recipe didn't just say so. You lay them in nice and flat, and voilà!

More threads.

Damn. And you think, How does that single line of instruction even make sense? "Fry celery leaves in oil until crisp." That scans about as sensically as "Soak until medium rare." But somehow your soul is on the line here, your manhood in the kitchen. Maybe the oil should be hotter?

Back in the car. Grin feebly at the same register woman. Four bunches. Cups upon cups of leaves. Into a really hot frying pan—for the love of Christ—again, swimming with new threads. You read the instruction one more time, then stare into the greening pool of oil. A breakthrough idea: Did Breton fishermen eat crisp celery leaves? I hardly think so. It's a big waste of time. What was the recipe writer thinking? Moving on. Crisp celery leaves are for silly people.

The very next line reads: "Score the carrots lengthwise with a channel knife." A channel knife? Is that just writerly pretense for a regular old knife or is this some kind of special tool that's actually needed? This chowder of mine occurred before the Internet, so an encounter with the unknown couldn't be quickly solved. Often I deal with my own ignorance by trying to outrun it. So I read ahead: "Add the remaining celery root . . ." But your celery was obviously sliced off right at the root. A vague sense that maybe "celery root" is wildly different from "celery" passes through your head.

But really, does it matter? Who's even heard of such a thing? Celery root. These chowder people, these chowderheads—they're such dainty chefs. In an effort to speed things up, you accidentally swipe a bowl—full of forty-five minutes of something painstakingly shredded and soaked—onto the ground in a ceramic explosion. A level of deep frustration sets in.

Now it's 9:00 p.m. and you look around your kitchen. Every pot is dirty and half-full of something started and abandoned, or it's shattered and in the trash. Every bit of counter space is somehow damp, evidence of a whole other tragedy that we'll just call "homemade carrot broth" and never speak of again.

The recessed window above the sink is now home to a near forest of de-nuded celery stalks. What recipe, you wonder, calls for ten bunches of celery?

Bowls and spoons are everywhere, and every surface seems to have become a magnet for carrot and potato peels. You yourself are somehow inexplicably soaked, as if you had just stepped off a whaling ship. Your future bride suddenly pokes her head in the door to coyly ask, "Sugar, can I help with dinner?"

And you find yourself not quite yourself, uttering the following, really, really loudly: "Oh, yeah, well, fuck you! You're the—I hate everybody. You caused this catastrophe. And if you hadn't—if only I—you. This shitty kitchen. How come you don't have a goddamn channel knife? Do you realize—chowder is stupid." Or sentiments to that effect. I have shortened it by four thousand words by editing out the repetitive obscenities. Funny thing is, the chowder tasted fine when we both sat down at the table to eat it. Of course, dining at 1:00 a.m. with a full day of hunger behind you would make old gum taste like paté.

■   ■   ■

When I was a little kid, kitchens weren't anything like what they are today. No one had a stage for a kitchen. Quite the opposite. The kitchen was a place of shame, always located in the back of the house. It was usually beat looking from overuse, with sagging cabinet doors, sunken floors, and scuffed linoleum. The kitchen was the last room in the house anyone spent remodeling money on.

In Charleston, South Carolina, where the houses are mostly antebellum, many kitchens had once been entirely separate outbuildings (as a fire precaution) and were connected only by narrow hallways. It's where servants worked, maybe a wife. The door to the kitchen signaled as much. It was a heavy wooden thing, painted white thirty years ago, that swung in both directions, functional like a restaurant's door or one to the furnace room— not ornamental and oaken like every other door in the house. The kitchen door had a chunk of plastic instead of a handle (framed by a fan of indelible grime) so you could push it open either way with a tray full of fresh food or dirty dishes, depending. This door and the area it opened onto was so dreadful that many families obscured the entrance with a folding screen, preferably one with a soothing Chinese landscape done on rice paper, so that the very entrance to the inferno was hidden from view.

At one friend's house where I spent a lot of time growing up in the early 1970s, the owner had a tiny lump in the carpet beneath his foot at the head of the table. With a tap of his toe, he could summon a servant from the bowels of this unwanted place to serve a tureen of, say, overcooked lima beans. In those days, it was impossible to avoid the general assumption that food was something the lower orders fetched up for the higher orders. If you ventured into the kitchen to have a discussion about how food got made with the black maids and carried on in conversation about Low Country crab dishes and red rice and okra gumbo, well, then you were considered an eccentric.

It wasn't as if good food wasn't appreciated, but by and large, food was something that came from the Piggly Wiggly and was cooked. Anything different typically meant that some of the men (and the occasional Annie Oakley–style gal) had gone hunting. Then the men might fry the venison in a mustard sauce, grill the dove breasts wrapped in bacon, or stew the duck meat in a half-day-long concoction called a purloo.

Outside of special occasions, the idea that a man might make a salad or cook a pot of rice insinuated provocative things we did not speak about. I would have to grow up and lose several closeted gay friends to self-imposed exile or AIDS before we'd ever begin to talk about such things.

But it's not as if, despite our repressed childhoods, we didn't experience the love of good food. That was always there: the how-to of it all, though, just wasn't much of a conversation. One of my favorite dishes of all time is red rice, a Gullah dish that pulls off the neat trick of getting long-grain white rice to take up a hefty tomato sauce as it would water or stock. When I was little, this dish was cooked all the time, not merely in my house but throughout the city. I'm not sure there is another dish that qualifies as more comforting comfort food for me—maybe shrimp and grits. My mental landscape of 1970s Charleston was charted in part by the landmarks of other people's red rice. My friend Lucas Daniels had some of the best red rice ever cooked. Because it's a dish that is arguably better cold than hot, his family kept a pot of it in the refrigerator, essentially, all the time.

We ate it as a break from playing outside. Sometimes I might ring the doorbell at his South Battery home to find out Lucas wasn't there. I'd go on in anyway, eat some red rice, and then head off to find him. Getting a bowl of red rice was hardly more of a bother than asking for a glass of water on a hot day.

But it never occurred to me to learn how to cook it. Red rice was . . . red, and so, something of a mystery. It simply emerged from the heated sweatshop of the kitchen, out from behind the folding screen. Why ask? But eventually, when I was sent away to school, I did ask. I wanted to be able to carry a few things with me, and one of them was how to cook red rice. How did one get it to come out fluffy and not gunky? When I asked Lucas's cook Delores how she cooked her red rice, I got only the universal smile of a chef: I'm not telling.

When I asked my own family cook back in those days, Annie Oliver, how she cooked her red rice, she just shrugged and said, "You put it all together." Gullah traditions were still considered state secrets and protected knowledge, stories held and transmitted on a need-to-know basis. Without explaining too much here, every white family I knew growing up employed a black woman as a cook. It was the early 1970s. She was either a young mother, like Delores, or a venerable ancient like Annie (who'd also raised my mother). My generation's struggle to understand just what really underlay our relationship to those cooks is part of the untold story of the civil rights epic—untold because it's so cringe inducing. And yet, without too much trouble, I could probably tell the whole racial history of the South through my attempt to learn how to cook really good red rice.

Of course, in those days, all recipes were considered secrets, regardless of race, creed, or color. People just didn't talk about food casually. That would come later. It was all very intimate and happened in that secret chamber behind the swinging door. Especially the everyday dishes. Teaching someone how to cook red rice implied a profound level of trust and love.

All popular dishes have a couple of little tricks that always get left out in the pointillist prose of recipes. In Charleston, the grand old white ladies of my grandmother's generation created a locally famous cookbook in 1950 called *Charleston Receipts*. It's an archeological wonder. Each page is decorated, at the turning corner, with a tiny silhouette of a black mammy in an apron, working at the kitchen table or presenting a tray of food. (Like I said, cringe inducing.)

Many of the recipes are accidental time capsules. The recipe for string beans lists its top ingredient as

1 package frozen French-cut string beans

And then it suggests this handy instruction: "Cook string beans by direction on package." Others are simply inscrutable and epigrammatic. As a result, the red rice recipe always left me with a pot of burnt red glop.

It took me almost twenty years of talking up red rice with old society ladies, black islanders, and a few drunken sailors to cadge enough of the secret cheats that will yield excellent red rice. The final tip, to do nothing at the end, came from another childhood friend, my godmother's son, Thomas Barnes. Here, as a public service, is my favorite way to cook South Carolina Low Country red rice (with no haiku and my love to Thomas).

Cook three or four pieces of really good hickory-smoked bacon in a cast-iron skillet. It should be smoked bacon, or what's the point? What you really want out of the back is, OK, bacon, but also: the smoke. So don't skimp. Buy the good bacon. Fry it at a low temperature for a while so that it slowly loses its fat and gets really crispy.

Pour off the fat until you have about a tablespoon or so of chunky bacon gunk in the pan, and in that, sauté a diced medium onion and half a green bell pepper. When they're soft, toss in a couple of pinches of salt and add a large can of diced tomatoes. Skinned fresh tomatoes are great, but only in high tomato season, late summer. Otherwise, go with canned. Many add tomato paste here (as in *Charleston Receipts*), but the problem with tomato paste is that it makes everything taste pasty. Skip that. Go with canned diced tomatoes—not whole not pureed—because the diced ones break down mostly but not entirely, giving the final result the perfect (I hate this word, but what can you do?) mouthfeel.

Simmer that concoction for ten more minutes; then add a cup and a half of rice—preferably Uncle Ben's parboiled long-grain rice. I don't quite understand why. There is something about how the parboiled works at taking up the tomato sauce concoction more easily than any other kind of rice. Anyway, there's about a decade's worth of Christmas-party chats with Mom's friends and creekside beers with acquaintances of friends invested in that little tip. And it works like a charm, so just do it and you'll be happy.

If the result is too stiff to stir, then add a splash or two of chicken broth. Most recipes suggest that you cook thereafter on the stove top. But don't do that. Instead, cover the skillet with tinfoil and put it in a 375°F oven for thirty minutes. Remove the skillet from the oven and put it on the back of the stove. Do not peek under the foil. No one knows what mystery is taking place under there, but it has something to do with liquid and rice, and like the spontaneous combustion of heavy-metal drummers, it's best left unsolved. As Thomas told me: "It's best not even to look at it." Remove the foil eventually—after ten minutes, say—and sprinkle the rice with bacon bits. All leftovers are better the next day, served either hot or cold, or you can fold them into an omelet like my nephew Jim does for a brilliant breakfast.

■   ■   ■

One day, not all that long ago, my twelve-year-old daughter, Yancey, announced that she and her friend Emma would cook dinner. I was having some friends over and had already put together my own menu. But no, she insisted, waving photocopies of recipes in my face. She and Emma would do it. They had already scoped out what ingredients were lacking in the kitchen. All I had to do was drive them to the store. Once I got them going, they shooed me from the kitchen, and thus began an afternoon that quickly swelled into family legend.

This production in the kitchen involved putting up a rampart of chairs to keep out unwanted spectators. Whenever any adult's orbit would wing near the kitchen, a squall of girlish gestures would erupt near the barricades, ordering him away. The entire Saturday afternoon took on the feeling of an earlier time, not that many years ago, when the kids would seal off a room and announce they were practicing to put on a play for the adults. Under no circumstances were we to peek.

Those plays were hilarious because the kids were trying to show off their ability to mimic the world as they knew it—the plot of a bedtime story or some recent event that struck them as crucial in their lives. What made them especially entertaining was the kindly recognition of just how bad they were at acting and writing and dialogue and improvising. The pleasure for the parents and the kids was always laughing generously at the boffo display of sheer ineptitude.

Translate this comedy to a room full of fire, sharp knives, whole chickens, and several jumbo canisters of (redundantly purchased) Costco oregano, and you have the makings of a tragedy, if not a fiasco.

But at the beginning of the evening, the two girls brought out a bewilderingly brilliant four-course meal, all made from scratch: gazpacho salad, chicken-barley soup, pork loin, chocolate mousse. When Yancey brought in the gazpacho salad, the room reacted to the bright array of color nestled on the Bibb lettuce. She said proudly, "Look how we plated it!"

We all thought: Way too much Food Network for this kid. But actually that wasn't it. The girls didn't really watch the Food Network. If anything, that whole *Iron Chef* vocabulary has simply permeated the culture, creating a generation with the descriptive powers of a sommelier and an easy ability to use "savory" and "umami" in a sentence. What accounted for the quality of the dinner was the fact that the girls had been watching us, really studying us, the adults, as we prepared meals.

I realized that the story of the generation raised in the postfeminist era—my generation—was one that could be told as a history of a single room, the modern kitchen.

The avoided place of my childhood had become a battleground in the 1970s, the place from which all women had to be emancipated. Now it had been reentered by men and women alike. Its repute as a ghetto for women's work was as remote to those kids as the reputation of colonial frontiersmen for being smelly. That room had been completely renovated—often literally, definitely metaphorically.

It had been remodeled, not only because we now admitted guests and friends there, but because a lot more was going on in there than the preparation of food. Today's kitchen is to our time what, say, the front parlor or salon was, at least in our imaginations, to the late nineteenth century. It is more than a place where people gather; it is a place where ideas are hatched, practiced, learned, and acted upon. It is a gathering spot for chance encounters and the millworks of family values. When I bought the house I currently live in, I found the old kitchen door in the basement. It was the exact same one from my childhood home—same plastic push guard beside the same fossilized handprint of generational grime. The previous owner had remodeled the kitchen and made it into one of the showcase rooms in the place. My kitchen now boasted panoramic views of a large green backyard and participated with the rest of the house via a wide, generous, inviting hallway. There was no door at all; rather, the space was merely another grand architectural staging area, on par with the living room.

For us, this reinvention of the kitchen was not a deliberate act. It just sort of happened after we brought our first and then second child home from the hospital. We ended up in the kitchen a lot. Almost all of the first two years of child rearing involves putting food into babies' mouths. Sometimes that food gets thrown across the room or splattered from beneath a slammed fist or reappears along projectile trajectories. The kitchen is unquestionably the best place to be in when any of these amazing events occur.

As a dad who spent a lot of time with the babies—when they were infants, my wife was in medical school and then a resident—I remember pondering one single conscious kitchen-related question: Was I going to spend the next few years eating Annie's mac and cheese and hot dogs? That's when I discovered Mark Bittman's Minimalist column in the newspaper, and the future became clear. With only a little more effort than it would take to produce crappy toddler crud, I could make meals I myself wanted to eat.

In other words, "I love to cook" would actually become: I love to cook.

So the center of gravity of my little family quickly became the kitchen. This was not a feminist pronouncement or a political decision. It had a lot more to do with easy cleanup than with anything so noble as an idea or an intention.

But soon enough, the simplicity of our location turned into all kinds of things. When the kids were two or three, I sat them down and gave them instructions on how to cut up a carrot with a knife. I showed them the secret of making grits (salt must go in before the grits are added, or all is lost). Naturally, pancakes and waffles were in abundant supply on a weekend morning. And precisely because Lisa, the resident, came home exhausted, she felt compelled to cook her mother's comfort foods—tuna fish casserole, chicken a la king, homemade chicken pot pie (for a Swanson refugee, the latter is a revelation). Our little family menu grew. Then, one summer, there was a trip to Paris. The taste of a sidewalk crepe became a critical moment in the life of my oldest daughter, Tarpley. It is now her own private Madeleine.

After we returned, she retrieved a recipe and became the house specialist. Soon thereafter, we purchased a crepe pan, and it was her crepe pan. Later, Yancey received her own block of kitchen knives. Even the equipment—

from my ancient cast-iron skillet dating back two generations, to Lisa's hand-thrown pots, to the kids' stuff—became a map of a family that lived in the kitchen and visited the other rooms in the house when time permitted.

In the years that followed, Tarpley also figured out the buttery secret of popovers. Then Yancey mixed some salad dressing, and somehow she got our favorite mustard-vinegar ratio perfect every time. So most nights, dinner became a big, noisy, jostling event—full of chores dictated by custom and history. Even stories of accidents became part of the epic tale. One afternoon, I grabbed a Cuisinart pot by the handle when it was accidentally parked over a low but hot blue flame. The kids saw Dad hold his hand under running water for an hour, squeezing out tears. Later, though, having the distinctive Cuisinart handle shape branded perfectly into my palm—including the nonblistered hole where one would hang up the pot—was not merely a puritan lesson in life's dangers but pretty funny to look at.

We stumbled upon little secrets. We figured out that broccoli with a dash of balsamic vinegar is surprisingly great. A visit to an Asian market found us taking home some bok choy. And a lifetime of cooking chicken had resulted in a foolproof method of cooking a basic but really great whole chicken. (Several tricks: Gash a lemon twenty-five times with a knife, stuff the chicken with a small handful of rosemary and tarragon, then shove the lemon in and sew the cavity shut. Cook the chicken at a blazing-hot temperature: twenty minutes at 500°F breast side down, fifteen minutes breast side up. Then turn the oven down to 350°F for thirty minutes. The insanely hot temps will seal the skin but also evaporate the lemon juice, which will force itself out, flavoring the meat with the herbs along the way.)

Slowly but surely, the whole family has emerged as able cooks. Last year, I flew home from some work I was doing the day after my birthday. I walked in to find that the two kids had cooked my favorite childhood dinner. That was their present.

Turns out cooking a meal is pretty good practice for just about any complex project. Planning ahead, anticipating mistakes, figuring out the little tricks that will have vast effects down the road, and getting to a result that can be described as beautiful is the basis of every decent meal but also the recipe for a good science-fair project, end-of-the-year term paper, or school play. Thomas Jefferson once said, "I'm a great believer in luck, and I find that the harder I work, the more I have of it." He could just as easily have been discussing a beautifully savory stew. Food, it turns out, is a gateway drug to aesthetics.

The meals we cook around here end up becoming some part of the discussion at dinner, but not in some supercilious or precious way. There are no foodies here, but there are people who like to cook and eat, so thoughts about how to make something better are appreciated.

It's in the kitchen that you realize how collaborative all food is. Even when you're alone, you're communing with some other cook via the recipe itself, deconstructing some other person's haiku written perhaps centuries ago. Some dishes—like an African American rice recipe prepared by a curious white boy—can only be cooked by adding a lot of honest history.

I have always enjoyed real barbecue. Slow-cooking a whole pig on a low-temp fire for twenty-four hours is magical not only because the meat tastes so good but because for a whole day, people can't help but stop by and pitch in with the best of intentions and often amazing advice. After I read Felipe Fernández-Armesto's *Near a Thousand Tables*, though, I learned that Nestor slow-cooks some beef barbecue in the *Odyssey*. That's the other conversation that's always happening with older dishes and ancient methods—one with the very roots of our being.

Mostly, though, the food in our kitchen happens in the present tense, in the here and now. Even when someone makes a mediocre dish—Lisa recently tried some fish thing in a tomato sauce and it ended up being merely OK—the criticisms aren't so hard to hear. They come from a different place than most disapproval, a place where we all know it could have been us there at the stove. Sometimes the alchemy just doesn't happen and you're stuck with a lump of lead. But each critique also comes with the sense that food is a common experience that needs group participation. So criticism comes couched in more helpful terms, empathetic terms, because in the kitchen it's easier to express dissent in the helpful language of cooking. Somehow in the kitchen, "This sucks" more often comes out as "Could have used more oregano in the sauce. What do you think?" So far, translating that more gracious conversational gambit to the other rooms of the house hasn't always worked out. But if that style of interaction makes the leap, it will be leaping from the kitchen.

The kitchen teaches us that the only way to make something better is to tweak it, talk about it, find some new trick, edit and rewrite, and call upon one's own ever-expanding experience. So often we've found that what's needed to boost something from merely OK to truly beautiful is just some small touch that really changes the dynamic participation of all the other elements of the dish and elevates the entire sense of the meal. It might be some little thing born of experience long ago, something that happens in the moment of cooking and easily gets lost when translated into the stenography of a recipe. Like crispy celery leaves.

# The Global South

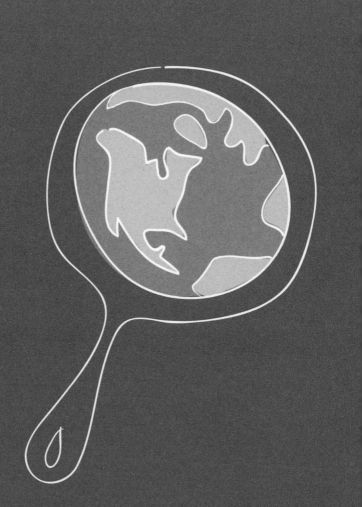

*Andrea Nguyen is the author of* Into the Vietnamese Kitchen *and* Asian Tofu. *A Saveur contributing editor, she also publishes Vietworldkitchen.com. This piece was adapted from a presentation she gave at the 2010 Southern Foodways Alliance Symposium on the Global South.*

# Bags, Butter, Surfboards, and Spice
## Viet-Cajun in Cali

**Andrea Nguyen**

Vietnamese people are into working for our food. Not only are we terrific at shucking, shrimping, and crabbing for a living, but on our off time we revel in picking at shells and bones to reveal delectable morsels. For example, if you and I were in Saigon right now and wanted to eat seafood, we might venture to a very casual storefront that specializes in shellfish. On the sidewalk, we'd inspect and select from the display of fresh mollusks, then choose our seasonings. The waiter would whisk our order off and return it cooked minutes later. We'd sit on plastic baby chairs at low tables to nibble on the feast while taxis and motorbikes zooming past provided a slight refreshing breeze in the tropical heat.

In Vietnamese, that's called *nhau*, and it describes hanging out for hours eating and chatting. In fact, there's a whole repertoire of celebratory nhau foods and *quan nhau* eateries that cater to people's gustatory needs. The recent Vietnamese-American crawfish phenomenon plugs right into people's penchant to nhau.

While there is no doubt that crawfish boils belong to the American South, the Asian craze over buttery, spicy boiled shellfish has people scratching their heads. I live in California, and in the sleepy, unassuming "Little Saigon" enclaves, there are restaurants full of boisterous diners, mopping their foreheads as they work through large plastic bags filled with chile-and-margarine-laden boiled crawfish, shrimp, crab, and sometimes even lobster. Typically, the only "vegetables" on the menu are corn on the cob, boiled potatoes, and French fries. These Viet-Cajun restaurants are decorated with bayou knick knacks, surfboards, graffiti, and pirate statues. Add to that thumping hip-hop music, flat-screen TVs airing sports events, and service-savvy wait staffs. These establishments are not what I grew up with in "Cali." They are definitely not your average mom-and-pop pho noodle soup shops or banh mi delis.

What are the roots of Viet-Cajun and how has it been transformed in California? How do the restaurants reflect the Vietnamese population in the United States? What are the implications for Vietnamese foodways?

## FROM IMMIGRATION TO MIGRATION

The fall of Saigon in April 1975 initiated a Vietnamese diaspora of huge dimensions. By and large, the fisherman population from South Vietnam did not arrive in the initial wave of immigrants. They were left behind and endured a lot of hardship, just like many others did, struggling to make ends meet under the Communist regime. Those who managed to leave were highly skilled in their trade, but many were not well educated and lacked the language skills to retrain in new careers and reinvent themselves in America. A large number of fishermen settled in the Gulf States, where they rebuilt their livelihoods and established robust Vietnamese-American fishing communities. Like many other immigrants to this country, the fishermen and their families absorbed the culture and foodways of their new environment. They spoke English with a Southern accent.

In the late 1980s and early 1990s, as economic opportunities in Louisiana started drying up for a lot of fishermen and their children, their story shifted from being one of immigration to being one of migration. Many headed to the closest Vietnamese-American enclave: Houston, home to one of the nation's largest "Little Saigon" communities. According to the 2000 census, roughly 64,000 Houstonians were of Vietnamese descent.

Starting from the early years, Vietnamese took a liking to crawfish. In fact, soon after seafood distributor and restaurateur Jim Gossen introduced crawfish to Houston in 1976, Vietnamese patrons were among his customers. By the early 2000s, author and food historian Robb Walsh was writing about the local Vietnamese crawfish scene in the *Houston Press*.

To Vietnamese people in California visiting family and friends in Texas, the Cajun-style Vietnamese crawfish restaurants in Houston, particularly at Hong Kong City Mall, were an exciting novelty. Pretty soon, in 2002 or 2003, Café Artist restaurant in Westminster, California—home to the biggest of all Little Saigons in America—began serving crawfish on Wednesdays. It was the first Viet restaurant to transplant the Southern crawfish boil to the broad, palm tree–lined avenues of Orange County, California. (Census 2000 estimates that within the Los Angeles–Orange County–Riverside area, there are 234,000 people of Vietnamese descent.)

Café Artist is a quan nhau joint where men typically go to drink and nosh. It planted the seed for Viet-Cajun in Cali, which possibly explains why it claims to be "the home of the Louisiana crawfish." The closest Louisiana-like bayou restaurant is about fifteen minutes away at Disneyland's Pirates of the Caribbean. Café Artist's brazen ownership of Cajun-style crawfish is a fine example of how Viet people pick up on the best ideas around them. It's the dynamic of Vietnamese culture, which, for the sake of survival and self-determination, has always absorbed and reinvented foreign concepts without hesitation.

News spreads quickly in the Vietnamese community; in 2004, Dada Ngo and her husband Sinh Nguyen opened the Boiling Crab, which spawned other Vietnamese-Cajun restaurants in California. Sinh was a crabber and shrimper whose family were fishermen in Vietnam and who resettled in Seadrift on the Texas Gulf Coast. He introduced weekend boils to Dada, who grew up in Kansas City. After the couple came out to California, they decided to pour all their savings into a restaurant that combined his fishing and shrimping expertise with her management skills.

"We wanted to serve crawfish in a crab-shack environment," Dada told me. The restaurant borrowed the plastic-bag approach from Houston's Hong Kong Food Market, as it kept the shellfish juicier and accommodated customer orders for different seasonings. They crafted their own spice blends and let guests dial in the heat levels according to taste. Vietnamese food is traditionally moderately spicy and hot. It is not for heat seekers, but Dada and Sinh understood that a chile-induced endorphin rush would contribute to the party atmosphere of their slightly irreverent, entertaining dining concept. It was a novel rendition of quan nhau that offered a "California-rization" of the bayou. Boiling Crab targeted twenty- to thirty-year-olds with provocative phrases such as, "You sucked what where?"

In delivering on the promise of a good time, the couple used fresh, quality seafood, bringing in live crawfish whenever possible. They charge premium prices; in the summer of 2010, a pound of crawfish cost between ten and twelve dollars at Boiling Crab. In the realm of Little Saigon dining, that's going upscale.

To differentiate Boiling Crab from other Little Saigon restaurants, Dada trained the mostly second-generation staff to provide professional American-style restaurant service. (Typical Vietnamese-style restaurant service means that you go in, sit down, and someone hands you a menu and promptly asks, "What do you want to order?" You have to make a quick decision or you may not see your waiter again for a while. It is not an easy-going experience.)

Initially, Boiling Crab had to teach customers how to peel and eat crawfish because most diners were new to mudbugs; there is no Vietnamese word for crawfish. They also fought against suggestions to add Viet favorites such as pho, fried rice, and boba drinks. "One customer asked if they could bring in their own seafood and we would cook it for them," Dada recounted with a certain rage. "I said, 'No! I have my own seafood, and it's really good, and it's really fresh.'" She also demurred at the suggestion that they host a weekly karaoke night. She and Sinh aimed to create a breakout restaurant in the Vietnamese community and they have wildly succeeded with a focused California-ized Cajun menu and theme. The only hint of Vietnamese food is the salt, pepper, and lime dipping sauce that comes with every order.

No wonder competitors with names like Claws and Crawfish Factory popped up like mushrooms overnight. They adopted Boiling Crab's business and marketing practices, using risqué phrases such as "Let the head suckin' begin" on menus and inviting customers to write on the walls. Despite the belligerent message, these new restaurants are overall pretty wholesome. It's not uncommon to see three generations of a family at one big table amidst a crowd that includes hipsters. They are all there because these Viet-Cajun restaurants are unusual and the food is tasty.

Over the years, a number of copycats have come and gone, but Boiling Crab has endured to build a chain of eleven restaurants in California and Texas. The Café Artist owners began wholesaling crawfish in Little Saigon and opened a to-go business. There are currently about a dozen Vietnamese-owned crawfish places within a three-mile radius in Orange County's Little Saigon. And they are all more or less doing well.

At San Jose's Boiling Crab, the manager told me that they go through 450 plastic bibs each day. Located in a sleepy strip mall, it is a seventy-five seat restaurant that opens from three o'clock in the afternoon to ten o'clock at night. One hot Wednesday summer afternoon, there was a one-and-a-half hour wait for a table when I arrived at 3:30 p.m. The restaurant takes no reservations.


REACTIONS AND ACCULTURATION

The crowd waiting outside the Boiling Crab was diverse and included mostly Asians with a few Latinos and whites. Most of them arrived in groups or were meeting friends at the restaurant. These diners seemed to know the routine, hence their early arrival. There was anticipation in the air, perhaps because people had to wait outside under the blazing sun and the restaurant blacked out its windows. You couldn't experience the fun, rowdy atmosphere until you were inside.

When I finally managed to snag a table, I felt triumphant, as if I'd been allowed into a special club. Guests at the next table revealed that it was their first time. What did they think of the food? "It's good, but it's messy," one woman said. A young couple nearby had the same response as they attacked a giant boiled lobster, piling refuse on paper towels torn from the roll set at each table. Viet-Cajun restaurants lack the accoutrements of Vietnamese dining.

I was there to meet my friend Holly Cao, who had grown up in Lafayette, Louisiana. Despite her Wharton MBA and professional demeanor, Holly professed to be expert at shelling crawfish and crab. It was part of her upbringing, she said. I wanted to get her Viet-Cajun reaction to the Cali-Cajun scene.

She handily slipped a plastic bib over her designer blouse, and as soon as the bag of lemon pepper crawfish arrived, she turned into a kid! Her hands worked like a little machine, barely moving as she peeled each one. She hardly looked down as her eyes were on the next crawfish to be shelled.

Beyond Holly's extreme manual dexterity was the fact that she took the crawfish out of the plastic bag, placing them on the table before shelling them. "No. No plastic bag," she said, shaking her head and lapsing into a Southern drawl. "In Louisiana, no plastic bag. We took 'em from the pot, we poured them on the table, we ate them. This is too mushy, it's got too much junk on it."

The other surprising thing was that she asked for mayonnaise and ketchup. When it arrived, she matter-of-factly started dipping crawfish in the condiments. When I asked about the mixture, Holly responded, "Well don't you know? Crawfish with mayo and ketchup; crab with salt, pepper, and lime."

For another Viet-Cajun perspective, I interviewed a man in his early thirties. Half Italian and half Vietnamese, Dallas Lee was born in Vietnam and adopted by a Vietnamese couple who lived in New Orleans. In his own words, he described himself as being "whitewashed." Dallas now lives in the Bay Area, but every year he returns to New Orleans to purchase about 150 pounds of fresh crawfish, which he has shipped out to California. He picks up special local sauces and seasonings for a big crawfish boil at his home. Given Holly's anti-plastic stance, I asked Dallas for his opinion of the bags, which seemed to be one of the markers of the transformation of the crawfish boil as it moved westward.

"You know what the bags are really good for?" he said with a certain jesting tone. "I think the bags are really only good for one thing: to put the trash in!" He didn't see a need for the bag. He also took offense to Vietnamese people putting crawfish pho and crawfish fried rice on menus. "If you mix Vietnamese food up too much with crawfish and present that as Cajun food to Asian people, you're giving a bad impression of Cajun food to Asians. That's a bad introduction, and I don't like it," he forcefully said.

Holly and Dallas identified with the South in ways that I had never seen Vietnamese people in other parts of the country identify with their region. Their strong allegiance to and defense of Southern foodways reflected the provenance of their upbringing.

In many ways, Viet-Cajun restaurants are also a weathervane for social change. For example, when I visited the Café Artist in Orange County's Little Saigon, I met a well-heeled group of five women in their twenties. It was Friday afternoon and they were all decked out, looking like the gals from *Sex and the City*. When they arrived, the ones who had never been there before said with surprise, "Oh my god! We're in a quan nhau! What are we doing here?" Because quan nhau are places where men traditionally gather, some of these women felt uncomfortable. But after the group sat down, they relaxed and ordered beers and food. (The crawfish, one of them told me, was to die for.) Diagonal to their table was a table of young men eyeing them. The fact that these girlfriends planned a get together at a quan nhau signaled a certain gender sea change in the community. They weren't going out for tea and cake.

At Claws, a young server and I chatted about how restaurant work fell outside the path to moneyed careers in medicine and law that so many young minorities pursue. When asked about what he thought of his job, he replied, "I never thought that I would enjoy serving people so much." He was seriously pondering a long-term career in the hospitality industry. In the past, Vietnamese people looked down on professional cooking and food service, perceiving it as manual labor.

My last conversation was with Uyen, a twenty-five-year-old woman who grew up in Little Saigon. I met her outside the original Boiling Crab location. Uyen said that she no longer has to leave Little Saigon to have a really great meal with her friends. For young people like her, the restaurants provided the opportunity to proudly bring non-Vietnamese friends to hip, happening restaurants in their own neighborhood.

"I know this is much more expensive than the four-dollar bowl of pho down the street," she said when we discussed the Viet-Cajun price tag of twenty to thirty dollars a head. "But it's worth it."

Fred Sauceman, head of university relations at East Tennessee State University, writes and speaks about the foodways of Appalachia. This story originally appeared in The Place Setting: Timeless Tastes of the Mountain South, from Bright Hope to Frog Level: Thirds.

# Ravioli and Country Music's First Family

## Fred Sauceman

Dale Jett inherited guitar licks and song lyrics from his grandparents, A. P. and Sara Carter. Bass fiddles fill the corners of the 150-year-old house he and his wife Teresa occupy on the banks of the Holston River's North Fork in Scott County, Virginia. Album covers bearing the serious countenances of his famous grandparents accent the wood-paneled room.

That much is to be expected. Hanging on the kitchen wall, though, is an implement Teresa describes as looking like "a spool bed with sticks on it." It's a ravioli roller, used to press out squares of dough to feed the First Family of Country Music.

Sara divorced A. P. in 1936, and in 1939 she married A. P.'s first cousin, Coy Bays. In 1943 she and Coy moved to California, where they met a family of Italian immigrants who fed them ravioli. Sara liked it so much that she convinced her hosts to teach her the technique.

Sara would eventually instruct her daughter Janette in the nuances of dough, filling, and sauce. And, in time, Janette would pass the recipe to her daughter-in-law, Teresa Jett. Along with the recipe came the ravioli roller and cutter Sara had used in California.

When the Carter family gets together for Thanksgiving and Christmas now, turkey and ham take a backseat to the storied ravioli.

"Janette gave me the recipe over the phone," remembers Teresa. "I had to call her back several times, because I thought the dough didn't look right. She told me if you can hardly roll it, you've got it right."

In one of those phone conversations, Janette directed a deviation from the original recipe: Leave out the chicken head when making the sauce. On her copy of the recipe, she punctuated that warning with three exclamation points.

Ravioli resonated with the Carters, Teresa believes, because it reminded Janette and the family of a favorite and more familiar mountain dish, tomato dumplings.

"Janette was the tomato dumpling queen," Teresa says.

The filling for Carter Family ravioli consists of chopped spinach, garlic, shredded cheese, diced chicken, eggs, and olive oil.

"You mash it all up together until it's a gooey mess," Teresa tells me. "Janette said it was right when it looked like goose droppings."

To the sauce, Teresa adds an extra shot of chicken broth, to substitute for the chicken head. Making the sauce involves browning beef, onions, parsley, garlic, and mushrooms and then cooking them in a pot with the broth and water, along with leftover chicken from the filling, salt, pepper, sugar, and fresh or home-canned tomatoes from the garden.

The dough is flour, egg, warm water, and salt. Teresa rolls it thinner than a pie crust, on an antique Murphy cabinet.

Although she hails from Defiance, Ohio, in the northwest corner of the state, Teresa is so ensconced in Carter Family culture that most folks assume she's a native Scott Countian. She took up playing the bass fiddle and often accompanies her husband Dale as he plays and sings his grandparents' music.

Yet Teresa had to overcome two childhood knuckle-rapped piano lessons and the embarrassment of her mother when she belted out the "Mabel, Black Label" beer commercial in front of the mirror at a Buster Brown shoe store. She says that put an end to her singing career, and she only sings now when Dale strongly insists. Teresa could never sing another note and still occupy an exalted place among the Carter Family, solely on the basis of her ravioli.

"Dale used to always order ravioli when we'd go out to an Italian restaurant," says Teresa. "But he always got disgusted when he got his plate. He refuses to order it now, because it never compares with Sara's."

David S. Shields is the McClintock Professor of Southern Letters at the University of South Carolina and the Chairman of the Carolina Gold Rice Foundation. An agricultural historian and food restorationist, he created the American Heritage Vegetables website in 2011.

# Prospecting for Oil

## David S. Shields

Of all the quests that early American farmers and horticulturists pursued, none was more enduring and consequential than the pursuit of culinary oils and fats—something less expensive and more suitable for salad dressing than melted lard. From Thomas Jefferson's failed attempts to grow olive trees in Albemarle County, Virginia, to David Wesson's labors in the laboratory to free cottonseed oil of its natural stink, the history of experiments is a fascinating chronicle of popular taste, economic ambition, and food chemistry. It begins in the attempt to acclimatize the best-tasting oil-producing plants of the Old World to the North American landscape and ends with the industrial synthesis of wholly new entities—Crisco and margarine—developed to be inoffensive to taste, even tasteless. These developments played out in little over a century, from 1773 to 1890, largely in the American South, and were greatly influenced by African American dietary needs.

Italian culinary evangelist Phillip Mazzei settled in the hill country of Virginia in 1773 to establish an American Tuscany of vineyards and olive groves. But the scant three years between the planting of his fields and the outbreak of the American Revolution thwarted both projects. Olive trees take at least ten years to mature and set fruit; Muscat vines need five to supply sufficient grapes for a crush. The location of Mazzei's land next to the plantation of Thomas Jefferson, then governor of Virginia, ensured that Mazzei's property would suffer spoilage at the hands of British invaders. The truth is, well before the British came to Charlottesville Mazzei knew that his olive groves would not flourish. He had seen most of the saplings die when the winter temperature dipped below fifteen degrees Fahrenheit in 1774. When Mazzei departed for Europe on a secret mission to secure arms for Virginia in 1779, he left without having fulfilled any of the major ambitions that had brought him to America. Even the vineyard Mazzei's workers had planted for Jefferson at Monticello would never produce a single vintage, falling victim to Virginia's rapacious raccoons, insects, and black rot.

One seed that Mazzei planted did bear fruit—the idea of diversified planting—in Jefferson's imagination. Mazzei's example had turned Jefferson, a rather traditional Virginia staple farmer with an interest in fruit trees, into a horticultural experimentalist inspired by any new plant or animal he encountered. In 1787, during a journey to northern Italy where he witnessed how fruit and oil grounded the diet of the Italian peasantry, Jefferson awoke to the virtues of Mazzei's cherished olive tree. His careful notation in his travel diary of the locales and elevations at which various cultivars flourished revealed that the winter temperatures in most of the United States precluded the olive's cultivation. Yet in the Lowcountry of South Carolina and Georgia, and in the territory of Florida (if and when it came under American control), conditions were roughly comparable to those in Italy. Jefferson contacted the one institution that might oversee the establishment of olives, the South Carolina Agricultural Society, which had organized in 1785. His letter commended olive oil particularly:

A pound of oil which can be bought for 3d. or 4d. sterling, is equivalent to many pounds of flesh by the quantity of vegetables, it will prepare and render fit and comfortable food. Notwithstanding the great quantity of oil made in France, they have not enough for their own consumption; and, there fore import from other countries. This is an article, of consumption of which, will always keep pace with the production. Raise it, and it begets its own demand. Little is carried to America, because Europe has it not to spare; we, therefore, have not learnt the use of it. But cover the Southern States with it, and every man will become a consumer of it, within whose reach it can be brought, in point of price.

Parts of Jefferson's letter must be explained—for instance, the claim that a pound of oil equaled many pounds of flesh in the preparation of vegetables. He spoke to his countrymen's propensity to fry vegetables in lard or bacon fat. The expense of raising a hog in terms of feed and growth rate, butchering and processing, far exceeded that of collecting and processing a crop of olives. Jefferson also confronted the question of demand. Since most Americans did not use olive oil, how could the olive become a profitable crop? He reassured planters that European demand, particularly in Revolutionary ally and trading partner France, exceeded supply; furthermore, he suggested that

Americans, once familiar with a cheap and available frying medium, would do as southern Europeans had traditionally done—embrace it as the most economical and convenient culinary fat.

Many of the historically minded planters who read Jefferson's letter would have known that the idea of planting olives in the Lowcountry dated from the time of Carolina's founding in 1670. John Locke, the secretary to the Lords Proprietors of Carolina, had composed a prospectus envisioning the colony as a quasi-Mediterranean haven of wine, olive oil, and silk. Olive cuttings from Portugal and Bermuda had been planted along the Ashley and Cooper rivers early in the 1670s; in 1678 colonial agent Richard Blom reported flourishing groves. Mitchell King, the antebellum historian of Carolina olive culture and himself an olive grower, recounted the legend of John Colleton sticking a wand of olive wood into the sandy loam of Charleston and having it sprout. Yet the colonial reports spoke of planting and growing, never of harvesting and pressing oil. Even a 1763 letter quoted by King remarking on olive trees in the city gardens suggests that they were novelties—specimens and conversation pieces. Governor Glen in 1747 did report the winter ice destroying one productive olive tree of a foot and a half girth. But olive oil never appeared on the customs list as an export commodity, and the local crop of olives appears entirely to have been pickled for home consumption.

The Society never reflected on why these early experiments with the olive had such desultory results. Perhaps the members knew that the obsessive concern with rice, corn, and indigo made the olive beside the point, particularly since the populace loved pork fat when it came to frying. This preference had at times a cultic extremity. In 1822 "Virginiansis Philoporcus" wrote to the American Farmer, proclaiming bacon fat ("that precious essence which titillates so exquisitely the papillae of the tongue") to be "far superior to all the oils that were ever discovered."

The disruption of Carolina agriculture wrought by the American Revolution, and the need to establish new commodities for the postwar free trade with all nations, made Carolina's elite planters willing to consider new ideas. Indeed, Henry Laurens, who spent part of the Revolution languishing in the Tower of London, secured an English horticulturist and a shipload of olive cuttings to plant at Mepkin and Charleston upon his return; according to John Adams, he harvested fifty to a hundred bushels of fruit a year. Jefferson's shipments to the Society did not arrive until 1791. These were allotted to interested members and planted at several locations in the Lowcountry.

Jefferson's olives did not transform the Lowcountry. Nor did Laurens's. Isolated trees (two in Beaufort, six in Charleston) grew to productive maturity and local renown, but Jefferson complained in a letter to James Ronaldson, dated January 12, 1813, that "It is now twenty-five years since I sent them two shipments (about 500 plants) of the Olive tree of Aix, the finest Olives in the world. If any of them still exist, it is merely as a curiosity in their gardens; not a single orchard of them has been planted." Cold snaps decimated the inland plantings, while humidity and the moisture of the Lowcountry soil caused most of the trees to fail. Like the colonial plantings, the post-Revolutionary olive experiment resulted in a scatter of hardy trees whose fruits were brined and consumed locally. What was true in Carolina was true in Georgia and Florida. In 1827 a reviewer in the *American Quarterly* of Grant Forbes's utopian *Sketches, Historical and Topographical, of the Floridas* responded to the author's vision of an olive-rich East Florida by observing that "Two olive trees, of very large size, and supposed to be of very great age, did grow near St. Augustine, and a few more were raised at New-Smyrna, but from what cause, none of them were fruitful." Not a single cruet of oil came from the South's olive trees until 1831, when John Couper of Cannon's Point, St. Simons Island, Georgia, produced some from his plantings.

Couper stood foremost among the generation of Southern experimentalists who turned to the olive as a possible way out of the soil exhaustion crisis of the 1820s. His letters on olive culture appeared in the first volume of the *Southern Agriculturist*, the journal founded by the South Carolina Agricultural Society to foster exchange among experimentalists in response to the political crisis over the United States tariff on cotton and the degradation of the region's topsoil. His name appeared first on the list of the "Report of the Union Agricultural Society of Georgia," proposing the olive as one "substitute for the rapidly depreciating staple, cotton." Couper, along with Robert Chisholm of Beaufort, South Carolina; W. L. Crawford of Darien, Georgia; Mitchell King of Charleston; Thomas Spalding of Sapelo Island, Georgia; J. H. Mey; and Judge Johnson, engaged in large-scale plantings in Beaufort and the Georgia Sea Islands. The most successful olive planter was Louisa Shaw, of Dungeness on Cumberland Island, Georgia, whose grove of six hundred trees produced throughout the nineteenth century and became a tourist venue.

If Jefferson had known of Shaw's activities, they would have warmed his heart. The youngest daughter of Revolutionary War hero General Nathaniel Greene, she planted the olives the South Carolina Agricultural Society had forwarded to her father. Under her vigilant care they flourished and expanded. Via reports in papers like the *Darien Gazette* their existence was known throughout the literate South. *American Farmer* in 1828 reprinted one such bulletin: "We are now informed on good authority, that 'olives of a very excellent quality,' have for several years been quite abundant on Cumberland Island, in the vicinity of Port St. Mary's, Geo. And that during the month of August last, many bushels of them were sold at the latter place, at seventy-five cents the bushel." Shaw's grove inspired hope in Couper, Spalding, and Chisholm that the olive could be made a merchantable commodity. Couper secured his two hundred trees from Provence and in May 1825 immediately planted the three-and-one-foot-long, branchless stems at Cannon's Point, St. Simons Island. Eighteen of the plantings died. Surprised at the slow growth, and realizing there would be no return on his land for years to come, Couper intercropped sweet potatoes in the grove, with good result. Although his attempt to expand his grove by cuttings failed, after a false start his experiments with planting from seed succeeded. J. H. Mey also had success growing olive from seed. Thomas Spalding, who secured his olive trees from Leghorn in Italy, complained about the cost, saying that at $2.50 apiece for purchase and transport, the importation of olives on a large scale was "too much for us to afford." He requested that the state "establish nursery grounds for the Olive tree," but Georgia declined to undertake this public work.

The experiments in olive culture nearly came to naught in 1835, when brutal February cold and ice destroyed most of the trees north of Cumberland Island. Couper was forced to cut his grove to the roots. Old Charleston trees, including a patriarch planted by Laurens on Lamboll Street, died. Yet Couper's roots sprouted shoots, the grove renewed, and the trees began bearing fruit in 1844. Once again planters were reminded that olives were a long-term project, with no expectation of quick returns. James Hamilton Couper, John Couper's son, reflected upon the course of his family's efforts in a letter to Charleston olive grower Mitchell King. He did not doubt that the olive could grow in the Lowcountry, regardless of the occasional freezes. Nor did he doubt that pickled olives would enjoy a ready reception.

> The question may be asked by those who have usually regarded olive oil as merely an article of household economy, of very limited use in North America, whether a ready sale of the oil can be depended on? They may believe with the late Abbe Correa, that our countrymen have "bacon stomachs," and that it will be very difficult, so far to conquer the obstinacy of established habit, as to induce them to substitute pure oil for rancid bacon. If the only use of this oil were for food, it would undoubtedly require time to introduce it into general consumption; but that time will effect it, there can be no doubt, from the intrinsic value of the commodity.

In 1845, according to the Report of the Secretary of the Treasury, 82,655 gallons of olive oil were imported into the United States. Some of this was used in soap manufacture and for machine oil. Despite the efforts of Mitchell King and J. Hamilton Couper, olive oil would not be produced in the South in more than experimental batches. In a letter to botanist Francis Peyre Porcher, Robert Chisolm of Beaufort (who exhibited sample vials of olive oil at the South Carolina Institute Fair on two occasions in the early 1850s) explained his view of the profitability of olive oil. Chisolm had planted his grove in 1833 with two types of Leghorn olives, a small, round oil olive and an oval-fruited one. He observed, "I do not think that the making of oil from the olive will be likely to prove sufficiently profitable to be pursued in this country for many years, and other crops will necessarily take the lead unless the price of labor or soil in Europe should be increased, when there will, consequently, become a greater demand." Porcher thought poppy seed oil would supply whatever culinary service olive oil might give. But ultimately another common Southern plant would provide a more economical culinary oil—benne, or sesame seed.

In 1808, when Thomas Jefferson, now president of the United States, despaired over the adoption of olive trees in the South, Governor John Milledge of Georgia sent him a bottle of benne oil. Jefferson found it equal to olive oil in its delicacy as a salad dressing and resolved to begin its production. The cultivation of benne seed became one of the president's important agricultural experiments of the early 1810s. There was an irony in this. Jefferson had imagined that the olive tree would be, first and foremost, a boon for African slaves in the South, providing them a fat that could be produced with less expense and greater volume than lard or bacon grease. (John Couper would echo this sentiment in a letter of 1830, when he remarked, "I am not of the opinion the Olive will be an object of great profit, but if we could introduce oil amongst our slaves, it would add much to their comforts.") Yet the slaves had brought with them the source of oil they needed in their diet, *Sesamum indicum*, or what the West African Mende called "benne."

Benne's wealth of oil (almost 50 percent of a seed's makeup) had been noted by agricultural writers repeatedly during the eighteenth century. As early as 1735 a "Mr. Garcia" announced in the *South Carolina Gazette* the establishment of a sesame oil press in Charleston. This press operated until the proprietor's death three years later. John Morel of Savannah in 1769 reported to the American Philosophical Society that "this seed makes oil equal in quality to Florence [olive oil], and some say preferable." Henry Laurens of South Carolina requested that his brother James "procure me as much Sesamum or Bene Seed as you possibly can, & encourage the planting it by all Negroes at each plantation." Throughout the 1790s the South Carolina Agricultural Society offered premiums to planters who could produce superior oil from sesame, olives, castor beans, sunflowers, cottonseed, or groundnuts (peanuts). Governor John Milledge and his neighbors began field cultivation of sesame around 1800, hoping to supply a native substitute for olive oil. His friend and colleague William Few moved to New York City and in 1804 began selling sesame oil pressed commercially in New Jersey. Pressing the sesame in a manner similar to that used to extract flaxseed oil, Milledge enthusiastically reported extracting three quarts of oil from a gallon of seed. Contemporaries observed that this yield was wishful, and that in most cases two quarts of oil could be expected. Thomas Marsh Forman of Maryland tasted the Georgia oil in 1812:

> At the home of my valued friend John McQueen, Esq. of Oatlands, the Bene plant was first made known to me. It was about the last of February, that dining with him, he requested my opinion of a bowl of fine Cabbage Lettuce; it deserved all the praise which I gave to the vegetable, as well as to the dressing, when Mr. McQueen smiling informed me, that the oil was of his own produce, from what made, and the value of the crop.

The West African method of extracting oil was designed for a household level of production and consumption. The seed was pounded by mortar and pestle. After "bruising the seed, and immersing them in boiling water . . . the oil rises to the top and is easily skimmed off. Good casks filled, or bottles filled, and well bunged, or corked are proper to preserve this oil which doubtless, will become rancid by heat, time, impurities, and air." Twenty-first-century chemical and nutritional analysis finds that of the culinary oils high in polyunsaturated omega-6, and with high smoke points, sesame oil is least prone to turn rancid, making it the most stable of healthy frying substances.

Benne oil kept as well as olive oil. It could be produced annually and abundantly, without a ten-year wait for productivity, and could be grown as far north as Maryland without much difficulty. It could also be pressed and extracted with less labor and mechanism than olive oil required. A simple iron press could do the job.

Many Southern farmers grew benne. Indeed, the amount of benne grown cannot be calculated with any certainty, because substantial slave-patch plantings went unnoted in plantation record books. Judging by surviving documents, planters rarely attempted benne production on a scale to create more than a modest, largely local market for oil (the maximum plantings tended to be fifty acres), yet a number of plantations engaged in artisanal production, using sesame in crop rotations with corn, sweet potatoes, and cowpeas, or with rice and sweet potatoes. A window on the small-scale world of sesame oil production and benne cake livestock feeding is found in the pages of Thomas Walter Peyre's plantation journal (1834–1859) at the South Carolina Historical Society. On Peyre's estate the benne press, like the brewhouse, was first a plantation resource, secondarily a production facility for market goods.

African American farming of benne can be imputed only by anecdotal reports, yet numerous records attest to benne's importance in the slave diet. Indeed a complex benne cookery adapted from African practices was recorded. In 1820 John S. Skinner, editor of the United States' most important agricultural journal, *American Farmer*, observed that

> The Bene vine or bush, has been produced for some time, in small quantities, in the southern states, from seed imported directly from Africa, or Asia—It abounds in the former, and in Bengal. Many of the blacks of the Mississippi, have continued the propagation of the seed of the Bene, and make soup of it after parching. The seed may be procured from them and from the blacks in the Carolinas and Georgia.

Skinner's note reveals several things: the African genesis of the plant, the broad geographic range yet relatively low acreage of its cultivation, and the black oversight of seed stock for benne. Skinner also provided a glimpse of its most notable culinary use—as the basis of benne soup.

Rich in oil and nutty in taste, benne can be eaten raw. Because it is highly nutritious (25 percent protein), it could provide sustenance with minimal preparation. But the African American population preferred to intensify the flavorful nuttiness of the seed by browning it in a skillet. Whether hulled or unhulled, seeds could be tossed onto the bottom of an ungreased dutch oven or iron skillet and stirred until lightly toasted—not scorched in any part. Parched benne had a host of uses. It could be eaten straight from the skillet, used as a condiment to flavor a pot of stew or greens, or pounded in a mortar and pestle to become a thickening agent or a base for pottage. Every surviving notice of the use of benne mash in cookery indicates that it was mixed with something else. The two basic partnering elements were wheat flour and cornmeal, cooked in salted water or stock.

Robert M. Goodwin of Skidaway Island, Georgia, observed in 1824 that for "negroes in this part of the country . . . it [benne] is thought . . . to be much better in soup than okra, and it is used by them in the same manner. I am told it is very good, but I have never tasted it." Calvin Jones noted the extensive use of benne in African American cookery in eastern North Carolina, observing that "among negroes who get little flesh meat, it is a valuable article." Meat rations on plantations tended to be restricted to three-and-one-half pounds of cured pork per week maximum. On small-scale farms there might be no ration, which meant that a slave had to hunt and trap during the off hours of labor to supply meat. Consequently, sesame served as an important dietary protein supplement. The sole surviving recipe for benne soup appeared as a variation of groundnut soup in Sarah Rutledge's 1847 *The Carolina Housewife*. Though attentive to vernacular cookery, Rutledge's collection was intended for a white readership with meat and seafood at its disposal. She added oysters to benne and flour to make a dish that survives in Lowcountry cuisine as "Brown Oyster and Benne Stew."

## Ground Nut Soup

To half a pint of shelled ground nuts, well beaten up, add two spoonsful of flour, and mix well. Put to them a pint of oysters, and a pint and a half of water. While boiling, throw in a seed pepper or two, if small.

## Bennie Soup

This is made exactly in the same manner except that instead of a half a pint of ground-nuts, a pint and a gill of bennie is mixed with the flour and the oysters.

Rutledge's soup can be considered an evolution of the basic benne soup cooked in the plantation quarters. All the ingredients for that more-basic soup were listed in Rutledge's recipe, but the mode of preparation was somewhat different, since she was concerned about preserving the quality of the oysters incorporated into the mix. The foundation soup called for

1 cup benne seed, enough sesame oil to cover the bottom of a cooking vessel, a handful of wheat flour, Salt & Pepper, onions, a quart of water. Toast benne seed in a dry skillet stirring constantly 2 minutes until browned, but not burnt. Empty contents of the skillet into a mortar and mash the seed into powder. In the same skillet cover the bottom with sesame oil [the African American way of making it is detailed below in the section on oil] and mix in flour. Stir and cook this until you form a brown roux. Fry one large roughly chopped onion. Add finely crushed benne, and then hot water, steadily, stirring constantly. Cook at a con-

stant medium until it is rich and thick and salt to taste. This is a hearty and flavorful soup.

Benne could be kept for winter use at a time when vegetables, apart from root vegetables, could be scarce. Commentators repeatedly remarked on the love of African Americans for onions, whether globe, spring, or wild leek. A chopped onion might be incorporated into the roux and allowed to become translucent before the benne was added, to give a sweet note to the soup and a pleasing texture. A seedpod of hot pepper was also a welcome addition. West Africans added cooked meats to benne soup when available. The foundation soup operated as a canvas for improvisation.

An 1824 article in *American Farmer* stated that "The Negroes in Georgia boil a handful of the seeds with their allowance of Indian Corn." Three years earlier, a North Carolinian had noted, "Mixed in due proportion with their hominy, it heightens its relish, and adds to its nutriment." Because whole seed takes longer to cook than cornmeal, it does not amalgamate well and can stick in one's teeth. The handful of benne cast into the hominy pot most likely had already been parched and pounded.

Hominy designated three things: small hominy was ground cornmeal; large hominy meant dried whole kernels of corn; and the word also referred to posole, a kind of dried whole-kernel corn soaked in lye to remove the kernel's outer hull. Native Americans throughout the Southeast boiled cornmeal, and English settlers learned to substitute cornmeal for the familiar oat and wheat pottages of their homeland. Because Africans ate millet stews, they, too, found the substitution of corn acceptable. A West African approach to mixing benne and hominy derives from the traditional practice of serving a groundnut or benne soup over a thick mash of cassava. In the Lowcountry hominy replaced cassava. It was prepared separately, spooned into a bowl, and benne soup was ladled over it. Usually pieces of precooked meat or greens were added to the liquid prior to serving.

In the 1770s Thomas Jefferson wrote that sesame "was brought to S. Carolina from Africa by the negroes. . . . They bake it in their bread, boil it with greens, enrich their broth" with it. His observation about the greens accords with longstanding practice among a number of West African peoples. Casting a handful of whole seed into a cooking pot of collards (the premier cold-weather green), turnip, beet, or mustard greens might be convenient, but it did not release all of the seed's oils. Mashing them beforehand rendered them luscious. In the second decade of the nineteenth century, when oil mills appeared on numbers of plantations, the mash cake left after pressing the sesame became a cooking condiment: "The oil cake is very pleasant at table, is eaten freely by horned cattle, swine, &c., and is often used when fresh to boil with other vegetables, rendering butter unnecessary." The use of benne mash as an oleo in boiling greens and root vegetables resembled North African practices of using tahini (sesame paste) as a condiment in vegetable cookery; it also mimicked the West African habit of adding mashed benne to one-pot preparations. The mixture of benne mash with greens remained as a feature of plantation cookery through the antebellum period.

Oily pressed seed cake fit into traditional (i.e., African) cooking practices, yet the demand for sesame oil in the white world of the marketplace was driven by a culinary vogue that nurtured a new taste—a hankering for uncooked greens, vegetables, and fruits. Until the end of the eighteenth century physicians contemplating the nature of human digestion viewed cooking as an externalized form of the digestive process, something that greatly aided the body's efficient uptake of the nutritional elements in food. Uncooked fruits and vegetables were not fully utilized by the body and, indeed, troubled the stomach and intestines, prompting dyspepsia, a gastrointestinal disorder that led to gas, stomachaches, blockage, and other sorts of internal distress. But in the 1790s old ideas about the function of cooking as a necessary supplement to digestion began to dissolve, as did fears of the dire consequences of dyspepsia. In Europe and, later, in the young United States, the fashion for salads composed of uncooked greens and vegetables spread. Celery rocketed into garden vogue, and lettuces became popular. Uncooked cabbage was shredded into slaws. These salads tasted best when lubricated by an acid (vinegar or lemon juice) and an oil. Melted lard would not do, nor would melted butter. It is no anomaly that the story of Jefferson's discovery of the virtues of benne oil has him eating it on a fresh salad. Jefferson was embracing two novelties simultaneously.

■　■　■

The final quarter of the [twentieth] century witnessed a revival of regional cuisines, traditional foodways, natural taste, and artisanal production. Olives found a home in California, and sesame in Texas, where production served an expanding market for oils. In 2008 the story came full circle. For the first time in a century benne became a crop in Georgia and the Carolinas, reintroduced by the Carolina Gold Rice Foundation and its affiliated growers. Sean Brock, chef of McCrady's restaurant in Charleston, South Carolina, embraced the ingredient and for his renovations of regional cooking won the 2010 James Beard Foundation Award as Best Chef in the Southeast. In Georgia, Dr. Mark L. Hanly and S. L. Davis planted olive groves and organized a group of twenty-four prospective orchardists and producers into the Georgia Olive Growers Association. Groves are now thriving in Blackshear and Appling counties. The first oil should issue from the presses in 2012.

*Valerie Erwin is the chef-owner of the Geechee Girl Rice Café in Philadelphia, Pennsylvania. This is an adaptation of the talk she delivered at the 2010 Southern Foodways Symposium on the Global South.*

# A Geechee Girl Speaks

## Valerie Erwin

I was born and raised in Philadelphia, my mother was born and raised in Philadelphia, and my father, who was born in Savannah, came to Philadelphia when he was sixteen. So in some ways I am thoroughly a product of the Northeast. Yet because of my family heritage—my mother's parents were from Charleston—I've always had an affinity for food from the South. And if your family, like mine, came from the Lowcountry, loving Southern food means loving rice.

Geechee Girl Rice Cafe, my Lowcountry restaurant in Philadelphia, is named for the Geechees, who live on the coast and on the islands of Georgia and Florida. They are the descendants of the enslaved Africans brought there from West Africa's Rice Coast. They have many of the same foodways and folkways as the Gullah people of South Carolina. Africans from rice-growing areas were particularly sought-after as slaves because of their agricultural expertise. Geechees were historically rice cultivators, and their descendants remain rice eaters.

My father taught me to cook. He learned from his grandmother. She must have been a very determined teacher, because my father had a thorough culinary knowledge by the time he arrived in Philadelphia at age sixteen to live with his uncle. My father's uncle was the pastor of the AME church to which my mother's family belonged. The Erwins, my father's family, are wonderful cooks. The Petersons, my mother's family—well, what my sister Lisa says is, "You know the Petersons don't cook." And of course that isn't, strictly speaking, true, but they never looked at cooking as the recreational activity that the Erwins did.

I learned from my father how to use a knife, the importance of planning, and how to taste carefully. He taught me, sometimes inadvertently, how to be an adventurous eater. I remember him bringing home scallops: white, gelatinous-looking, almost alive-looking. I had no intention of eating them. But once they were fried, they looked delicious: golden and crispy, and I was in this unfortunate position of having adamantly declared that I'd never eat those nasty white scallops, and wanting desperately to eat the golden-brown ones. So I learned not to prejudge food, or at least not to do it out loud.

My mother was a skilled and careful cook, but my father was the celebrity cook in our family. He was the source of the fancy and sometimes unusual food in our home, but it was my mother who made all my favorites, like crackly fried chicken, yellow layer cake with chocolate icing, and a perfectly cooked pot of rice.

When I read Judith Carney's book *Black Rice*, a parallel struck me between rice eaters in West Africa, in the Lowcountry, and in my own family. Judith says that the Africans in Africa and in America considered rice culture "women's work." It was that way in my house, too. My father was immensely talented. He could fix a car and rewire a house. He could make ravioli from scratch. But he was, by his own assessment, a dismal failure at cooking rice, even though he expected it on the table every single night. When his grandmother wanted to teach him to cook—and to sew—my father protested that those were things that his wife would do. Apparently, he was overly optimistic, because according to my father, my mother didn't know how to cook when they got married. He thought she could cook, but it turned out that all she knew how to make was cake. And rice.

We ate rice every day. I didn't question it, but I knew, even as a child, that it wasn't universal. Once I had dinner at a neighbor's house, and when my parents asked how the meal was, I said, "It was fine, but Mrs. Jackson forgot the rice." When I was charged with the task of making dinner for the family and inspiration proved elusive, my father would give his best menu-planning advice: "Put on a pot of rice, and then decide what to make to go with it." Occasionally we had a complicated rice dish.

My mother would make red rice, the Lowcountry version of Spanish rice: crisp bacon with onions, celery, and peppers fried in the drippings, made into a pilaf with rice and tomatoes. Or a supper dish that she said she and my father invented of rice sautéed with onions and peppers and served with scrambled eggs. My mother made Hoppin' John on New Year's Day: black-eyed peas intensely flavored with ham and cooked up with rice so that it was perfectly fluffy. There was, to my consternation, always a hog jowl in the pot, teeth and all. But most of the time, we had plain rice: rice with gravy, rice with beans, rice with stew. A pot of white rice at the ready to serve as a foil for whatever else we ate.

I never intended to be a chef. In fact, my career plan, such as it was, could be boiled down to "avoid manual labor." At Geechee Girl, I cook six days a week, seven meals a week—so that plan didn't go that well. But my love of food and cooking eventually led to my working in restaurants. I had the usual culinary trajectory for someone who started working in the late '70s: Continental, International, French, New American. I loved everything I learned during those years, but I always felt a nagging disconnect between what was in my soul and what was on the plate. The first time I made Osso Bucco a la Milanese, my immediate reaction was that it tasted just like my father's neckbones and tomatoes. I remember that era as the "everybody makes Osso Bucco, but nobody makes neckbone" years. Or, in an analogy even closer to my heart, "everybody wants fresh, handmade pasta, but Uncle Ben's rice is just fine." When I was in a position to make menu choices, I'd serve some of the food I loved: ham and red-eye gravy, fried fish rolled in cornmeal—but not rice. Neither the customers nor my employers seemed ready. And the quality of rice in every restaurant I'd worked at was abysmal.

I opened Geechee Girl Rice Cafe in 2003 out of a confluence of circumstances. I wanted a nice restaurant in my neighborhood; someone I knew was selling a nearby turn-key operation; I had run out of places where I really wanted to work. The restaurant had a small dining room and a minimally equipped kitchen, so we'd have to do a simple concept. It was my sister Alethia's idea: "We could call it Geechee Girl," she said, "and serve rice." I wasn't looking to preserve a culture; I was looking to cook. But a few things happen when you put the words "Geechee" and "rice" into the name of your business. People with Lowcountry roots come in to talk. People for whom "Geechee" had been a pejorative term are thrilled to see it rehabilitated. People who've vacationed on the Sea Islands have a sense of nostalgia. Expat Southerners want a little taste of home. People from other places where rice is the staple grain—which is just about everywhere except Northern Europe—love the idea of a rice restaurant. People from Africa or the Caribbean see our logo—a turbaned black woman winnowing rice—and wonder where we're from. In fact, everyone wonders where we're from. I think they're all a bit disappointed that my sisters and I are from North Philadelphia.

I design our menu to pay tribute to tradition, but not to be bound by it. For a cook, taste trumps tradition every time. And for a businessperson, salability wins over authenticity. But that being said, I am more aware each year of the responsibility I've assumed for preserving Lowcountry cuisine. So now, although my mother made Hoppin' John only on New Year's Day, we serve it every day. Just like in my house when we were growing up, at Geechee Girl we serve a lot of plain rice: rice with gravy, rice with beans, rice with stew. We serve traditional Lowcountry rice dishes like red rice and purloo.

I feel a particularly close culinary kinship with the food of the African diaspora. We serve curried goat from the Caribbean and peanut chicken stew from West Africa. We search for home cooks from around the world who are willing to partner with us in presenting special dinners, and over the years, these partnerships have been a great source of menu ideas. I struggle sometimes with the decision to keep rice in the restaurant's name. When people see the word "rice," they sometimes think we're vegetarians, or that we only serve rice. How ridiculous is that?! The word remains because of how fundamental rice was to my ancestors. They grew it, they ate it, they were captured and sold in its service.

I'm proud of my part in introducing Lowcountry cooking to a wider audience, and I treasure making foods that act as a thread back to Africa. I look around my city, and I see a shocking dearth of black restaurant owners. I see an even more shocking dearth of black employees in restaurant dining rooms. I search for opportunities to expand my business for one fundamental reason: If we have more, we can do more. I want to take our food and our message to a larger audience.

I believe that the South is more than a location. It is history; it is memory; it is culture. And for me, most of all, it is food.

Iain Haley Pollock's debut collection of poems, Spit Back a Boy, won the 2010 Cave Canem Poetry Prize.

# My Stove's in Good Condition

**Iain Haley Pollock**

Because she thought I wanted it,

    for dinner Naomi wants catfish,
        catfish on the range spitting oil, its smoke
            spicing the house with pepper, black & cayenne.

From speakers in the living room, ragtime piano,

    a winking old blues by Lil Johnson,
        Lil Johnson singing about her stove but fooling
            with more than pots & pans: When my wood gets
            too hot . . .

I check the crisp on the fish & flip, then shuffle in my
    slippers

    to the front windows, looking for Naomi to pull up at the
    house,
        brick house down the street from the Poplar Bridge,
        built in '22 & crumbling over the freight rail line.

No sign of her little blue car,

    just the 32 bus ferrying riders from North Philly,
        North Philly to graveyard shifts downtown,
        guards & clerks & cleaners in the lit cabin

like relatives waiting in a hospice room:

a man presses his forehead against a window,
window pushing up the brim of his cap: a gray woman
slouches down & pillows her head on plastic bags
stuffed

with plastic bags & piled on the next seat. Watching for
Naomi,

I'd lost the fish & music, then again the crackling,
crackling of cornmeal & pepper, of Lil Johnson
& her lusty blues: Nothin to be waitin on, let's get
drunk

and truck. A month since we lay curled & sweaty in bed:

on the way back to the kitchen, I turn down the music,
music that growled like hunger, growled like the dull
ache
of hunger filling the body, pushing out til the mind

pricks with hunger, is consumed with hunger—

so much hunger in these blues:
blues so much hunger:
hunger so much blues:
so much

blues:
hunger:
hunger:
so much:
blues:
hunger so much:
blues:
so much:
blues:
hunger:
blues

Bill Smith is the chef at Crook's Corner in Chapel Hill, North Carolina. He is at
work on a memoir.

# Pancho at the Flor de Celaya

## Bill Smith

The Flor de Celaya is a chicharroneria in the sprawling Mercado de Abastos,
or wholesale market, in the city of Celaya, in the Mexican state of Guana-
juato. My buddy Francisco (a.k.a. Pancho) works there now. Pancho was the
second person to whom I taught baking in Spanish. This was years ago and
now that he's gone back home I go to visit him whenever I can. He is just
one of many friends I have in Celaya. The friendships always quickly pick
up where they left off, as if we'd never been away from one another. I'm sure
the wives and girlfriends hate to hear that I'm coming. As soon as we get in
each other's sights, the Peter Pan Syndrome kicks in. All my friends will go
missing drunk at least one night while I'm in town. I'm in town at least twice
a year.

A chicharroneria is a place that makes pork rinds, and the Flor de Celaya
job is a new one for Pancho. The place is nuts from morning until closing
time. It isn't very big, yet there are several sales people, a guy at the fryer, a
presser at his side, a boss or two, and for some reason people drinking beer
and playing cards right in the middle of everything. I am always given a stool
and a beer the minute I show up. It's a good thing that I don't live any closer,
because I am easily bewitched by this vibe, and if I were there any more often
I would eventually just never leave. The store has an open front and a high
ceiling. In the loft above are stored heavy bales of imported American pork
skins. They have already been blanched once in hot oil in the city of Toluca,
about four hours to the southwest. At first glance, they could be mistaken for
bundles of cardboard ready for recycling. They are unrefrigerated and drip
cold grease. As needed, a whole bale is thrown into the cauldron of boiling
oil that has been bricked in against the left wall, where the skins break apart
and are miraculously transformed into fluffy, crispy clouds. At this point

they weigh nothing. If you order a kilo, you leave with a garbage bag full. I'm thinking I should be able to do this back in Chapel Hill. After all, people make them in iron pots in their front yards all over Mexico. Pork rinds and a Coca-Cola could be a first course.

I have known and loved Pancho for many years now. As is often the case with immigrant workers, he started as a dishwasher and worked his way up—in his instance, to be my baker. Although he had no context for American-style desserts, he learned quickly. When he was forced to return home suddenly because of serious flooding in Celaya, he took a Kitchenaid mixer with him. As a sideline he began making pineapple upside-down cakes, which he sold to a neighborhood school for their cafeteria. In the restaurant kitchen I have an old beat-up set of clear plastic measuring cups sized from one cup to four quarts. Since Mexico uses metrics and the system of wet-dry measure we use in the United States really doesn't make any sense, I converted all of our recipes both into Spanish and into a format where the plastic measuring cups will work for everything. I am always careful to have backup sets of plastic measuring cups. I still have the first notebook of recipes, translucent with grease, ink beginning to wick out into the paper. It has sentimental value.

Pancho is a complicated man. Like a lot of my Mexican friends, he married very young because that is what everyone around him did. No one expected or looked for other options. Then, when he came to the United States, he saw people—people his age especially—who had made other choices. He realized that maybe he wanted other choices too and thus became a citizen of two worlds, old and new, first and second. He loved his wife and children but regretted lost opportunities. His wife, the pretty and intelligent Silvia, could never really understand the differences that he now saw. They have separated but are friendly.

I am content when I get to sit in the melee of the Flor de Celaya on my stool drinking beer way too early in the day as the fire roars and the chicharrones crackle. The men swear and sing and hump each other all day long. They exclaim over shapely women and declare that everyone else who works with them is *joto*, or gay. These things aren't ever said with any kind of meanness. They are merely pointing out a list of possibilities, all of them tantalizing. These are working-class people, like the people I come from. I guess this is why I fit in so well, even though reading back over this paragraph it doesn't seem like I would.

We don't really ever do much when I'm in Celaya. It's odd in a way. We just sort of bask in each other's presence, usually in bars but also in homes. Together with another friend, Rambo, we prowl this sprawling, gritty town most evenings, windows rolled down and radio blaring. People will feed you without notice here and don't seem to mind. One evening last fall, Pancho's mother fixed us posole at ten thirty at night. There couldn't have been five minutes' notice, yet it appeared as if she had been expecting us all day. Rambo's mother usually asks me over at least once a visit. It always seems to be somebody's birthday, so she's entertaining anyway. I try to arrive at the time she tells me but guests come and go all evening. There are always lots of children in tow. She just gets up and cooks whenever somebody new shows up. This makes for a sort of swarming, chaotic dinner party. It's really fun, but it would drive me crazy. She is a great cook. I never leave her house without at least one new menu idea.

Holy Week is one of the best times to visit Latin America, especially if you have friends in the meat selling business, because in observance of Lent, they get a few extra days off since people are fasting. The Palm Sunday processions seem especially happy. In the pictures I've taken, people's faces are radiant. I miss my friends but I am always glad to come and see them here. They provided a level of humor and common sense to my kitchen that I think might be missing in others. I have adopted this attitude as my own. They have helped make a very difficult job a great deal easier by their example of insouciant but good work. It would be impossible now for me to disentangle myself from their influences even if I wanted to. And, of course, I don't.

# Acknowledgments

"Why Chile con Queso Matters," by Alison Cook. Originally published in the *Houston Chronicle*, December 24, 2009. Reprinted by permission of the author.

"The Ceremony," by Molly O'Neill. Originally published in *One Big Table: A Portrait of American Cooking, 600 Recipes from the Nation's Best Home Cooks, Farmers, Fishermen, Pit-Masters, and Chefs* (New York: Simon and Schuster, 2010). Reprinted by permission of the author.

"In Sorrow's Kitchen," by Jessica B. Harris. Originally published in *High on the Hog: A Culinary Journey from Africa to America* (New York: Bloomsbury, 2011). Reprinted by permission of the author.

"Blood-Bought Luxuries," by Frederick Douglass. Originally published in *My Bondage and My Freedom* (1855). Reprinted in *Lapham's Quarterly* food issue, summer 2011. Work is in the public domain.

"Green Goddess: Why We Love Collard Greens," by Lonnée Hamilton. Originally published in *Saveur* 133 (November 2010). Reprinted by permission of the author.

"The Fatback Collective" by Wright Thompson. Originally published in *Garden & Gun*, Fall 2011. Reprinted by permission of the author.

"I Was a Texas Rib Ranger," by Brett Martin. Published here for the first time by permission of the author.

"Fire in the Hole," by Jon Fasman. Originally published in the *Economist*, December 16, 2010. © The Economist Newspaper Limited, London, December 16, 2010. Reprinted with permission of The Economist Newspaper Limited.

"Carlo Silvestrini on the Hog Slaughter," by Greg Alan Brownderville. Originally published in *Gravy* 39 (Winter 2011). Reprinted by permission of the author.

"An Oyster by Any Other Name," by Elizabeth Engelhardt. Originally published in *Southern Spaces*, April 18, 2011. Reprinted by permission of the author.

"Adventures of a Boudin Junkie," by Sara Roahen. Originally published in *Garden & Gun*, February/March 2009. Reprinted by permission of the author.

"Boy & Egg," by Naomi Shihab Nye. Originally published in *Fuel* (Rochester, N.Y.: BOA Editions, 1998). Reprinted by permission of the author.

"As ConAgra Pulls Out, Workers Face Uncertainty," by Sarah Nagem. Originally published in the *Raleigh News & Observer*, May 22, 2011. Reprinted with permission of The News & Observer of Raleigh, North Carolina.

"Reviving Red Snapper," by Barry Estabrook. Originally published in *Gastronomica* 10, no. 3 (2010). Reprinted by permission of the author.

"Flooded," by Jennifer Justus. Originally published on the author's blog, *A Nasty Bite*, May 9, 2010. Reprinted by permission of the author.

"Reconsidering the Oyster," by Paul Greenberg. Originally published in the *Times* of London, April 14, 2011. Reprinted by permission of the author.

"The Collins Oyster Family," photographs by David Grunfeld / *Times-Picayune*. © 2010 The Times-Picayune. All rights reserved. Reprinted with permission. Originally appeared May 30, 2010.

"A Paradise Lost," by Bob Marshall. This piece is adapted from the author's four-part series on Delacroix in the *Times-Picayune*, August 2010. Adapted and reprinted by permission of the author.

"Mr. Leroy and the French Club," by Francis Lam. Originally published on Gourmet .com, May 5, 2009. Reprinted by permission of the author.

"Wendell Berry's Wisdom," by Michael Pollan. Originally published in the *Nation*, September 21, 2009, and as an introduction to *Bringing It to the Table: On Farming and Food* by Wendell Berry (Berkeley: Counterpoint Press, 2009). Reprinted by permission of the author.

"Tom Pritchard, Local Culinary Rock Star and Stuff of Legend," by Ben Montgomery. Originally published in the *St. Petersburg Times*, January 11, 2009. Reprinted with permission of the *St. Petersburg Times*.

"Home Grown," by Jane Black. Originally published in the *Washington Post*, August 25, 2010. Reprinted by permission of the author.

"Blood and Water," by Kim Severson. From *Spoon Fed: How Eight Cooks Saved My Life* by Kim Severson, copyright © 2010 by Kim Severson. Used by permission of Riverhead Books, an imprint of Penguin Group (USA) Inc.

"A Force of Nature," by Andrea Weigl. Originally published in the *Raleigh News & Observer*, February 20, 2011. Reprinted with permission of The News & Observer of Raleigh, North Carolina.

"St. Francine at the Café Max," by John Dufresne. Originally published in *Alimentum* 8. Reprinted by permission of the author.

"Eula Mae Doré," by Edward Behr. Originally published in the *Art of Eating* 34 (Spring 1995). Reprinted by permission of the author.

"How *Not* to Hire a Chef," by Tim Carman. Originally published in *Washington City Paper*, May 22, 2009. Reprinted by permission of the author.

"A Rapping Drag Queen and Her Fried Chicken," by Ben Westhoff. This piece is adapted from the author's book *Dirty South: OutKast, Lil Wayne, Soulja Boy, and the Southern Rappers Who Reinvented Hip-Hop* (Chicago: Chicago Review Press, 2011). Adapted and reprinted by permission of the author.

"Past and Presence," by Wayne Curtis. Originally published in *Imbibe* magazine, May/June 2009. Reprinted by permission of the author.

"Whiskey and Geography," by Charles D. Thompson Jr. Originally published in *Spirits of Just Men: Mountaineers, Liquor Bosses, and Lawmen in the Moonshine Capital*

*of the World* (Champaign: University of Illinois Press, 2011). Reprinted by
permission of University of Illinois Press.

"Cheerwine," by Lucid Olason. Originally published in *Put a Egg on It / Tasty Zine* 3.
Reprinted by permission of the author.

"Corncob Wine," by Matt and Ted Lee. Originally published in *The Lee Bros. Southern
Cookbook* (New York: W. W. Norton, 2006). Reprinted by permission of the
authors.

"The Wild Vine," by Todd Kliman. This piece is adapted from the author's book *The
Wild Vine: A Forgotten Grape and the Untold Story of American Wine* (New York:
Clarkson Potter, 2010). Adapted and reprinted by permission of the author.

"Empire State South: Athens Star Chef Hugh Acheson Brings Atlanta Its Latest
Southern Sensation," by Bill Addison. Originally published in *Atlanta* magazine,
December 2010. Reprinted by permission of the author.

"Real Cajun," by Donald Link. From *Real Cajun: Rustic Home Cooking from Donald
Link's Louisiana*, by Donald Link and with Paula Disbrowe. Copyright © 2009 by
Donald Link. Used by permission of Clarkson Potter Publishers, an imprint of the
Crown Publishing Group, a division of Random House, Inc.

"No Daily Specials," by Calvin Trillin. Copyright © by Calvin Trillin. Originally
appeared in the *New Yorker*. Reprinted by permission of Lescher & Lescher, Ltd.
All rights reserved.

"Pie + Design = Change," by John T. Edge. From the *New York Times Magazine*,
October 10, 2010. © 2010 The New York Times. All rights reserved. Used by
permission and protected by the Copyright Laws of the United States. The
printing, copying, redistribution, or retransmission of the material without express
written permission is prohibited.

"The Origin Myth of New Orleans Cuisine," by Lolis Eric Elie. Originally published
in the *Oxford American* 68 (March 2010). Reprinted by permission of the
author.

"Where Are All the Black Chefs?" by John Kessler. Originally published in the *Oxford
American* 68 (March 2010). Reprinted by permission of the author.

"Homesick Restaurants: How Dallas Became a Dining Nowhereville," by Hanna Raskin.
Originally published in the *Dallas Observer*, December 9, 2010. Reprinted by
permission of Village Voice Media, LLC.

"An Open Letter to Kim Severson," by Besha Rodell. Originally published in *Omnivore
Atlanta*, the food and drink blog of *Creative Loafing Atlanta*, March 14, 2011.
Reprinted by permission of the author.

"Family Pieces," by Martha Foose. Originally published in *A Southerly Course: Recipes
and Stories from Close to Home* (New York: Clarkson Potter, 2011). Reprinted by
permission of the author.

"Putting Food on the Family," by Jack Hitt. Originally published in *Man with a Pan:
Culinary Adventures of Men Who Cook for Their Families*, edited by John Donahue.
© 2011 by John Donahue. Reprinted by permission of Algonquin Books of Chapel
Hill. All rights reserved.

"Bags, Butter, Surfboards, and Spice: Viet-Cajun in Cali," by Andrea Nguyen. Originally
delivered as a talk at the 2010 Southern Foodways Alliance Symposium, Oxford,
Miss. Adapted and reprinted by permission of the author.

"Ravioli and Country Music's First Family," by Fred Sauceman. Originally published in *The Place Setting: Timeless Tastes of the Mountain South, From Bright Hope to Frog Level—Thirds* (Macon, Ga.: Mercer University Press, 2009). Reprinted by permission of the author.

"Prospecting for Oil," by David S. Shields. This piece originally appeared in a different form in *Gastronomica* 10, no. 4 (2010). Adapted and reprinted by permission of the author.

"A Geechee Girl Speaks," by Valerie Erwin. Originally delivered as a talk at the 2010 Southern Foodways Alliance Symposium, Oxford, Miss. Adapted and reprinted by permission of the author.

"My Stove's in Good Condition," by Iain Haley Pollock. Originally published in *Spit Back a Boy* (Athens: University of Georgia Press, 2011). Reprinted by permission of the author.

"Pancho at the Flor de Celaya," by Bill Smith. Published here for the first time by permission of the author.

# The Southern Foodways Alliance

The Southern Foodways Alliance, founded in 1999, documents, studies, and celebrates the diverse food cultures of the changing American South.

We set a common table where black and white, rich and poor—all who gather—may consider our history and our future in a spirit of reconciliation.

A member-supported nonprofit, based at the University of Mississippi, we collect oral histories, produce documentary films, sponsor scholarship, stage symposia, and publish compendiums of great writing. In the *Atlantic Monthly*, Corby Kummer dubbed the SFA "this country's most intellectually engaged (and probably most engaging) food society."

## DOCUMENT

Documentary projects are central to the SFA's mission. Oral history interviews and documentary films not only capture the stories of our region for future generations, they illuminate people and place. Since the formal inception of our documentary initiative in 2005, we have collected over five hundred stories—stories about barbecue and boudin, tamales and tupelo honey.

We catalog the bulk of our oral history archive online. Additionally, we share these stories through podcasts, smart phone apps, and various social media platforms.

Each year, the SFA produces several films in concert with the University of Mississippi's Center for Documentary Projects.

Our subjects range from goat cheese artisans to fried pie cooks, from buttermilk producers to barbecue pit masters. All films may be streamed through our website. By way of our Potlikker Film Festivals we take those films on the road. Look for screenings (and potlikker shots) in your area.

## STUDY

The SFA is the foremost national resource focused on the study and living history of Southern foodways. As an institute of the Center for the Study of Southern Culture, at the University of Mississippi, we take seriously our charge to contribute to cultural studies dialogues about food.

Academic rigor underscores our work. We host an academic lecture series that focuses on foodways topics. We aid students by offering internships and graduate assistantships. In the fall of 2011, we welcomed our first post-doctoral teaching fellow.

## CELEBRATE

By way of symposia on food culture, field trips to the region's great food cities, compelling Stir the Pot dinners, and Potlikker Film Festivals, the SFA celebrates the diverse food cultures of the American South.

For a look at our coming calendar, or a look back at past events, visit www.southernfoodways.org.

## SFA FOUNDING MEMBERS

Ann Abadie, Oxford, Miss.
Kaye Adams, Birmingham, Ala.
Jim Auchmutey, Atlanta, Ga.
Marilou Awiakta, Memphis, Tenn.
Ben Barker, Durham, N.C.
Ella Brennan, New Orleans, La.
Ann Brewer, Covington, Ga.
Karen Cathey, Arlington, Va.
Leah Chase, New Orleans, La.
Al Clayton, Jasper, Ga.
Mary Ann Clayton, Jasper, Ga.
Shirley Corriher, Atlanta, Ga.
Norma Jean Darden, New York, N.Y.

Crescent Dragonwagon, Eureka Springs, Ark.
Nathalie Dupree, Social Circle, Ga.
John T. Edge, Oxford, Miss.
John Egerton, Nashville, Tenn.
Lolis Eric Elie, New Orleans, La.
John Folse, Donaldsonville, La.
Terry Ford, Ripley, Tenn.
Psyche Williams Forson, Beltsville, Md.
Damon Lee Fowler, Savannah, Ga.
Vertamae Grosvenor, Washington, D.C.
Jessica B. Harris, Brooklyn, N.Y.

Cynthia Hizer, Covington, Ga.
Portia James, Washington, D.C.
Martha Johnston, Birmingham, Ala.
Sally Belk King, Richmond, Va.
Sarah Labensky, Columbus, Miss.
Edna Lewis, Atlanta, Ga.
Rudy Lombard, Chicago, Ill.
Ronni Lundy, Louisville, Ky.
Louis Osteen, Charleston, S.C.
Marlene Osteen, Charleston, S.C.
Timothy W. Patridge, Atlanta, Ga.
Paul Prudhomme, New Orleans, La.
Joe Randall, Savannah, Ga.
Marie Rudisill, Hudson, Fla.

Dori Sanders, Clover, S.C.
Richard Schweid, Barcelona, Spain
Ned Shank, Eureka Springs, Ark.
Kathy Starr, Greenville, Miss.
Frank Stitt, Birmingham, Ala.
Pardis Stitt, Birmingham, Ala.
Marion Sullivan, Mt. Pleasant, S.C.
Van Sykes, Bessemer, Ala.
John Martin Taylor, Charleston, S.C.
Toni Tipton-Martin, Austin, Tex.
Jeanne Voltz, Pittsboro, N.C.
Charles Reagan Wilson, Oxford, Miss.

## ABOUT JOHN T. EDGE

John T. Edge (www.johntedge.com) is the director of the Southern Foodways Alliance. He writes a monthly column, "United Tastes," for the *New York Times*, is a contributing editor at *Garden and Gun*, and a longtime columnist for the *Oxford American*. His work for *Saveur* and other magazines has been featured in six editions of the *Best Food Writing* compilation. He has been nominated for four James Beard Foundation awards, including the M. F. K. Fisher Distinguished Writing Award. In 2009, he was inducted into Beard's Who's Who of Food and Beverage in America. He is a coeditor of the *Southern Foodways Alliance Community Cookbook*.